THE BABY READER

*56 Selections from World Literature
about Babies and their Mothers,
Fathers, Admirers and Adversaries*

EDITED BY

MARIE WINN

SIMON AND SCHUSTER *New York*

Copyright © 1973 by Marie Winn
All rights reserved
including the right of reproduction
in whole or in part in any form
Published by Simon and Schuster
Rockefeller Center, 630 Fifth Avenue
New York, New York 10020

First printing

SBN 671-21439-X
Library of Congress Catalog Card Number: 72-90403
Designed by Dorothy S. Kaiser
Manufactured in the United States of America

To Allan

ACKNOWLEDGMENTS

The editor wishes to express her thanks to Richard Hart, head of the Humanities Department of the Enoch Pratt Library in Baltimore, Maryland, for his encouragement and valuable suggestions; to the staff of the Enoch Pratt for use of its admirable collection; to the staff of the New York Public Library.

The editor also wishes to thank Janet Malcolm, Literary Consultant of Babies for Peace, for her indispensable aid in every stage of the making of this book.

CONTENTS

IX. Early Learnings

INTRODUCTION

Babies are an acquired taste. Most people don't think they're particularly interesting until they have one of their own. Why people go ahead and have babies before they feel any real interest in them is a good question. The tax deduction cannot be the whole answer either. But a taste for babies, once acquired, is uncommonly strong. Other interests fade in its wake. House plants wilt and pampered pets go into a decline. And while the enthusiasm for babies seems to wane and finally disappear as the baby metamorphoses into a child, it is only lying dormant, biding its time and preparing to surface again at the first signs of grandparenthood.

When I had my first baby I was caught unawares by this sudden preoccupation with babies. I had heard about maternal instinct and expected to be (and indeed was) filled with tender emotions for *my* baby, but the idea of *babies* as an area of particular interest had never occurred to me. I hardly expected to find myself interested in nothing *but* babies. But that is what happened. I think most mothers and not a few fathers enjoy this harmless form of monomania when they have their first baby.

I didn't entirely abandon my old habits as a new mother. I had always done a lot of reading, and now I found that when I wasn't taking care of the baby, playing with the baby, talking to the baby or talking about the baby, I still wanted to read. The trouble was that I really didn't want to read about anything besides babies.

For a while I had no problem. There was always Dr. Spock. I read and reread that famous book during the first weeks of motherhood. It positively sustained me, and I grew to understand that when new mothers jokingly refer to their dog-eared copies of Dr. Spock as "the bible" they aren't entirely kidding. When I wasn't communing with Dr. Spock, I scoured the magazines for reading matter about babies and gratefully studied such articles as "Cradle Cap: Scourge of the Scalp" or "A New Look at Diaper Rash."

But there came a time when Dr. Spock was virtually committed

13

to memory, when the scourge of cradle cap had been successfully vanquished and *no* look seemed more promising than a new look at the ever-present diaper rash—when, in short, I was beginning to consider myself a fairly competent mother—it was about then that I began to feel the need for something more satisfying to read. Baby mania, however, had not by any means run its course—I still wanted to read about babies. But having the arrival of the diaper service magazine herald the high point of the month's literary activity began to depress me, for some reason. Wasn't there anything better to read about babies?

I cast a wistful look at our bookshelves, a whole wall of books; nothing seemed to appeal. Then as I glanced past the worn red copy of Tolstoy's *War and Peace* something stirred in my memory. Didn't Natasha eventually marry Pierre and have a *baby*? I faintly remembered a part of the novel that described Natasha as a wife and mother; I more distinctly remembered disliking that part of the book.

I found Natasha's baby in the first Epilogue of *War and Peace*. There it was, a real baby, and I read about it and Natasha's feelings, worries, and joys as a new mother with the greatest pleasure. Why had I neglected this wonderful little part of the book? I wondered, and an answer occurred to me: without a taste for babies a reader might be left unmoved by Tolstoy's domestic details about the ordinary life of a mother and baby.

I began to suspect that there might be other babies lurking about in unexpected places, in novels, stories or poems, in anthropology, sociology or psychology books, perhaps—good, meaty babies that might better fulfill my need to read about babies than the diaper service magazine. It became something of a hobby, searching for babies in literature. And I began to uncover a wealth of good babies, most of them probably skimmed over by the general reader, as I had done with Natasha and her baby in my first reading of *War and Peace*. But as a new mother, I now read about them with a new enjoyment. After a time I began to search for good writings about babies with a greater purpose: to collect them in a book for the pleasure of other new mothers.

I was guided by a few simple principles in choosing pieces to include in this collection. First, I wanted *good* writings—after all I was starting off with Tolstoy, and to include mediocre writings in a collection with great writings is always an affront. Next, the piece had to include a *real* baby, as it were, or describe a *real* feeling about babies. There are numbers of stage babies in literature, inanimate bundles of padding that exist only to forward a plot. Indeed, most babies in pre-twentieth-century fiction fall into this category. Tolstoy and Dickens provide exceptions in the nineteenth century, Smollett in the eighteenth—few others. But stage babies don't interest the mother of a real baby—only an infant with similarities to her own will satisfy her. Occasionally I stretched this principle a bit; Rabelais' outlandish and funny infant Gargantua scarcely qualifies as a "real" baby. And yet, just as any good parody reveals something about the nature of its subject, so the portrait of the prodigious baby gives an insight into the physical realities of infancy: the baby Gargantua behaves like a baby and does all the basic things real babies do, only in his case, just a little more so.

For similar reasons I have excluded some well-known babies in literature who are babies in name only. I pounced upon a story by F. Scott Fitzgerald called "The Baby Party," only to find that the "babies" in the story walked, talked, and indulged in social dancing! These were not babies, no matter what you called them. I decided to use walking and talking as the real boundary that separates infancy from childhood—the final accomplishment of these skills, that is. The process of learning to walk and talk is another matter; indeed, that is a major business of babies and comes up often in many of these selections.

The major business of new mothers, meanwhile, is to raise their babies well. This book will not offer much practical help for specific problems a new mother may come across. There's always Dr. Spock for that. But in reading about how babies are raised in an Israeli kibbutz or on a primitive South Sea Island, or in reading a fifteenth-century physician's advice on baby care or a twentieth-century psychoanalyst's theories about how babies adapt to their societies, in reading the insights of great writers and poets into the deepest feelings of new mothers and fathers and even the feelings of babies themselves—a new mother may gain a better perspective on herself as a mother. This may be as useful, in the long run, as the knowledge gained from the child-care manuals.

Here they are, then, the babies. Here are funny babies, infuriating babies, clever babies, hungry babies, sleeping babies, faraway babies, famous babies, obscure babies—and their mothers, fathers, uncles, neighbors, brothers, sisters, and baby-sitters. Many of them have been hiding for years, sometimes centuries, in various literary nooks and crannies, skimmed and skipped and generally unloved. This can't be good for babies. Surely these babies, like real ones, will thrive on the attention and affection they will now receive, exposed at last to the most appreciative audience they'll ever find: the mothers and fathers of real babies.

Part I

THE MATERNAL INSTINCT

A MOST DIFFICULT METAMORPHOSIS

From THE EVENING STAR

Colette

Already a famous novelist and stage figure, Colette faced the idea of her first child at the age of forty with serious misgivings. "Intelligent cats are usually bad mothers," she brooded, and continued acting a strenuous stage role at night and working on her unfinished novel by day. At last the play was abandoned, and in the competition between the book and the birth the maternal instinct triumphed. The novel suffered a hasty and unsatisfying ending, as the novelist found herself transformed into a mother.

I was forty, and I remember greeting the certitude of the belated child's presence with serious mistrust, while saying nothing about it. Physical apprehension had nothing to do with my behavior; I was simply afraid that at my age I would not know how to give a child the proper love and care, devotion and understanding. Love—so I believed—had already hurt me a great deal by monopolizing me for the past twenty years.

It is neither wise nor good to start a child with too much thought. Little used to worrying about the future, I found myself for the first time preparing for an exact date that it would have been quite enough to think about only four weeks beforehand. I meditated, I tried to think clearly and reasonably, but I was struck

19

by the recollection that intelligent cats are usually bad mothers, sinning by inadvertence or by excess of zeal, constantly moving their kittens from place to place, holding them by the nape of the neck, pinched between their teeth, hesitating where to deposit them. What a comfortable nest that sagging seat of an armchair! However, less so than under the down quilt, perhaps? But surely the acme of comfort would be the second drawer of the commode?

During the first three months I told almost no one of my condition or my worries. I did tell Charles Sauerwein and was struck by his comment. "Do you know what you're doing?" he exclaimed. "You're behaving as a man would, you're having a masculine pregnancy! You must take it more lightheartedly than this. Come, put on your hat, we'll go to the Poirée-Blanche and have some strawberry ice cream."

Fortunately I changed, without realizing it at first. Soon everyone around me began to exclaim how well I looked and how cheerful I was. The half-hidden and involuntary smile of pregnant women showed even through my makeup as the Optimistic Owl— for I was serenely continuing to play my part in *L'Oiseau de Nuit*, which involved some skillful pugilistics, mean uppercuts, and some rough and tumble clinches, on the table, under the table . . . A masculine pregnancy? Yes, and one might even say the pregnancy of a champion, for I had the taut, well-muscled body of an athlete . . .

Then, in the fourth month, one of the actors in the company, Georges Wague, reminded me of "the Geneva affair"—our plan to take our act to Geneva, and I realized that would be halfway between the fifth and sixth months . . . Hurriedly I confessed everything, and left behind me two dismayed friends, my two partners, Wague and Christine Kerf, contemplating the ruins of "the Geneva affair."

Insidiously, unhurriedly, the beatitude of pregnant females spread through me. I was no longer subjected to any discomfort, any unease. This purring contentment, this euphoria—how give a name either scientific or familiar to this state of preservation?— must certainly have penetrated me, since I have not forgotten it and am recalling it now, when life can never again bring me plenitude . . .

One gets tired of keeping to oneself all the unsaid things—in the present case my feeling of pride, of banal magnificence, as I ripened my fruit. My recollection of all this is linked with "the Geneva affair," for not long after breaking up our "turn," I summoned Wague and Christine Kerf and, strong in my newfound health and spirits, I reorganized our trio and our project for starting out on the road. Georges Wague hid his emotion by calling me an egg-laying hoot owl and predicting that my child would be dayblind. On the day settled upon, we left for Switzerland, and I celebrated my new importance by taking, at the hotel, the best room.

The lake cradled its swans on their reflection, the Alpine snows were softening, capped by mists, and I smiled at everything—the Swiss bread, the honey, the Swiss coffee . . .

"Beware of special cravings," said Wague. "What do you now have for breakfast, since you've gone astray?"

"Exactly what I had before the fault: *café au lait.*"

"Good, I'll order your breakfast when I go down for mine. Is it for eight o'clock?"

"Yes, for eight o'clock . . ."

Next morning at eight there was a knock at my door and a frightfully affected little voice murmured: "It's the chambermaid!"

If you've never seen a strapping, dark-skinned young fellow, all seasoned muscle, half naked under a shirtwaist borrowed from Kerf, a red ribbon tying his black hair at the temples, and got up in a tailormade skirt, you cannot imagine how a pregnant and jolly woman can laugh. Serious, her dark hair draped on her shoulders— strange ornament for a female boy-impersonator—Kerf followed, bringing a little tin filter coffeepot and preceded by the aroma of fresh coffee.

What good comrades they were! In order that I might have a breakfast unlike the hotel slop, they had filtered fresh ground coffee and boiled a half liter of milk on a portable alcohol stove— and this they did every morning, buying the fresh rolls and butter at night and keeping them fresh by setting them out on the windowsill. I was pleased and touched, but when I tried to thank them, Wague put on a refrigerated-Basque look. "We're not doing this for your sake," he said. "We're merely trying to keep down our expenses." And Kerf added: "It's not for your sake, it's for your baby's."

At night, on stage, during the well-regulated rough-and-tumble, I felt a careful arm being insinuated between my back and the table, helping my effort, which in appearance it was paralyzing.

Every night I bade farewell, more or less, to one of the happiest periods of my life, knowing well how I was going to regret it. But the cheerfulness, the purring contentment, the euphoria submerged everything and over me reigned the sweet animal innocence and unconcern arising from my added weight and the muffled appeals of the new life being formed within me.

The sixth month, the seventh month . . . Suitcases to pack, the departure for Limoges, a lightheartedness that disdained rest . . . But how heavy I became, especially at night! When climbing back up the road winding around the hill toward my lodgings, I let my two shepherd dogs, Bagheera and Son, haul me, by pulling on their two leashes. The first strawberries, the first roses . . . Can I regard my pregnancy as anything but one long festival? We forget the anguish of the labor pains but do not forget the long and singular festival; I have certainly not forgotten any detail. I especially remember how at odd hours sleep overwhelmed me and how I was seized again, as in my infancy, by the need to sleep on the ground, on the grass, on the sun-warmed hay. A unique and healthy craving.

When I had almost reached my term, I looked like a rat dragging a stolen egg. Feeling unwieldy, I sometimes was too tired out to lie down, and would sit in a comfortable armchair to exhaust the resources of a book or newspaper before going to bed. One night I had read a newspaper dry, skipping nothing, not even the racing forecasts or the name of the proprietor, and even going so far as to read the serial story. It was a high-class story, full of counts and marquises, and carriage horses that, noble beasts, only knew how to gallop and always seemed to be racing hell for leather:

Feverishly the Count paced up and down in his study. His black velvet smoking jacket accentuated his natural pallor. He pressed a bell; a footman appeared.

"Request Madame la Comtesse to rejoin me here," the Count commanded curtly.

After a short while, Yolande entered. She had lost none of her energy, but one guessed that she was feeling faint. The Count handed her the fatal letter which fluttered in his twitching fingers.

"Madame," he said through clenched teeth, "are you ready to reveal the name of the author of this letter?"

Yolande did not at once reply. Standing straight and white as a lily, she took a step forward and articulated, heroically:

"That goddamned swine, Ernest!"

I reread the last line to dispel the hallucination. Yes, I had read it correctly. Was it the vengeance of a printer who had been dismissed? A gross practical joke? The retort of the Countess gave me the strength to laugh and go to my bed, upon which the June wind had scattered, through the open french window, the flowers of an acacia.

Beneath the weight and beneath the fatigue, my long festival was not yet interrupted. I was borne on a shield of privileges and attentions. "Take this armchair! No, it's too low, take this other one instead." "I've made a strawberry tart for you." "Here is the pattern for the booties, you begin by casting on fifteen stitches . . ."

Neither fifteen nor ten. I would neither embroider a bib nor cut out a vest, nor gloat over white woolies. When I tried to visualize my little babe, I saw it naked, not all dressed up. It had to be content with a plain and practical English layette, without any frills or lace or smocking, and even that was bought—out of superstition—at the very last minute.

The "masculine pregnancy" did not lose all its rights; I was working on the last part of L'Entrave. The child and the novel were both rushing me, and the Vie Parisienne, which was serializing my unfinished novel, was catching up with me. The baby showed signs that it would win the race, and I screwed on the cap of my fountain pen.

My long festival came to an end on a cloudless day in July. The imperious child, on its way to its second life, maltreated a body no less eager than itself. In my little garden surrounded by other gardens, sheltered from the sun, provided with books and newspapers, I waited. I listened to the neighbors' cocks crowing and to the accelerated beating of my heart. When no one was looking, I took down the garden hose and gave the thirsty garden—which I would not be able to succor the next day or the following days—a token watering.

What followed . . . What followed doesn't matter, and I will give it no place here. What followed was the prolonged scream that issues from all women in childbed. If I like, this very day, to hear its echo, I need only open the window overlooking the Palais-Royal: from beneath the arcade rises the humble clamor of a neighbor woman who is pushing out into the world her sixth child. What followed was a restorative sleep and selfish appetite. But what followed was also, once, an effort to crawl toward me made by my bundled-up little larva that had been laid down for a moment on my bed. What animal perfection! The little creature guessed, she sensed the presence of my forbidden milk, and blindly struggled toward that blocked source. Never did I cry more brokenheartedly. Dreadful it is to ask in vain, but small is that hurt when compared with the pain of not giving . . .

What followed was the contemplation of a new person who had appeared in the house without coming from the outside. What followed, strange thing, was the proud and positive refusal of the Beauceron bitch ever to enter the room where the cradle stood. For a long time I tried to weaken this pensive enemy who wanted no rival in my heart. I even went so far as to hold out my sleeping baby girl, one little hand dangling, her naked feet pink as a rose, and say, "Look at her, lick her, take her, I give her to you," but the bitch consented only to a hurt silence and gazed at me briefly with golden eyes that were soon averted.

Did I bring sufficient love to my contemplation? I dare not state it with certainty. But I did have the habit—and still have—of marveling. I exercised it on the assemblage of wonders that constitute a newborn child. Her fingernails, transparent as the convex carapace of the pink prawn, and the tender soles of the feet that had come to us without touching the ground . . . The feathery lashes, lowered on the cheek, interposed between the terrestrial landscapes and the azure dream of the eye . . . The little private parts, almond just barely incised, bivalve exactly shut, lip to lip . . .

But I did not call it love, this detailed admiration I devoted to my daughter, nor did I feel it so. I watched and waited. I studied the delightful authority of my young nurse, who treated the small body with its clenched fists as if it were a lump of dough, rolling and flouring it, holding it upside down with one hand . . . But such spectacles, which I had waited so many years to witness, did not stir me to emulation or give me a dazzled maternal feeling. I began to wonder when I would experience my second and most difficult metamorphosis. Finally I had to yield to the evidence: it would take more than one admonitory sign to change me into an ordinary mother. I would have to wait for the sum-total results of a series of admonitions and premonitions, both true and false: the secret and jealous rebellions, the feeling of pride at controlling a life of which I was the humble creditor, the sensation, rather treacherous, of giving a lesson in modesty to the other kind of love. As a matter of fact, I was not reassured on the score of my maternal endowments until language blossomed on the entrancing lips, until understanding, affection, and the spirit of mischief transformed a run-of-the-mill baby into a girl, and the girl into my girl, my daughter.

In the competition between the book and the birth, it was the novel, thank God, which got the worst of it. Conscientiously I went back to work on the unfinished *L'Entrave*, but it could not recover from the blows dealt by the weak and triumphant infant. Please note, O my hypothetical readers, how skimped is that ending, how insufficient the corridor through which I wanted my pared-down heroes to pass. Observe, too, the empty tone of a conclusion in which those heroes do not believe, an ending like a subdominant chord—the cadence a musician would call plagal— too hurriedly struck.

Since then, I have tried to rewrite the ending of *L'Entrave*, but have never succeeded. Between the interruption of the work and its resumption, I had performed the laborious delectation of procreating. My jot of virility saved me from the danger to which the writer promoted to the status of happy and loving parent is exposed, a danger that can turn him into a mediocre author, thenceforth preferring the rewards of a visible and material growth: the cult of children, of plants, of breeding life in some form or other. An old boy of forty under the surface of the still young woman that I was, kept a sharp watch on the safety of a perhaps precious part of me.

When I was a young girl, if I ever happened to occupy myself with some needlework, Sido always shook her soothsayer's head and commented, "You will never look like anything but a boy who is sewing." She would now have said, "You will never be anything but a writer who gave birth to a child," for she would not have failed to see the accidental character of my maternity.

LIFE, LIFE, LIFE!

From MY LIFE

Isadora Duncan

Isadora Duncan lived an extraordinary life and wielded an extraordinary influence on her times. Her flamboyant rejection of the accepted morality (in an era before illegitimate babies became fashionable) and her freedom from convention have made her a symbol to all who fight stuffiness and hypocrisy. Did she, then, take to motherhood in some new and liberated way? Did her "Art" still come first in this new experience she shared with all mothers everywhere? Here is her description from her autobiography, My Life.

Ah, but the baby! The baby was astonishing; formed like a Cupid, with blue eyes and long, brown hair, that afterwards fell out and gave place to golden curls. And, miracle of miracles, that mouth sought my breast and bit with toothless gums, and pulled and drank the milk that gushed forth. What mother has ever told the feeling when the babe's mouth bites at her nipple, and the milk gushes from her breast? This cruel, biting mouth, like the mouth of a lover, and our lover's mouth, in turn, reminding us of the babe.

Oh, women, what is the good of us learning to become lawyers, painters or sculptors, when this miracle exists? Now I knew this tremendous love, surpassing the love of man. I was stretched and bleeding, torn and helpless, while the little being sucked and howled. Life, life, life! Give me life! Oh, where was my Art? My Art or any Art? What did I care for Art! I felt I was a God, superior to any artist.

During the first weeks, I used to lie long hours with the baby in my arms, watching her asleep; sometimes catching a gaze from her eyes; feeling very near the edge, the mystery, perhaps the knowledge of Life. This soul in the newly created body which answered my gaze with such apparently old eyes—the eyes of Eternity—gazing into mine with love. Love, perhaps, was the answer of all. What words could describe this joy? What wonder that I, who am not a writer, cannot find any words at all!

AN ASTONISHED MELANCHOLY

From THE SECOND SEX

Simone de Beauvoir

A basic book in any Woman's Liberation book-shelf is The Second Sex *by Simone de Beauvoir, a monumental consideration of every aspect of the female sex from prehistoric times to the present, and from infancy to old age. The following passage is from the chapter on the nature of motherhood.*

The first relations of the mother with her newborn child are variable. Some women suffer from the emptiness they now feel in their bodies: it seems to them that their treasure has been stolen. In her poems Cecile Sauvage expresses this feeling: "I am the hive whence the swarm has departed," and also: "He is born, I have lost my young beloved, now he is born, I am alone."

At the same time, however, there is an amazed curiosity in every young mother. It is strangely miraculous to see and to hold a living being formed within oneself and issued forth from oneself. But just what part has the mother had in the extraordinary event that brings into the world a new existence? She does not know. The newborn would not exist had it not been for her, and yet he leaves her. There is an astonished melancholy in seeing him outside, cut off from her. And almost always disappointment. The woman would like to feel the new being as surely *hers* as is her own hand; but everything he experiences is shut up inside him; he is opaque, impenetrable, apart; she does not even recognize him because she does not know him. She has experienced her pregnancy without him: she has no past in common with this little stranger. She expected that he would be at once familiar; but no, he is a new-comer, and she is surprised at the indifference with which she receives him. In the reveries of her pregnancy he was a mental image with infinite possibilities, and the mother enjoyed her future maternity in thought; now he is a tiny, finite individual, and he is there in reality—dependent, delicate, demanding. Her quite real joy in his finally being there is mingled with regret to find him no more than that.

A NEW SORT OF WARMTH

From TALKING TO WOMEN

Nell Dunn

To get to the heart of what modern young women think and feel about their lives as women, novelist Nell Dunn interviewed five articulate representatives of her sex and discussed with them all aspects of life and especially love. Inevitably the conversation turned to the feelings that accompany motherhood, within and without the framework of marriage.

NELL. . . . girls often each time they have a child, they're sort of rewarmed, afire I feel. I felt this very much about having my second child, suddenly so warm and marvelous and having become before that rather calm and logical and practical and you know, interested in a whole lot of things but I suddenly felt full of a new sort of warmth toward life and people. Very much sort of flushed with it, and I remembered very much what it was like having the first child, that it was this sort of sudden—as if one had suddenly been poured full of a new warm liquid.

PADDY. It is like that. Particularly if one has a happy relationship with the father of the child and he's entering into it; sometimes people seem to complain so much about pregnancy and seem rather bothered by the whole process.

NELL. Having a child on one's own must be very rough.

PADDY. And having a child within a very conventional marriage must be rather rough. This isn't very relevant but I've just remem-

30

bered a girl who had two children—and she just said a remark like, "Oh well, what poor David had to bear with me during pregnancy" or something, so I said "Didn't he enjoy it?" and she said "Good heavens, no, what man would?" I think Frank thought a lot of me when I was pregnant, he really loved me, you know, more than at any time.

NELL. Yes, one is gentle, soft, and sitting about and making soup and calm as opposed to rushing around like a whirlwind half the time, and more slowed down. You become very much nicer I think. I never understand why men don't want their women to have babies.

PADDY. I think some do get just a bit repulsed by the physical thing because the women do, they get repulsed as they get fat and the men do too.

NELL. Yes but that's so wrong. Really it's so wrong. And this is of course an interesting thing about sex being important. Where I think it's important is I think it's important because it gives one physical confidence and therefore makes one beautiful and this is very true when one is having a baby of the man who one feels loves one's body, is that one feels beautiful. And in a way becomes beautiful. And this is very true that if pregnant women look unloved, they look horrible.

PADDY. They look awkward. Or miserable.

NELL. It's marvelous. It's very interesting this thing of women liking or not liking being pregnant. I don't resent it at all, I mean I tend to get a bit bored toward the end.

PADDY. Yes, I think I did a little bit. But I enjoyed it—I would more willingly go into pregnancy and indeed having a baby, than having another child there all the time, you know what I mean, the whole process of having a baby is marvelous.

NELL. It's the coping with the child afterwards?

PADDY. Yes, remembering you've got a human being until death, you know.

NELL. Did it worry you before you had a child, suddenly thinking of the emotional responsibility?

PADDY. A little bit but not all that much. I felt quite confident having the first one. I think having had one—one obviously doesn't know what it's like until one has had one—would perhaps prevent me from rushing into having a second one. Just the practical problems of coping and help to look after it and a bit the responsibility

of the life I suppose. If you've got one I don't suppose that two is very much different.

NELL. One has to organize for one, one organizes for two, I agree I don't think it makes too much difference.

PADDY. People often say to me they think it's immoral practically just to have one child, that's something I don't quite understand. I think people are so independent human beings that they're not going to be bugged by the fact that one has no brothers and sisters, something like that.

ALL WOMEN FEEL EXACTLY THAT

From THE MILLSTONE

Margaret Drabble

A particular type of young woman who emerges in the works of English novelist Margaret Drabble undeniably exists in real life today, and perhaps has existed among women at all times. Rosamund Stacey is a perfect example of the type: clever, cool, somewhat asexual and yet very desirable to men (perhaps for that very reason). It is only in her role as a mother and in her feelings toward her baby that her feminine feelings emerge in full strength.

. . . the midwife asked me if I would like to see the child. "Please," I said gratefully, and she went away and came back with my daughter wrapped up in a small gray bloodstained blanket, and with a ticket saying Stacey round her ankle. She put her in my arms and I sat there looking at her, and her great wide blue eyes looked at me with seeming recognition, and what I felt it is pointless to try to describe. Love, I suppose one might call it, and the first of my life.

I had expected so little, really. I never expect much. I had been told of the ugliness of newborn children, of their red and wrinkled faces, their waxy covering, their emaciated limbs, their hairy cheeks, their piercing cries. All I can say is that mine was beautiful and in my defense I must add that others said she was beautiful too. She was not red nor even wrinkled, but palely soft, each feature delicately reposed in its right place, and she was not bald

33

but adorned with a thick, startling crop of black hair. One of the nurses fetched a brush and flattened it down and it covered her forehead, lying in a dense fringe that reached to her eyes. And her eyes, that seemed to see me and that looked into mine with deep gravity and charm, were a profound blue, the whites white with the gleam of alarming health. When they asked if they could have her back and put her back in her cradle for the night, I handed her over without reluctance, for the delight of holding her was too much for me. I felt as well as they that such pleasure should be regulated and rationed.

When they had removed her, they wheeled me off to a ward and put me to bed and gave me some sleeping pills and assured me I would fall asleep at once and be out till the morning. But I didn't, I lay awake for two hours, unable to get over my happiness. I was not much used to feeling happiness: satisfaction, perhaps, or triumph, and at times excitement and exhilaration. But happiness was something I had not gone in for for a long time, and it was very nice, too nice to waste in sleep. I dozed off at about half past four but was awakened at half past five with cups of tea and the sight of all the other mothers giving their babies breakfast.

I tried to explain the other day to somebody . . . about how happy I had felt, but he was very contemptuous of my descriptions. "What you're talking about," he said, "is one of the most boring commonplaces of the female experience. All women feel exactly that, it's nothing to be proud of, it isn't even worth thinking about."

I denied hotly that all women felt it, as I knew hardly a one who had been as enraptured as I, and then I contradicted my own argument by saying that anyway, if all other women did feel it, then that was precisely what made it so remarkable in my case, as I could not recall a single other instance in my life when I had felt what all other women feel. . . .

Octavia was an extraordinarily beautiful child. Everyone said so, in shops and on buses and in the park, wherever we went. I took her to Regent's Park as often as I could face getting the pram up and down in the lift. It was a tolerable summer, and we both got quite brown. I was continually amazed by the way in which I could watch for hours nothing but the small movements of her hands, and the fleeting expressions of her face. She was a very

happy child, and once she learned to smile, she never stopped; at first she would smile at anything, at parking meters and dogs and strangers, but as she grew older she began to favor me, and nothing gave me more delight than her evident preference. I suppose I had not really expected her to dislike and resent me from birth, though I was quite prepared for resentment to follow later on, but I certainly had not anticipated such wreathing, dazzling gaiety of affection from her whenever I happened to catch her eye. Gradually I began to realize that she liked me, that she had no option to liking me, and that unless I took great pains to alienate her she would go on liking me, for a couple of years at least. It was very pleasant to receive such uncritical love, because it left me free to bestow love; my kisses were met by small warm rubbery unrejecting cheeks and soft dovey mumblings of delight.

A MOTHER'S WEAKNESS

From "THREE YEARS"

Anton Chekhov

Most mothers are aware of the "weakness" Yulia describes in a short story by Chekhov, and most mothers are no more successful than Yulia in avoiding it.

"Mothers see something extraordinary in their children; that is ordained by nature," said Yulia. "A mother will stand for hours together by the baby's cot looking at its little ears and eyes and nose, and fascinated by them. If anyone else kisses her baby the poor thing imagines that it gives him immense pleasure. And a mother talks of nothing but her own baby. I know that weakness in mothers, and I keep a watch over myself, but my Olga really is exceptional. How she looks at me when I'm nursing her! How she laughs! She's only eight months old, but, upon my word, I've never seen such intelligent eyes in a child of three."

Part II

FATHERS FROM ADAM ON UP

EXTRACTS FROM ADAM'S DIARY

From THE $3,000 BEQUEST

Mark Twain

Adam's troubles begin with the arrival of a new creature who talks too much and calls herself "Eve." His troubles are compounded when Eve takes up with a persuasive serpent. But all previous problems seem to fade when Eve presents him with a brand-new creature that he cannot seem to identify . . . a noisy little creature that makes Eve behave in a most peculiar way.

Monday.—This new creature with the long hair is a good deal in the way. It is always hanging around and following me about. I don't like this; I am not used to company. I wish it would stay with the other animals. . . . Cloudy to-day, wind in the east; think we shall have rain. . . . *We?* Where did I get that word?—I remember now—the new creature uses it.

Tuesday.—Been examining the great waterfall. It is the finest thing on the estate, I think. The new creature calls it Niagara Falls—why, I am sure I do not know. Says it *looks* like Niagara Falls. That is not a reason, it is mere waywardness and imbecility. I get no chance to name anything myself. The new creature names everything that comes along, before I can get in a protest. And always that same pretext is offered—it *looks* like the thing. There is the dodo, for instance. Says the moment one looks at it one sees at a glance that it "looks like a dodo." It will have to keep that name, no doubt. It wearies me to fret about it, and it does no good, anyway. Dodo! It looks no more like a dodo than I do.

Wednesday.—Built me a shelter against the rain, but could not have it to myself in peace. The new creature intruded. When I tried to put it out it shed water out of the holes it looks with, and wiped it away with the back of its paws, and made a noise such as some of the other animals make when they are in distress. I wish it would not talk; it is always talking. That sounds like a cheap fling at the poor creature, a slur; but I do not mean it so. I have never heard the human voice before, and any new and strange sound intruding itself here upon the solemn hush of these dreaming solitudes offends my ear and seems a false note. And this new sound is so close to me; it is right at my shoulder, right at my ear, first on one side and then on the other, and I am used only to sounds that are more or less distant from me.

Friday.—The naming goes recklessly on, in spite of anything I can do. I had a very good name for the estate, and it was musical and pretty—GARDEN OF EDEN. Privately, I continue to call it that, but not any longer publicly. The new creature says it is all woods and rocks and scenery, and therefore has no resemblance to a garden. Says it *looks* like a park, and does not look like anything *but* a park. Consequently, without consulting me, it has been new-named—NIAGARA FALLS PARK. This is sufficiently high-handed, it seems to me. And already there is a sign up:

KEEP OFF

THE GRASS

My life is not as happy as it was.

Saturday.—The new creature eats too much fruit. We are going to run short, most likely. "We" again—that is *its* word; mine, too, now, from hearing it so much. Good deal of fog this morning. I do not go out in the fog myself. The new creature does. It goes out in all weathers, and stumps right in with its muddy feet. And talks. It used to be so pleasant and quiet here.

Sunday.—Pulled through. This day is getting to be more and more trying. It was selected and set apart last November as a day of rest. I had already six of them per week before. This morning found the new creature trying to clod apples out of that forbidden tree.

Monday.—The new creature says its name is Eve. That is all right, I have no objections. Says it is to call it by, when I want it to come. I said it was superfluous, then. The word evidently raised me in its respect; and indeed it is a large, good word and will bear repetition. It says it is not an It, it is a She. This is probably doubtful; yet it is all one to me; what she is were nothing to me if she would but go by herself and not talk.

Tuesday.—She has littered the whole estate with execrable names and offensive signs:

> THIS WAY TO THE WHIRLPOOL
> THIS WAY TO GOAT ISLAND
> CAVE OF THE WINDS THIS WAY

She says this part would make a tidy summer resort if there was any custom for it. Summer resort—another invention of hers—just words, without any meaning. What is a summer resort? But it is best not to ask her, she has such a rage for explaining.

Friday.—She has taken to beseeching me to stop going over the Falls. What harm does it do? Says it makes her shudder. I wonder why; I have always done it—always liked the plunge, and coolness. I supposed it was what the Falls were for. They have no other use that I can see, and they must have been made for something. She says they were only made for scenery—like the rhinoceros and the mastodon.

I went over the Falls in a barrel—not satisfactory to her. Went over in a tub—still not satisfactory. Swam the Whirlpool and the Rapids in a fig-leaf suit. It got much damaged. Hence, tedious complaints about my extravagance. I am too much hampered here. What I need is change of scene.

Saturday.—I escaped last Tuesday night, and traveled two days, and built me another shelter in a secluded place, and obliterated my tracks as well as I could, but she hunted me out by means of a beast which she has tamed and calls a wolf, and came making that pitiful noise again, and shedding that water out of the places she looks with. I was obliged to return with her, but will presently emigrate again when occasion offers. She engages herself in many foolish things; among others, to study out why the animals called lions and tigers live on grass and flowers, when, as she says, the sort of teeth they wear would indicate that they were intended to eat each other. This is foolish, because to do that would be to kill each other, and that would introduce what, as I understand it, is called "death"; and death, as I have been told, has not yet entered the Park. Which is a pity, on some accounts.

Sunday.—Pulled through.

Monday.—I believe I see what the week is for: it is to give time to rest up from the weariness of Sunday. It seems a good idea. . . . She has been climbing that tree again. Clodded her out of it. She said nobody was looking. Seems to consider that a sufficient justification for chancing any dangerous thing. Told her that. The word justification moved her admiration—and envy, too, I thought. It is a good word.

Tuesday.—She told me she was made out of a rib taken from my body. This is at least doubtful, if not more than that. I have not missed any rib. . . . She is in much trouble about the buzzard; says grass does not agree with it; is afraid she can't raise it; thinks it was intended to live on decayed flesh. The buzzard must get along the best it can with what it is provided. We cannot overturn the whole scheme to accommodate the buzzard.

Saturday.—She fell in the pond yesterday when she was looking at herself in it, which she is always doing. She nearly strangled, and said it was most uncomfortable. This made her sorry for the creatures which live in there, which she calls fish, for she continues to fasten names on to things that don't need them and don't come when they are called by them, which is a matter of no consequence to her, she is such a numskull, anyway; so she got a lot of them out and brought them in last night and put them in my bed to keep warm, but I have noticed them now and then all day and I don't see that they are any happier there than they were before, only quieter. When night comes I shall throw them outdoors. I will not sleep with them again, for I find them clammy and unpleasant to lie among when a person hasn't anything on.

Sunday.—Pulled through.

Tuesday.—She has taken up with a snake now. The other animals are glad, for she was always experimenting with them and bothering them; and I am glad because the snake talks, and this enables me to get a rest.

Friday.—She says the snake advises her to try the fruit of that tree, and says the result will be a great and fine and noble education. I told her there would be another result, too—it would introduce death into the world. That was a mistake—it had been better to keep the remark to myself; it only gave her an idea—she could save the sick buzzard, and furnish fresh meat to the despondent lions and tigers. I advised her to keep away from the tree. She said she wouldn't. I foresee trouble. Will emigrate.

Wednesday.—I have had a variegated time. I escaped last night, and rode a horse all night as fast as he could go, hoping to get clear out of the Park and hide in some other country before the trouble should begin; but it was not to be. About an hour after sun-up, as I was riding through a flowery plain where thousands of animals were grazing, slumbering, or playing with each other, according to their wont, all of a sudden they broke into a tempest of frightful noises, and in one moment the plain was a frantic commotion and every beast was destroying its neighbor. I knew what it meant— Eve had eaten that fruit, and death was come into the world . . . The tigers ate my horse, paying no attention when I ordered them to desist, and they would have eaten me if I had stayed—which I didn't, but went away in much haste. . . . I found this place, outside the Park, and was fairly comfortable for a few days, but she has found me out. Found me out, and has named the place Tonawanda—says it *looks* like that. In fact I was not sorry she came, for there are but meager pickings here, and she brought some of those apples. I was obliged to eat them, I was so hungry. It was against my principles, but I find that principles have no real force except when one is well fed. . . . She came curtained in boughs and bunches of leaves, and when I asked her what she meant by such nonsense, and snatched them away and threw them down, she tittered and blushed. I had never seen a person titter and blush before, and to me it seemed unbecoming and idiotic. She said I would soon know how it was myself. This was correct. Hungry as I was, I laid down the apple half-eaten—certainly the best one I ever saw, considering the lateness of the season—and arrayed myself in the discarded boughs and branches, and then spoke to her with some severity and ordered her to go and get some more and not make such a spectacle of herself. She did it, and after this we crept down to where the wild-beast battle had been, and collected some skins, and I made her patch together a couple of suits proper for public occasions. They are uncomfortable, it is true, but stylish, and that is the main point about clothes. . . . I find she is a good deal of a companion. I see I should be lonesome and depressed without her, now that I have lost my property. Another thing, she says it is ordered that we work for our living hereafter. She will be useful. I will superintend.

Ten Days Later.—She accuses *me* of being the cause of our disaster! She says, with apparent sincerity and truth, that the Serpent assured her that the forbidden fruit was not apples, it was chestnuts. I said I was innocent, then, for I had not eaten any chestnuts. She said the Serpent informed her that "chestnut" was a figurative term meaning an aged and moldy joke. I turned pale at that, for I have made many jokes to pass the weary time, and some of them could have been of that sort, though I had honestly supposed that they were new when I made them. She asked me if I had made one just at the time of the catastrophe. I was obliged to admit that I had made one to myself, though not aloud. It was this. I was thinking about the Falls, and I said to myself, "How wonderful it is to see that vast body of water tumble down there!" Then in an instant a bright thought flashed into my head, and I let it fly, saying, "It would be a deal more wonderful to see it tumble *up* there!"—and I was just about to kill myself with laughing at it when all nature broke loose in war and death and I had to flee for my life. "There," she said, with triumph, "that is just it; the Serpent mentioned that very jest, and called it the First Chestnut, and said it was coeval with the creation." Alas, I am indeed to blame. Would that I were not witty; oh, that I had never had that radiant thought!

Next Year.—We have named it Cain. She caught it while I was up country trapping on the North Shore of the Erie; caught it in the timber a couple of miles from our dug-out—or it might have been four, she isn't certain which. It resembles us in some ways, and may be a relation. That is what she thinks, but this is an error, in my judgment. The difference in size warrants the conclusion that it is a different and new kind of animal—a fish, perhaps, though when I put it in the water to see, it sank, and she plunged in and snatched it out before there was opportunity for the experiment to determine the matter. I still think it is a fish, but she is indifferent about what it is, and will not let me have it to try. I do not understand this. The coming of the creature seems to have changed her whole nature and made her unreasonable about experiments. She thinks more of it than she does of any of the other animals, but is not able to explain why. Her mind is disordered— everything shows it. Sometimes she carries the fish in her arms half the night when it complains and wants to get to the water. At such times the water comes out of the places in her face that she looks out of, and she pats the fish on the back and makes soft sounds with her mouth to soothe it, and betrays sorrow and solicitude in a hundred ways. I have never seen her do like this with any other fish, and it troubles me greatly. She used to carry the young tigers around so, and play with them, before we lost our property, but it was only play; she never took on about them like this when their dinner disagreed with them.

Sunday.—She doesn't work, Sundays, but lies around all tired out, and likes to have the fish wallow over her; and she makes fool noises to amuse it, and pretends to chew its paws, and that makes it laugh. I have not seen a fish before that could laugh. This makes me doubt. . . . I have come to like Sunday myself. Superintending all the week tires a body so. There ought to be more Sundays. In the old days they were tough, but now they come handy.

Wednesday.—It isn't a fish. I cannot quite make out what it is. It makes curious devilish noises when not satisfied, and says "googoo" when it is. It is not one of us, for it doesn't walk; it is not a bird, for it doesn't fly; it is not a frog, for it doesn't hop; it is not a snake, for it doesn't crawl, I feel sure it is not a fish, though I cannot get a chance to find out whether it can swim or not. It merely lies around, and mostly on its back, with its feet up. I have not seen any other animal do that before. I said I believed it was an enigma; but she only admired the word without understanding it. In my judgment it is either an enigma or some kind of a bug. If it dies, I will take it apart and see what its arrangements are. I never had a thing perplex me so.

Three Months Later.—The perplexity augments instead of diminishing. I sleep but little. It has ceased from lying around, and goes about on its four legs now. Yet it differs from the other four-legged animals, in that its front legs are unusually short, consequently this causes the main part of its person to stick up uncomfortably high in the air, and this is not attractive. It is built much as we are, but its method of traveling shows that it is not of our breed. The short front legs and long hind ones indicate that it is of the kangaroo family, but it is a marked variation of the species, since the true kangaroo hops, whereas this one never does. Still it is a curious and interesting variety, and has not been catalogued before. As I discovered it, I have felt justified in securing the credit of the discovery by attaching my name to it, and hence have called it *Kangaroorum Adamiensis.* . . . It must have been a young one when it came, for it has grown exceedingly since. It must be five times as big, now, as it was then, and when discontented it is able to make from twenty-two to thirty-eight times the noise it made at first. Coercion does not modify this, but has the contrary effect. For this reason I discontinued the system. She reconciles it by persuasion, and by giving it things which she had previously told me she wouldn't give it. As already observed, I was not at home when it first came, and she told me she found it in the woods. It seems odd that it should be the only one, yet it must be so, for I have worn myself out these many weeks trying to find another one to add to my collection, and for this one to play with; for surely then it would be quieter and we could tame it more easily. But I find none, nor any vestige of any; and strangest of all, no tracks. It has to live on the ground, it cannot help itself; therefore, how does it get about without leaving a track? I have set a dozen traps, but they do no good. I catch all small animals except that one; animals that merely go into the trap out of curiosity, I think, to see what the milk is there for. They never drink it.

Three Months Later.—The Kangaroo still continues to grow, which is very strange and perplexing. I never knew one to be so long getting its growth. It has fur on its head now; not like kangaroo fur, but exactly like our hair except that it is much finer and softer, and instead of being black is red. I am like to lose my mind over the capricious and harassing developments of this unclassifiable zoological freak. If I could catch another one—but that is hopeless; it is a new variety, and the only sample; this is plain. But I caught a true kangaroo and brought it in, thinking that this one, being lonesome, would rather have that for company than have no kin at all, or any animal it could feel a nearness to or get sympathy from in its forlorn condition here among strangers who do not know its ways or habits, or what to do to make it feel that it is among friends; but it was a mistake—it went into such fits at the sight of the kangaroo that I was convinced it had never seen one before. I pity the poor noisy little animal, but there is nothing I can do to make it happy. If I could tame it—but that is out of the question; the more I try the worse I seem to make it. It grieves me to the heart to see it in its little storms of sorrow and passion. I wanted to let it go, but she wouldn't hear of it. That seemed cruel and not like her; and yet she may be right. It might be lonelier than ever; for since I cannot find another one, how could *it* ?

Five Months Later.—It is not a kangaroo. No, for it supports itself by holding to her finger, and thus goes a few steps on its hind legs, and then falls down. It is probably some kind of a bear; and yet it has no tail—as yet—and no fur, except on its head. It still keeps on growing—that is a curious circumstance, for bears get their growth earlier than this. Bears are dangerous—since our catastrophe—and I shall not be satisfied to have this one prowling about the place much longer without a muzzle on. I have offered to get her a kangaroo if she would let this one go, but it did no good—she is determined to run us into all sorts of foolish risks, I think. She was not like this before she lost her mind.

A Fortnight Later.—I examined its mouth. There is no danger yet: it has only one tooth. It has no tail yet. It makes more noise now than it ever did before—and mainly at night. I have moved out. But I shall go over, mornings, to breakfast, and see if it has more teeth. If it gets a mouthful of teeth it will be time for it to go, tail or no tail, for a bear does not need a tail in order to be dangerous.

Four Months Later.—I have been off hunting and fishing a month, up in the region that she calls Buffalo; I don't know why, unless it is because there are not any buffaloes there. Meantime the bear has learned to paddle around all by itself on its hind legs, and says "poppa" and "momma." It is certainly a new species. This resemblance to words may be purely accidental, of course, and may have no purpose or meaning; but even in that case it is still extraordinary, and is a thing which no other bear can do. This imitation of speech, taken together with general absence of fur and entire absence of tail, sufficiently indicates that this is a new kind of bear. The further study of it will be exceedingly interesting. Meantime I will go off on a far expedition among the forests of the north and make an exhaustive search. There must certainly be another one somewhere, and this one will be less dangerous when it has company of its own species. I will go straightway; but I will muzzle this one first.

Three Months Later.—It has been a weary, weary hunt, yet I have had no success. In the mean time, without stirring from the home estate, she has caught another one! I never saw such luck. I might have hunted these woods a hundred years, I never would have run across that thing.

Next Day.—I have been comparing the new one with the old one, and it is perfectly plain that they are the same breed. I was going to stuff one of them for my collection, but she is prejudiced against it for some reason or other; so I have relinquished the idea, though I think it is a mistake. It would be an irreparable loss to science if they should get away. The old one is tamer than it was and can laugh and talk like the parrot, having learned this, no doubt, from being with the parrot so much, and having the imitative faculty in a highly developed degree. I shall be astonished if it turns out to be a new kind of parrot; and yet I ought not to be astonished, for it has already been everything else it could think of since those first days when it was a fish. The new one is as ugly now as the old one was at first; has the same sulphur-and-raw-meat complexion and the same singular head without any fur on it. She calls it Abel.

Ten Years Later.—They are *boys*; we found it out long ago. It was their coming in that small, immature shape that puzzled us; we were not used to it. There are some girls now. Abel is a good boy, but if Cain had stayed a bear it would have improved him. After all these years, I see that I was mistaken about Eve in the beginning; it is better to live outside the Garden with her than inside it without her. At first I thought she talked too much; but now I should be sorry to have that voice fall silent and pass out of my life. Blessed be the chestnut that brought us near together and taught me to know the goodness of her heart and the sweetness of her spirit!

UNEXPECTED FEELINGS

From ANNA KARENINA

Leo Tolstoy

Into the story of Anna's unhappy marriage and ill-fated love affair in Anna Karenina, *Tolstoy intertwines a story of a happy marriage.*

The happy couple are Anna's cousin Kitty and her husband Levin. Their joys in the common experiences of married life, as in the following description of Levin's feelings as a new father, are a powerful contrast to Anna's increasing misery in her search for happiness outside the bounds of conventional morality.

At ten o'clock the old prince, Sergey Ivanovitch, and Stepan Arkadyevitch were sitting at Levin's. Having inquired after Kitty, they had dropped into conversation upon other subjects. Levin heard them, and unconsciously, as they talked, going over the past, over what had been up to that morning, he thought of himself as he had been yesterday till that point. It was as though a hundred years had passed since then. He felt himself exalted to unattainable heights, from which he studiously lowered himself so as not to wound the people he was talking to. He talked, and was all the time thinking of his wife, of her condition now, of his son, in whose existence he tried to school himself into believing. The whole world of woman, which had taken for him since his marriage a new value he had never suspected before, was now so exalted that he could not take it in in his imagination. He heard

49

them talk of yesterday's dinner at the club, and thought: "What is happening with her now? Is she asleep? How is she? What is she thinking of? Is he crying, my son Dmitri?" And in the middle of the conversation, in the middle of a sentence, he jumped up and went out of the room.

"Send me word if I can see her," said the prince.

"Very well, in a minute," answered Levin, and without stopping, he went to her room.

She was not asleep, she was talking gently with her mother, making plans about the christening.

Carefully set to rights, with hair well-brushed, in a smart little cap with some blue in it, her arms out on the quilt, she was lying on her back. Meeting his eyes, her eyes drew him to her. Her face, bright before, brightened still more as he drew near her. There was the same change in it from earthly to unearthly that is seen in the face of the dead. But then it means farewell, here it meant welcome. Again a rush of emotion, such as he had felt at the moment of the child's birth, flooded his heart. She took his hand and asked him if he had slept. He could not answer, and turned away, struggling with his weakness.

"I have had a nap, Kostya!" she said to him; "and I am so comfortable now."

She looked at him, but suddenly her expression changed.

"Give him to me," she said, hearing the baby's cry. "Give him to me, Lizaveta Petrovna, and he shall look at him."

"To be sure, his papa shall look at him," said Lizaveta Petrovna, getting up and bringing something red, and queer, and wriggling. "Wait a minute, we'll make him tidy first," and Lizaveta Petrovna laid the red wobbling thing on the bed, began untrussing and trussing up the baby, lifting it up and turning it over with one finger and powdering it with something.

Levin, looking at the tiny, pitiful creature, made strenuous efforts to discover in his heart some traces of fatherly feeling for it. He felt nothing towards it but disgust. But when it was undressed and he caught a glimpse of wee, wee, little hands, little feet, saffron-colored, with little toes, too, and positively with a little big toe different from the rest, and when he saw Lizaveta Petrovna closing the wide-open little hands, as though they were soft springs, and putting them into linen garments, such pity for the little creature came upon him, and such terror that she would hurt it, that he held her hand back.

Lizaveta Petrovna laughed.

"Don't be frightened, don't be frightened!"

When the baby had been put to rights and transformed into a firm doll, Lizaveta Petrovna dandled it as though proud of her handiwork, and stood a little away so that Levin might see his son in all his glory.

Kitty looked sideways in the same direction, never taking her eyes off the baby. "Give him to me! give him to me!" she said, and even made as though she would sit up.

"What are you thinking of, Katerina Alexandrovna, you mustn't move like that! Wait a minute. I'll give him to you. Here we're showing papa what a fine fellow we are!"

And Lizaveta Petrovna, with one hand supporting the wobbling head, lifted up on the other arm the strange, limp, red creature, whose head was lost in its swaddling-clothes. But it had a nose, too, and slanting eyes and smacking lips.

"A splendid baby!" said Lizaveta Petrovna.

Levin sighed with mortification. This splendid baby excited in him no feeling but disgust and compassion. It was not at all the feeling he had looked forward to.

He turned away while Lizaveta Petrovna put the baby to the unaccustomed breast.

Suddenly laughter made him look round. The baby had taken the breast.

"Come, that's enough, that's enough!" said Lizaveta Petrovna, but Kitty would not let the baby go. He fell asleep in her arms.

"Look, now," said Kitty, turning the baby so that he could see it. The aged-looking little face suddenly puckered up still more and the baby sneezed.

Smiling, hardly able to restrain his tears, Levin kissed his wife and went out of the dark room. What he felt towards this little creature was utterly unlike what he had expected. There was nothing cheerful and joyous in the feeling; on the contrary, it was a new torture of apprehension. It was the consciousness of a new sphere of liability to pain. And this sense was so painful at first, the apprehension lest this helpless creature should suffer was so intense, that it prevented him from noticing the strange thrill of senseless joy and even pride that he had felt when the baby sneezed.

THE BEDTIME STORY

From "INCEST," in The Same Door

John Updike

Dinner is ready on the table. The baseball game is at its most exciting on the radio. The father is exhausted from the day's work. Then an ominous creaking of springs is heard from the crib in the nursery . . .

In this passage from a long story by John Updike, the author re-creates a most familiar situation in the life of any young American family, trained by Spock and dedicated to the proposition that a small baby reigns supreme.

Having lifted her into the crib and seen her root the bottle in her mouth, he dropped the fuzzy pink blanket over her and left quickly, gently closing the doors and sealing her into the darkness that was to merge with sleep. It was no doubt this quickness that undid the process. Though the child was drugged with heated milk, she still noticed a slight.

He suspected this at the time. When, their own meal barely begun, the crib springs creaked unmistakably, he said, "Son of a bitch." Stan Lomax, on their faint radio, was giving an account of Williams' latest verbal outrage; Lee was desperate to hear every word. Like many Americans he was spiritually dependent on Ted Williams. He asked his wife, "God damn it, doesn't that kid do anything in the day? Didn't you take her to the park? Why isn't she worn out?"

52

The one answer to this could be his own getting up, after a silence, and going in to wait out the baby's insomnia. The hollow goodness of the act, like a gift given to a beggar with embarrassment, infuriated his tongue: "I work like a fool all day and come home and run the kid up and down until my legs ache and I have a headache and then I can't even eat my pork chop in peace."

In the aquarium of the dark room his child's face floated spectrally, and her eyes seemed discrete pools of the distant, shy power that had put them all there, and had made these walls, and the single tree outside, showing the first stages of leaf under the yellow night sky of New York. "Do you want to go on the big bed?"

"Big—bed!"

"O.K."

"Ogay."

Adjusting to the lack of light, he perceived that the bottle, nested in a crumpled sheet, was drained. Little Jane had been standing in her crib, one foot on the edge, as in ballet school. For two weeks she had been gathering nerve for the time she would climb the crib's wall and drop free outside. He lifted her out, breathing "Ooh, *heavy*," and took her to the wide low bed made of two beds. She clung to the fuzzy blanket—with milk, her main soporific.

Beside her on the bed, he began their story. "Once upon a time, in the big, big woods—" She flipped ecstatically at the known cadence. "Now you relax. There was a tiny little creature name of Barry Mouse."

"Mouff!" she cried, and sat straight up, as if she had heard one. She looked down at him for confirmation.

"Barry Mouse," he said. "And one day when Barry Mouse was walking through the woods, he came to a great big tree, and in the top of the great big tree what do you think there was?"

At last she yielded to the insistent pressure of his hand and fell back, her heavy blond head sinking into the pillow. He repeated, "What do you think there was?"

"Owl."

"That's right. Up at the top of the tree there was an owl, and the owl said, 'I'm going to eat you, Barry Mouse.' And Barry Mouse said, 'No, no.' So Owl said, 'O.K, then why don't you *hop* on my *back* and we'll *fly* to the *moon*?" And so Barry Mouse hopped on Owl's back and away they went—"

Jane turned on her side, so her great face was an inch from his. She giggled and drummed her feet against his abdomen, solidly. Neither Lee nor his wife, who shared the one bedtime story, had ever worked out what happened on the moon. Once the owl and the mouse were aloft, their imaginations collapsed. Knowing his voice daren't stop now, when her state was possibly transitional and he felt as if he were bringing to his lips an absolutely brimful glass of liquid, he continued with some nonsense about cinnamon trees and Chinese maidens, no longer bothering to keep within her vocabulary. She began touching his face with her open mouth, a sure sign she was sleepy. "Hey," he murmured when one boneless moist kiss landed directly on his lips.

"Jane is so sleepy," he said, "because Daddy is sleepy, and Mommy is sleepy, and Bear is ssleepy, and Doll is sssleepy. . . ."

She lay quiet, her face in shadow, her fine straight yellow hair fanned across the pillow. Neither he nor his wife was blond; they had brown hair, rat color. There was little blondness in either family: just Jane's Aunt Ruth, and Lee's sister Margaret, eight years older than he and married before he had left grade school. She had been the fetching one of the children and he the bright one. So he imagined, though his parents loved them all impeccably.

Presuming his daughter asleep, he lifted himself on one elbow. She kicked his belly, rolled onto her back, and said in a voice loud with drowsiness, "Baaiy Mouff."

Stroking her strange hair, he began again, "Once upon a time, in the deep, deep woods, there lived a little creature," and this time succeeded.

As he lowered her into her crib, her eyes opened. He said, "O.K.?"

She pronounced beautifully, "O.K."

OH YOU POOR, WRETCHED FELLOW

From "THE ESTATE OF MARRIAGE," Luther's Works, Volume 45

Martin Luther

Rumor would have it that only modern American fathers are sufficiently downtrodden to be obliged to change a baby's diaper and take a turn with the night feeding. Here is an excerpt from the sixteenth century finally disproving that notion. (It is only fair to mention that Martin Luther was not really a misogynist, nor was he attacking marriage. The remainder of the essay exhorts the reader to consider all the onerous duties of child care as services to God.)

Alas, must I rock the baby, wash its diapers, make its bed, smell its stench, stay up nights with it, take care of it when it cries, heal its rashes and sores, and on top of that care for my wife, provide for her, labor at my trade, take care of this and take care of that, do this and do that, endure this and endure that, and whatever else of bitterness and drudgery married life involves? What, should I make such a prisoner of myself? Oh you poor, wretched fellow, have you taken a wife? Fie, fie upon such wretchedness and bitterness! It is better to remain free and lead a peaceful, carefree life.

BUT THOU, MY BABE

From FROST AT MIDNIGHT

Samuel Taylor Coleridge

Looking at his new baby, what father has not felt something of what Coleridge expresses in this fragment from "Frost at Midnight"—a feeling that everything no longer possible for himself still lies ahead for this new creature.

Dear Babe, that sleepest cradled by my side,
Whose gentle breathings, heard in this deep calm,
Fill up the interspersed vacancies
And momentary pauses of the thought!
My babe so beautiful it thrills my heart
With tender gladness, thus to look at thee,
And think that thou shalt learn far other lore,
And in far other scenes! For I was reared
In the great city, pent 'mid cloisters dim,
And saw nought lovely but the sky and stars.
But *thou*, my babe! shalt wander like a breeze
By lakes and sandy shores, beneath the crags
Of ancient mountains, and beneath the clouds,
Which image in their bulk both lakes and shores
And mountain crags: so shalt thou see and hear
The lovely shapes and sounds intelligible
Of that eternal language, which thy God
Utters, who from eternity doth teach
Himself in all, and all things in himself.
Great universal Teacher! he shall mould
Thy spirit, and by giving make it ask.

DOMBEY AND SON

From DOMBEY AND SON

Charles Dickens

Dickens' novel Dombey and Son *opens with a literary* tour de force: *an amazing comparison between a father of eight-and-forty years and a son of eight-and-forty minutes!*

Dombey sat in the corner of the darkened room in the great armchair by the bedside and Son lay tucked up warm in a little basket bedstead, carefully disposed on a low settee immediately in front of the fire and close to it, as if his constitution were analogous to that of a muffin, and it was essential to toast him brown while he was very new.

Dombey was about eight-and-forty years of age. Son about eight-and-forty minutes. Dombey was rather bald, rather red, and though a handsome well-made man, too stern and pompous in appearance to be prepossessing. Son was very bald, and very red, and, though (of course) an undeniably fine infant, somewhat crushed and spotty in his general effect, as yet. On the brow of Dombey, Time and his brother Care had set some marks, as on a tree that was to come down in good time—remorseless twins they are for striding through their human forests, notching as they go—while the countenance of Son was crossed and recrossed with a thousand little creases, which the same deceitful Time would take delight in smoothing out and wearing away with the flat part of his scythe, as a preparation of the surface for his deeper operations.

Dombey, exulting in the long-looked-for event, jingled and jingled the heavy gold watch-chain that depended from below his trim blue coat, whereof the buttons sparkled phosphorescently in the feeble rays of the distant fire. Son, with his little fists curled up and clenched, seemed, in his feeble way, to be squaring at existence for having come upon him so unexpectedly.

"The house will once again, Mrs. Dombey," said Mr. Dombey, "be not only in name but in fact Dombey and Son; Dom-bey and Son!" The words had such a softening influence that he appended a term of endearment to Mrs. Dombey's name (though not without some hesitation, as being a man but little used to that form of address) and said, "Mrs. Dombey, my—my dear."

A transient flush of faint surprise overspread the sick lady's face as she raised her eyes towards him.

"He will be christened Paul, my—Mrs. Dombey—of course."

She feebly echoed, "Of course," or rather expressed it by the motion of her lips, and closed her eyes again.

"His father's name, Mrs. Dombey, and his grandfather's! I wish his grandfather were alive this day!" And again he said "Dom-bey and Son," in exactly the same tone as before.

Those three words conveyed the one idea of Mr. Dombey's life. The earth was made for Dombey and Son to trade in, and the sun and moon were made to give them light. Rivers and seas were formed to float their ships; rainbows gave them promise of fair weather; winds blew for or against their enterprises; stars and planets circled in their orbits to preserve inviolate a system of which they were the centre. Common abbreviations took new meanings in his eyes, and had sole reference to them: A.D. had no concern with Anno Domini, but stood for Anno Dombei—and Son.

He had risen, as had his father before him, in the course of life and death, from Son to Dombey, and for nearly twenty years had been the sole representative of the firm. Of those years he had been married ten—married, as some said, to a lady with no heart to give him; whose happiness was in the past, and who was content to bind her broken spirit to the dutiful and meek endurance of the present. Such idle talk was little likely to reach the ears of Mr. Dombey, whom it nearly concerned; and probably no one in the world would have received it with such utter incredulity as he, if it had reached him. Dombey and Son had often dealt in hides, but never in hearts. They left that fancy ware to boys and girls and boarding-schools and books. Mr. Dombey would have reasoned that a matrimonial alliance with himself *must*, in the nature of things, be gratifying and honourable to any woman of common sense; that the hope of giving birth to a new partner in such a house could not fail to awaken a glorious and stirring ambition in the breast of the least ambitious of her sex; that Mrs. Dombey had entered on that social contract of matrimony—almost necessarily part of a genteel and wealthy station, even without reference to the perpetuation of family firms—with her eyes fully open to these advantages; that Mrs. Dombey had had daily practical knowledge of his position in society; that Mrs. Dombey had always sat at the head of his table, and done the honours of his house in a remarkably ladylike and becoming manner; that Mrs. Dombey must have been happy; that she couldn't help it.

Or, at all events, with one drawback. Yes. That he would have allowed. With only one; but that one certainly involving much. They had been married ten years, and until this present day, on which Mr. Dombey sat jingling and jingling his heavy gold watch-chain in the great arm-chair by the side of the bed, had had no issue.

—To speak of; none worth mentioning. There had been a girl some six years before, and the child, who had stolen into the chamber unobserved, was now crouching timidly in a corner whence she could see her mother's face. But what was a girl to Dombey and Son! In the capital of the House's name and dignity, such a child was merely a piece of base coin that couldn't be invested—a bad boy—nothing more.

Mr. Dombey's cup of satisfaction was so full at this moment, however, that he felt he could afford a drop or two of its contents, even to sprinkle on the dust in the bypath of his little daughter.

So he said, "Florence, you may go and look at your pretty brother, if you like, I dare say. Don't touch him!"

The child glanced keenly at the blue coat and stiff white cravat, which, with a pair of creaking boots and a very loud ticking watch, embodied her idea of a father; but her eyes returned to her mother's face immediately, and she neither moved nor answered.

Next moment, the lady had opened her eyes and seen the child; and the child had run towards her; and, standing on tiptoe, the better to hide her face in her embrace, had clung about her with a desperate affection very much at variance with her years.

"Oh, Lord bless me!" said Mr. Dombey, rising testily, "a very ill-advised and feverish proceeding this, I am sure. I had better ask Doctor Peps if he'll have the goodness to stop upstairs again perhaps. I'll go down. I needn't beg you," he added, pausing for a moment at the settee before the fire, "to take particular care of this young gentleman, Mrs. ——"

"Blockitt, sir?" suggested the nurse, a simpering piece of faded gentility, who did not presume to state her name as a fact, but merely offered it as a mild suggestion.

"Of this gentleman, Mrs. Blockitt."

"No, sir, indeed. I remember when Miss Florence was born—"

"Aye, aye, aye," said Mr. Dombey, bending over the basket bedstead, and slightly bending his brows at the same time. "Miss Florence was all very well, but this is another matter. This young gentleman has to accomplish a destiny. A destiny, little fellow!" As he thus apostrophized the infant he raised one of his hands to his lips, and kissed it; then, seeming to fear that the action involved some compromise of his dignity, went, awkwardly enough, away.

PATERNITY IS A GREAT EXPERIENCE

From THE AUTOBIOGRAPHY OF BERTRAND RUSSELL 1914–1944

Letter from Joseph Conrad to Bertrand Russell

A letter from the novelist Joseph Conrad to the philosopher Bertrand Russell upon the occasion of the birth of Russell's first baby reveals that even great men are flattered by the simple honor of acquiring a namesake.

My Dear Russell:

Jessie must have sent yesterday our congratulations and words of welcome to the "comparative stranger" who has come to stay with you (and take charge of the household as you will soon discover). Yes! Paternity is a great experience of which the least that can be said is that it is eminently worth having—if only for the deepened sense of fellowship with all men it gives one. It is the only experience perhaps whose universality does not make it common but invests it with a sort of grandeur on that very account. My affection goes out to you both, to him who is without speech and thought as yet and to you who have spoken to men profoundly with effect and authority about the nature of the mind. For your relation to each other will have its poignant moments arising out of the very love and loyalty binding you to each other.

Of all the incredible things that come to pass this—that there should be one day a Russell bearing mine for one of his names is surely the most marvelous. Not even my horoscope could have disclosed that for I verily believe that all the sensible stars would have refused to combine in that extravagant manner over my cradle. However it has come to pass (to the surprise of the Universe) and all I can say is that I am profoundly touched—more than I can express—that I should have been present to your mind in that way and at such a time.

Please kiss your wife's hand for me and tell her that in the obscure bewildered masculine way (which is not quite unintelligent however) I take part in her gladness. Since your delightful visit here she was much in our thoughts—and I will confess we felt very optimistic. She has justified it fully and it is a great joy to think of her with two men in the house. She will have her hands full presently. I can only hope that John Conrad has been born with a disposition towards indulgence which he will consistently exercise towards his parents. I don't think that I can wish you anything better and so with my dear love to all three of you, I am

always yours,
JOSEPH CONRAD

BABY'S BATH

From TALES OF THE FIVE TOWNS

Arnold Bennett

> *Mr. Blackshaw had gone to extreme lengths to arrange to be home in time for his baby's bath . . . and then the tragedy occurred that brought him to the very depths of despair (or was it the very heights of comedy?).*

Mrs. Blackshaw had a baby. It would be an exaggeration to say that the baby interested the entire town, Bursley being an ancient, *blasé* sort of borough of some thirty thousand inhabitants. Babies, in fact, arrived in Bursley at the rate of more than a thousand every year. Nevertheless, a few weeks after the advent of Mrs. Blackshaw's baby, when the medical officer of health reported to the Town Council that the births for the month amounted to ninety-five, and that the birth-rate of Bursley compared favourably with the birth-rates of the sister towns, Hanbridge, Knype, Longshaw, and Turnhill—when the medical officer read these memorable words at the monthly meeting of the Council, and the *Staffordshire Signal* reported them, and Mrs. Blackshaw perused them, a blush of pride spread over Mrs. Blackshaw's face, and she picked up the baby's left foot and gave it a little peck of a kiss. She could not help feeling that the real solid foundation of that formidable and magnificent output of babies was her baby. She could not help feeling that she had done something for the town—had caught the public eye.

As for the baby, except that it was decidedly superior to the

63

average infant in external appearance and pleasantness of disposition, it was, in all essential characteristics, a typical baby—that is to say, it was purely sensuous and it lived the life of the senses. It was utterly selfish. It never thought of anyone but itself. It honestly imagined itself to be the centre of the created universe. It was convinced that the rest of the universe had been brought into existence solely for the convenience and pleasure of it—the baby. When it wanted anything, it made no secret of the fact, and it was always utterly unscrupulous in trying to get what it wanted. If it could have obtained the moon, it would have upset all the astronomers of Europe and made *Whitaker's Almanack* unsaleable without a pang. It had no god but its stomach. It never bothered its head about higher things. It was a bully and a coward, and it treated women as beings of a lower order than men. In a word, it was that ideal creature, sung of the poets, from which we gradually sink and fall away as we grow older.

At the age of six months it had quite a lot of hair, and a charming rosy expanse at the back of its neck, caused through lying on its back in contemplation of its own importance. It didn't know the date of the Battle of Hastings, but it knew with the certainty of absolute knowledge that it was the master of the house, and that the activity of the house revolved round it.

Now, the baby loved its bath. In any case its bath would have been an affair of immense and intricate pomp; but the fact that it loved its bath raised the interest and significance of the bath to the nth power. The bath took place at five o'clock in the evening, and it is not too much to say that the idea of the bath was immanent in the very atmosphere of the house. When you have an appointment with the dentist at five o'clock in the afternoon, the idea of the appointment is immanent in your mind from the first moment of your awakening. Conceive that an appointment with the dentist implies heavenly joy instead of infernal pain, and you will have a notion of the daily state of Mrs. Blackshaw and Emmie (the nurse) with regard to the baby's bath.

Even at ten in the morning Emmie would be keeping an eye on the kitchen fire, lest the cook might let it out. And shortly after noon Mrs. Blackshaw would be keeping an eye on the thermometer in the bedroom where the bath occurred. From four o'clock onwards the clocks in the house were spied on and overlooked like suspected persons; but they were used to that, because the baby had his sterilized milk every two hours. I have at length allowed you to penetrate the secret of his sex.

And so at five o'clock precisely the august and exciting ceremony began in the best bedroom. A bright fire was burning (the month being December), and the carefully-shaded electric lights were also burning. A large bath-towel was spread in a convenient place on the floor, and on the towel were two chairs facing each other, and a table. On one chair was the bath, and on the other was Mrs. Blackshaw with her sleeves rolled up, and on Mrs. Blackshaw was another towel, and on that towel was Roger (the baby). On the table were zinc ointment, vaseline, scentless eau de Cologne, Castile soap, and a powder-puff.

Emmie having pretty nearly filled the bath with a combination of hot and cold waters, dropped the floating thermometer into it, and then added more waters until the thermometer indicated the precise temperature proper for a baby's bath. But you are not to imagine that Mrs. Blackshaw trusted a mere thermometer. No. She put her arm in the water up to the elbow. She reckoned the sensitive skin near the elbow was worth forty thermometers.

Emmie was chiefly an audience. Mrs. Blackshaw had engaged her as nurse, but she could have taught a nigger-boy to do all that she allowed the nurse to do. During the bath Mrs. Blackshaw and Emmie hated and scorned each other, despite their joy. Emmie was twice Mrs. Blackshaw's age, besides being twice her weight, and she knew twice as much about babies as Mrs. Blackshaw did. However, Mrs. Blackshaw had the terrific advantage of being the mother of that particular infant, and she could always end an argument when she chose, and in her own favour. It was unjust, and Emmie felt it to be unjust; but this is not a world of justice.

Roger, though not at all precocious, was perfectly aware of the carefully-concealed hostility between his mother and his nurse, and often, with his usual unscrupulousness, he used it for his own ends. He was sitting upon his mother's knees toying with the edge of the bath, already tasting its delights in advance. Mrs. Blackshaw undressed the upper half of him, and then she laid him on the flat of his back and undressed the lower half of him, but keeping some wisp of a garment round his equatorial regions. And then she washed his face with a sponge and the Castile soap, very gently, but not half gently enough for Emmie, nor half gently enough for Roger, for Roger looked upon this part of the business as insulting and superfluous. He breathed hard and kicked his feet nearly off.

"Yes, it's dreadful having our face washed, isn't it?" said Mrs. Blackshaw, with her sleeves up, and her hair by this time down. "We don't like it, do we? Yes, yes."

Emmie grunted, without a sound, and yet Mrs. Blackshaw heard her, and finished that face quickly and turned to the hands.

"Potato-gardens every day," she said. "Evzy day-day. Enough of that, Colonel!" (For, after all, she had plenty of spirit.) "Fat little creases! Fat little creases! There! He likes that! There! Feet! Feet! Feet and legs! Then our back! And then *whup* we shall go into the bath! That's it. Kick! Kick your mother!"

And she turned him over.

"Incredible bungler!" said the eyes of the nurse. "Can't she turn him over neater than that?"

"Harridan!" said the eyes of Mrs. Blackshaw. "I wouldn't let you bath him for twenty thousand pounds!"

Roger continued to breathe hard, as if his mother were a horse and he were rubbing her down.

"Now! Zoop! Whup!" cried his mother, and having deprived him of his final rag, she picked him up and sat him in the bath, and he was divinely happy, and so were the women. He appeared a gross little animal in the bath, all the tints of his flesh shimmering under the electric light. His chest was superb, but the rolled and creased bigness of his inordinate stomach was simply appalling, not to mention his great thighs and calves. The truth was, he had grown so that if he had been only a little bit bigger, he would have burst the bath. He resembled an old man who had been steadily eating too much for about forty years.

His two womenfolk now candidly and openly worshipped him, forgetting sectarian differences.

And he splashed. Oh! he splashed. You see, he had learnt how to splash, and he had certainly got an inkling that to splash was wicked and messy. So he splashed—in his mother's face, in Emmie's face, in the fire. He pretty well splashed the fire out. Ten minutes before, the bedroom had been tidy, a thing of beauty. It was now naught but a wild welter of towels, socks, binders— peninsulas of clothes nearly surrounded by water.

Finally his mother seized him again, and, rearing his little legs up out of the water, immersed the whole of his inflated torso beneath the surface.

"Hallo!" she exclaimed. "Did the water run over his mouf? Did it?"

"Angels and ministers of grace defend us! How clumsy she is!" commented the eyes of Emmie.

"There! I fink that's about long enough for this kind of wevver," said the mother.

"I should think it was! There's almost a crust of ice on the water now!" the nurse refrained from saying.

And Roger, full of regrets, was wrenched out of the bath. He had ceased breathing hard while in the water, but he began again immediately he emerged.

"We don't like our face wiped, do we?" said his mother on his behalf. "We want to go back into that bath. We like it. It's more fun than anything that happens all day long! Eh? That old dandruff's coming up in fine style. It's a peeling off like anything."

And all the while she wiped him, patted eau de Cologne into him with the flat of her hand, and rubbed zinc ointment into him, and massaged him, and powdered him, and turned him over and over and over, till he was thoroughly well basted and cooked. And he kept on breathing hard.

Then he sneezed, amid general horror!

"I told you so!" the nurse didn't say, and she rushed to the bed where all the idol's beautiful, clean, aired things were lying safe from splashings, and handed a flannel shirt, about two inches in length, to Mrs. Blackshaw. And Mrs. Blackshaw rolled the left sleeve of it into a wad and stuck it over his arm, and his poor little vaccination marks were hidden from view till next morning. Roger protested.

"We don't like clothes, do we?" said his mother. "We want to tumble back into our tub. We aren't much for clothes anyway. We'se a little Hottentot, aren't we?"

And she gradually covered him with one garment or another until there was nothing left of him but his head and his hands and feet. And she sat him up on her knees, so as to fasten his things behind. And then it might have been observed that he was no longer breathing hard, but giving vent to a sound between a laugh and a cry, while sucking his thumb and gazing round the room.

"That's our little affected cry that we start for our milk, isn't it?" his mother explained to him.

And he agreed that it was.

And before Emmie could fly across the room for the bottle, all ready and waiting, his mouth, in the shape of a perfect rectangle, had monopolized five-sixths of his face, and he was scarlet and bellowing with impatience.

He took the bottle like a tiger his prey, and seized his mother's hand that held the bottle, and he furiously pumped the milk into that insatiable gulf of a stomach. But he found time to gaze about the room too. A tear stood in each roving eye, caused by the effort of feeding.

"Yes, that's it," said his mother. "Now look round and see what's happening. Curiosity! Well, if you *will* bob your head, I can't help it."

"Of course you can!" the nurse didn't say.

Then he put his finger into his mouth side by side with the bottle, and gagged himself, and choked, and gave a terrible— excuse the word—hiccough. After which he seemed to lose interest in the milk, and the pumping operations slackened and then ceased.

"Goosey!" whispered his mother, "getting seepy? Is the sand-man throwing sand in our eyes? Old Sandman at it? Sh—" . . . He had gone.

Emmie took him. The women spoke in whispers. And Mrs. Blackshaw, after a day spent in being a mother, reconstituted herself a wife, and began to beautify herself for her husband.

II

Yes, there was a Mr. Blackshaw, and with Mr. Blackshaw the tragedy of the bath commences. Mr. Blackshaw was a very important young man. Indeed, it is within the mark to say that, next to his son, he was the most important young man in Bursley. For Mr. Blackshaw was the manager of the newly-opened Municipal Electricity Works. And the Municipal Electricity had created more excitement and interest than anything since the 1887 Jubilee, when an ox was roasted whole in the market-place and turned bad in the process. Had Bursley been a Swiss village, or a French country town, or a hamlet in Arizona, it would have had its electricity fifteen years ago, but being only a progressive English borough, with an annual value of a hundred and fifty thousand pounds, it struggled on with gas till well into the twentieth century. Its great neighbour Hanbridge had become acquainted with electricity in the nineteenth century.

All the principal streets and squares, and every decent shop that Hanbridge competition had left standing, and many private houses, now lighted themselves by electricity, and the result was splendid and glaring and coldly yellow. Mr. Blackshaw developed into the hero of the hour. People looked at him in the street as though he had been the discoverer and original maker of electricity. And if the manager of the gasworks had not already committed murder, it was because the manager of the gasworks had a right sense of what was due to his position as vicar's churchwarden at St. Peter's Church.

But greatness has its penalties. And the chief penalty of Mr. Blackshaw's greatness was that he could not see Roger have his nightly bath. It was impossible for Mr. Blackshaw to quit his arduous and responsible post before seven o'clock in the evening. Later on, when things were going more smoothly, he might be able to get away; but then, later on, his son's bath would not be so amusing and agreeable as it then, by all reports, was. The baby was, of course, bathed on Sunday nights, but Sunday afternoon and evening Mr. Blackshaw was obliged to spend with his invalid mother at Longshaw. It was on the sole condition of his weekly presence thus in her house that she had consented not to live with the married pair. And so Mr. Blackshaw could not witness Roger's bath. He adored Roger. He understood Roger. He weighed, nursed, and fed Roger. He was "up" in all the newest theories of infant rearing. In short, Roger was his passion, and he knew everything of Roger except Roger's bath. And when his wife met him at the front door of a night at seven-thirty and launched instantly into a description of the wonders, delights, and excitations of Roger's latest bath, Mr. Blackshaw was ready to tear his hair with disappointment and frustration.

"I suppose you couldn't put it off for a couple of hours one night, May?" he suggested at supper on the evening of the particular bath described above.

"Sidney!" protested Mrs. Blackshaw, pained.

Mr. Blackshaw felt that he had gone too far, and there was a silence.

"Well!" said Mr. Blackshaw at length, "I have just made up my mind. I'm going to see that kid's bath, and, what's more, I'm going to see it tomorrow. I don't care what happens."

"But how shall you manage to get away, darling?"

"You will telephone to me about a quarter of an hour before you're ready to begin, and I'll pretend it's something very urgent, and scoot off."

"Well, that will be lovely, darling!" said Mrs. Blackshaw. "I *would* like you to see him in the bath, just once! He looks so—"

And so on.

The next day, Mr. Blackshaw, that fearsome autocrat of the Municipal Electricity Works, was saying to himself all day that at five o'clock he was going to assist at the spectacle of his wonderful son's bath. The prospect inspired him. So much so that every hand on the place was doing its utmost in fear and trembling, and the whole affair was running with the precision and smoothness of a watch.

From four o'clock onwards, Mr. Blackshaw, in the solemn, illuminated privacy of the managerial office, safe behind glass partitions, could no more contain his excitement. He hovered in front of the telephone, waiting for it to ring. Then, at a quarter to five, just when he felt he couldn't stand it any longer, and was about to ring up his wife instead of waiting for her to ring him up, he saw a burly shadow behind the glass door, and gave a desolate sigh. That shadow could only be thrown by one person, and that person was his Worship the Mayor of Bursley. His Worship entered the private office with mayoral assurance, pulling in his wake a stout old lady whom he introduced as his aunt from Wolverhampton. And he calmly proposed that Mr. Blackshaw should show the mayoral aunt over the new Electricity Works!

Mr. Blackshaw was sick of showing people over the Works. Moreover, he naturally despised the Mayor. All permanent officials of municipalities thoroughly despise their mayors (up their sleeves). A mayor is here today and gone tomorrow, whereas a permanent official is permanent. A mayor knows nothing about anything except his chain and the rules of debate, and he is, further, a tedious and meddlesome person—in the opinion of permanent officials.

So Mr. Blackshaw's fury at the inept appearance of the Mayor and the mayoral aunt at this critical juncture may be imagined. The worst of it was, he didn't know how to refuse the Mayor.

Then the telephone-bell rang.

"Excuse me," said Mr. Blackshaw, with admirably simulated politeness, going to the instrument. "Are you there? Who is it?"

"It's me, darling," came the thin voice of his wife far away at Bleakridge. "The water's just getting hot. We're nearly ready. Can you come now?"

"By Jove! Wait a moment!" exclaimed Mr. Blackshaw, and then turning to his visitors, "Did you hear that?"

"No," said the Mayor.

"All those three new dynamos that they've got at the Hanbridge Electricity Works have just broken down. I knew they would. I told them they would!"

"Dear, dear!" said the Mayor of Bursley, secretly delighted by this disaster to a disdainful rival. "Why! They'll have the town in darkness. What are they going to do?"

"They want me to go over at once. But, of course, I can't. At least, I must give myself the pleasure of showing you and this lady over our Works first."

"Nothing of the kind, Mr. Blackshaw!" said the Mayor. "Go at once. Go at once. If Bursley can be of any assistance to Hanbridge in such a crisis, I shall be only too pleased. We will come tomorrow, won't we, auntie?"

Mr. Blackshaw addressed the telephone.

"The Mayor is here, with a lady, and I was just about to show them over the Works, but his Worship insists that I come at once."

"Certainly," the Mayor put in pompously.

"Wonders will never cease," came the thin voice of Mrs. Blackshaw through the telephone. "It's very nice of the old thing! What's his lady friend like?"

"Not like anything. Unique!" replied Mr. Blackshaw.

"Young?" came the voice.

"Dates from the 'thirties," said Mr. Blackshaw. "I'm coming." And he rang off.

"I didn't know there was any electric machinery as old as that," said the mayoral aunt.

"We'll just look about us a bit," the Mayor remarked. "Don't lose a moment, Mr. Blackshaw."

And Mr. Blackshaw hurried off, wondering vaguely how he should explain the lie when it was found out, but not caring much. After all, he could easily ascribe the episode to the trick of some practical joker.

III

He arrived at his commodious and electrically lit residence in the very nick of time, and full to overflowing with innocent paternal glee. Was he not about to see Roger's tub? Roger was just ready to be carried up-stairs as Mr. Blackshaw's latchkey turned in the door.

"Wait a sec!" cried Mr. Blackshaw to his wife, who had the child in her arms, "I'll carry him up."

And he threw away his hat, stick, and overcoat and grabbed ecstatically at the infant. And he had got perhaps half-way up the stairs, when lo! the electric light went out. Every electric light in the house went out.

"Great Scott!" breathed Mr. Blackshaw, aghast.

He pulled aside the blind of the window at the turn of the stairs, and peered forth. The street was as black as your hat, or nearly so.

"Great Scott!" he repeated. "May, get candles."

Something had evidently gone wrong at the Works. Just his luck! He had quitted the Works for a quarter of an hour, and the current had failed!

Of course, the entire house was instantly in an uproar, turned upside down, startled out of its life. But a few candles soon calmed its transports. And at length Mr. Blackshaw gained the bedroom in safety, with the offspring of his desires comfortable in a shawl.

"Give him to me," said May shortly. "I suppose you'll have to go back to the Works at once?"

Mr. Blackshaw paused, and then nerved himself; but while he was pausing, May, glancing at the two feeble candles, remarked: "It's very tiresome. I'm sure I shan't be able to see properly."

"No!" almost shouted Mr. Blackshaw. "I'll watch this kid have his bath or I'll die for it! I don't care if all the Five Towns are in darkness. I don't care if the Mayor's aunt has got caught in a dynamo and is suffering horrible tortures. I've come to see this bath business, and dashed if I don't see it!"

"Well, don't stand between the bath and the fire, dearest," said May coldly.

Meanwhile, Emmie, having pretty nearly filled the bath with a combination of hot and cold water, dropped the floating thermometer into it and then added more waters until the thermometer indicated the precise temperature proper for a baby's bath. But you are not to imagine that Mrs. Blackshaw trusted a mere thermometer—

She did not, however, thrust her bared arm into the water this time. No! Roger, who never cried before his bath, was crying, was indubitably crying. And he cried louder and louder.

"Stand where he can't see you, dearest. He isn't used to you at bath-time," said Mrs. Blackshaw still coldly. "Are you, my pet? There! There!"

Mr. Blackshaw effaced himself, feeling a fool. But Roger continued to cry. He cried himself purple. He cried till the veins stood out on his forehead and his mouth was like a map of Australia. He cried himself into a monster of ugliness. Neither mother nor nurse could do anything with him at all.

"I think you've upset him, dearest," said Mrs. Blackshaw even more coldly. "Hadn't you better go?".

"Well—" protested the father.

"I think you had better go," said Mrs. Blackshaw, adding no term of endearment, and visibly controlling herself with difficulty.

And Mr. Blackshaw went. He had to go. He went out into the unelectric night. He headed for the Works, not because he cared two-pence, at that moment, about the accident at the Works, whatever it was; but simply because the Works was the only place to go to. And even outside in the dark street he could hear the rousing accents of his progeny.

People were talking to each other as they groped about in the road, and either making jokes at the expense of the new Electricity Department, or frankly cursing it with true Five Towns directness of speech. And as Mr. Blackshaw went down the hill into the town his heart was as black as the street itself with rage and disappointment. He had made his child cry!

Someone stopped him.

"Eh, Mester Blackshaw!" said a voice, and under the voice a hand struck a match to light a pipe. "What's th' maning o' this eclipse as you'm treating uz to?"

Mr. Blackshaw looked right through the inquirer—a way he had when his brain was working hard. And he suddenly smiled by light of the match.

"*That child wasn't crying because I was there*," said Mr. Blackshaw with solemn relief. "*Not at all! He was crying because he didn't understand the candles. He isn't used to candles, and they frightened him."*

And he began to hurry towards the Works.

At the same instant the electric light returned to Bursley. The current was resumed.

"That's better," said Mr. Blackshaw, sighing.

A POET'S WELCOME TO HIS LOVE-BEGOTTEN DAUGHTER

(THE FIRST INSTANCE THAT ENTITLED HIM TO THE VENERABLE APPELATION OF FATHER)

Robert Burns

The "wean" (wee one) of this humorous lyric by the Scottish poet Robert Burns was the poet's daughter Elizabeth, born in November, 1784 to Elizabeth Paten, a servant at the Burns' family farm of Lochlie. A few translations of unfamiliar words in the Scottish dialect follow, but the joyful, hopeful, generous feelings of a new father emerge clearly even without translation.

Thou's welcome, wean! Mishanter[1] fa' me
If thoughts o' thee or yet thy mammie
Shall ever daunton[2] me or awe me,
       My sweet, wee lady,
Or if I blush when thou shalt ca' me
       Tyta or daddie!

What tho' they ca' me fornicater,
An' tease my name in kintra clatter?[3]
The mair they talk, I'm kend[4] the better;
       E'en let them clash!
An auld wife's tongue's a feckless[5] matter
       To gie ane fash.[6]

Welcome, my bonny, sweet, wee dochter!
Tho' ye come here a wee unsought for,
And tho' your comin I hae fought for
                    Baith kirk and queir;[7]
Yet by my faith, ye're no unwrought for—
                    That I shall swear!

Sweet fruit o' monie a merry dint,
My funny toil is no a'tint;[8]
Tho' thou cam to the warl' asklent,[9]
                    Which fools may skeff at,
In my last plack[10] thy part's be in't
                    The better half o't.

Tho' I should be the waur[11] bestead
Thou's be as braw[12] and bienly clad,[13]
And thy young years as nicely bred
                    Wi' education,
As onie brat o' wedlock's bed
                    In a' thy station.

Wee image o' my bonie Betty,
As fatherly I kiss and daut[14] thee,
As dear and near my heart I set thee,
                    Wi' as guid will,
As a' the priests had seen me get thee
                    That's out o' Hell.

Gude grant that thou may ay inherit
Thy mither's looks an' gracefu' merit
An' thy poor, worthless daddie's spirit
                    Without his failins!
'Twill please me mair to see thee heir it
                    Than stocket mailins.[15]

And if thou be what I wad hae thee,
An' tak the counsel I shall gie thee,
I'll never rue my trouble we' thee—
                    The cost nor shame o't
But be a loving father to thee,
                    And brag the name o't.

1. mishanter—misfortune
2. daunton—to daunt
3. kintra clatter—country gossip
4. kend—known
5. feckless—weak, futile
6. To gie ane fash—to make one worry
7. kirk and queir—church and choir
8. no a'tint—not a loss
9. asklent—irregularly
10. plack—the smallest Scottish coin
11. waur—worse
12. braw—fine, handsome
13. bienly clad—well-dressed
14. daut—fondle
15. stocket mailins—stocked farms

Part III

A LIFE BEGINS

ADAM

From WELCOME TO THE MONKEY HOUSE

Kurt Vonnegut, Jr.

"It's the most wonderful thing in the world," said the father to the doctor who had just safely delivered the baby: a fairly universal sentiment for first fathers. But there is a distinct possibility, in this early story by Kurt Vonnegut, Jr., that this time indeed it was the most wonderful thing in the world.

It was midnight in a Chicago lying-in hospital.

"Mr. Sousa," said the nurse, "your wife had a girl. You can see the baby in about twenty minutes."

"I know, I know, I know," said Mr. Sousa, a sullen gorilla, plainly impatient with having a tiresome and familiar routine explained to him. He snapped his fingers. "Girl! Seven, now. Seven girls I got now. A houseful of women. I can beat the stuffings out of ten men my own size. But, what do I get? Girls."

"Mr. Knechtmann," said the nurse to the other man in the room. She pronounced the name, as almost all Americans did, as colorless Netman. "I'm sorry. Still no word on your wife. She is keeping us waiting, isn't she?" She grinned glassily and left.

Sousa turned on Knechtmann. "Some little son of a gun like you, Netman, you want a boy, bing! You got one. Want a football team, bing, bing, bing, eleven, you got it." He stomped out of the room.

The man he left behind, all alone now, was Heinz Knechtmann,

81

a presser in a dry-cleaning plant, a small man with thin wrists and a bad spine that kept him slightly hunched, as though forever weary. His face was long and big-nosed and thin-lipped, but was so overcast with good-humored humility as to be beautiful. His eyes were large and brown, and deep-set and long-lashed. He was only twenty-two, but seemed and felt much older. He had died a little as each member of his family had been led away and killed by the Nazis, until only in him, at the age of ten, had life and the name of Knechtmann shared a soul. He and his wife, Avchen, had grown up behind barbed wire.

He had been staring at the walls of the waiting room for twelve hours now, since noon, when his wife's labor pains had become regular, the surges of slow rollers coming in from the sea a mile apart, from far, far away. This would be his second child. The last time he had waited, he had waited on a straw tick in a displaced-persons camp in Germany. The child, Karl Knechtmann, named after Heinz's father, had died, and with it, once more, had died the name of one of the finest cellists ever to have lived.

When the numbness of weary wishing lifted momentarily during this second vigil, Heinz's mind was a medley of proud family names, gone, all gone, that could be brought to life again in this new being—if it lived. Peter Knechtmann, the surgeon; Kroll Knechtmann, the botanist; Friederich Knechtmann, the playwright. Dimly recalled uncles. Or if it was a girl, and if it lived, it would be Helga Knechtmann, Heinz's mother, and she would learn to play the harp as Heinz's mother had, and for all Heinz's ugliness, she would be beautiful. The Knechtmann men were all ugly, the Knechtmann women were all lovely as angels, though not all angels. It had always been so—for hundreds and hundreds of years.

"Mr. Netman," said the nurse, "it's a boy, and your wife is fine. She's resting now. You can see her in the morning. You can see the baby in twenty minutes."

Heinz looked up dumbly.

"It weighs five pounds nine ounces." She was gone again, with the same prim smile and officious, squeaking footsteps.

"Knechtmann," murmured Heinz, standing and bowing slightly to the wall. "The name is Knechtmann." He bowed again and gave a smile that was courtly and triumphant. He spoke the name with an exaggerated Old World pronunciation, like a foppish footman announcing the arrival of nobility, a guttural drum roll, unsoftened for American ears. *"KhhhhhhhhhhhhhhhNECHT!mannnnnnnnn."*

"Mr. Netman?" A very young doctor with a pink face and close-cropped red hair stood in the waiting-room door. There were circles under his eyes, and he spoke through a yawn.

"Dr. Powers!" cried Heinz, clasping the man's right hand between both of his. "Thank God, thank God, thank God, and thank you."

"Um," said Dr. Powers, and he managed to smile wanly.

"There isn't anything wrong, is there?"

"Wrong?" said Powers. "No, no. Everything's fine. If I look down in the mouth, it's because I've been up for thirty-six hours straight." He closed his eyes, and leaned against the doorframe. "No, no trouble with your wife," he said in a faraway voice. "She's made for having babies. Regular pop-up toaster. Like rolling off a log. Schnip-schnap."

"She is?" said Heinz incredulously.

Dr. Powers shook his head, bringing himself back to consciousness. "My mind—conked out completely. Sousa—I got your wife confused with Mrs. Sousa. They finished in a dead heat. Netman, you're Netman. Sorry. Your wife's the one with pelvis trouble."

"Malnutrition as a child," said Heinz.

"Yeah. Well, the baby came normally, but, if you're going to have another one, it'd better be a Caesarean. Just to be on the safe side."

"I can't thank you enough," said Heinz passionately.

Dr. Powers licked his lips, and fought to keep his eyes open. "Uh huh. 'S O.K.," he said thickly. " 'Night. Luck." He shambled out into the corridor.

The nurse stuck her head into the waiting room. "You can see your baby, Mr. Netman."

"Doctor—" said Heinz, hurrying out into the corridor, wanting to shake Powers' hand again so that Powers would know what a magnificent thing he'd done. "It's the most wonderful thing that ever happened." The elevator doors slithered shut between them before Dr. Powers could show a glimmer of response.

"This way," said the nurse. "Turn left at the end of the hall, and you'll find the nursery window there. Write your name on a piece of paper and hold it against the glass."

Heinz made the trip by himself, without seeing another human being until he reached the end. There, on the other side of a large glass panel, he saw a hundred of them cupped in shallow canvas buckets and arranged in a square block of straight ranks and files.

Heinz wrote his name on the back of a laundry slip and pressed it to the window. A fat and placid nurse looked at the paper, not at Heinz's face, and missed seeing his wide smile, missed an urgent invitation to share for a moment his ecstasy.

She grasped one of the buckets and wheeled it before the window. She turned away again, once more missing the smile.

"Hello, hello, hello, little Knechtmann," said Heinz to the red prune on the other side of the glass. His voice echoed down the hard, bare corridor, and came back to him with embarrassing loudness. He blushed and lowered his voice. "Little Peter, little Kroll," he said softly, "little Friederich—and there's Helga in you, too. Little spark of Knechtmann, you little treasure house. Everything is saved in you."

"I'm afraid you'll have to be more quiet," said a nurse, sticking her head out from one of the rooms.

"Sorry," said Heinz. "I'm very sorry." He fell silent, and contented himself with tapping lightly on the window with a fingernail, trying to get the child to look at him. Young Knechtmann would not look, wouldn't share the moment, and after a few minutes the nurse took him away again.

Heinz beamed as he rode on the elevator and as he crossed the hospital lobby, but no one gave him more than a cursory glance. He passed a row of telephone booths and there, in one of the booths with the door open, he saw a soldier with whom he'd shared the waiting room an hour before.

"Yeah, Ma—seven pounds six ounces. Got hair like Buffalo Bill. No, we haven't had time to make up a name for her yet . . . That you, Pa? Yup, mother and daughter doin' fine, just fine. Seven pounds six ounces. Nope, no name. . . . That you, Sis? Pretty late for you to be up, ain't it? Doesn't look like anybody yet. Let me talk to Ma again. . . . That you, Ma? Well, I guess that's all the news from Chicago. Now, Mom, Mom, take it easy—don't worry. It's a swell-looking baby, Mom. Just the hair looks like Buffalo Bill, and I said it as a joke, Mom. That's right, seven pounds six ounces. . . ."

There were five other booths, all empty, all open for calls to anyplace on earth. Heinz longed to hurry into one of them breathlessly, and tell the marvelous news. But there was no one to call, no one waiting for the news.

But Heinz still beamed, and he strode across the street and into a quiet tavern there. In the dank twilight there were only two men, tête-à-tête, the bartender and Mr. Sousa.

"Yes, sir, what'll it be?"

"I'd like to buy you and Mr. Sousa a drink," said Heinz with a heartiness strange to him. "I'd like the best brandy you've got. My wife just had a baby!"

"That so?" said the bartender with polite interest.

"Five pounds nine ounces," said Heinz.

"Huh," said the bartender. "What do you know."

"Netman," said Sousa, "wha'dja get?"

"Boy," said Heinz proudly.

"Never knew it to fail," said Sousa bitterly. "It's the little guys, all the time the little guys."

"Boy, girl," said Heinz, "it's all the same, just as long as it lives. Over there in the hospital, they're too close to it to see the wonder of it. A miracle over and over again—the world made new."

"Wait'll you've racked up seven, Netman," said Sousa. "*Then* you come back and tell me about the miracle."

"You got seven?" said the bartender. "I'm one up on you. I got eight." He poured three drinks.

"Far as I'm concerned," said Sousa, "you can have the championship."

Heinz lifted his glass. "Here's long life and great skill and much happiness to—to Peter Karl Knechtmann." He breathed quickly, excited by the decision.

"*There's* a handle to take ahold of," said Sousa. "You'd think the kid weighed two hundred pounds."

"Peter is the name of a famous surgeon," said Heinz, "the boy's great-uncle, dead now. Karl was my father's name."

"Here's to Pete K. Netman," said Sousa, with a cursory salute.

"Pete," said the bartender, drinking.

"And here's to *your* little girl—the new one," said Heinz.

Sousa sighed and smiled wearily. "Here's to her. God bless her."

"And now, *I'll* propose a toast," said the bartender, hammering on the bar with his fist. "On your feet, gentlemen. Up, up, everybody up."

Heinz stood, and held his glass high, ready for the next step in camaraderie, a toast to the whole human race, of which the Knechtmanns were still a part.

"Here's to the White Sox!" roared the bartender.

"Minoso, Fox, Mele," said Sousa.

"Fain, Lollar, Rivera!" said the bartender. He turned to Heinz. "Drink up, boy! The White Sox! Don't tell me you're a Cub fan."

"No," said Heinz, disappointed. "No—I don't follow baseball, I'm afraid." The other two men seemed to be sinking away from him. "I haven't been able to think about much but the baby."

The bartender at once turned his full attention to Sousa. "Look," he said intensely, "they take Fain off of first, and put him at third, and give Pierce first. Then move Minoso in from left field to shortstop. See what I'm doing?"

"Yep, yep," said Sousa eagerly.

"And then we take that no-good Carrasquel and . . ."

Heinz was all alone again, with twenty feet of bar between him and the other two men. It might as well have been a continent.

He finished his drink without pleasure, and left quietly.

At the railroad station, where he waited for a local train to take him home to the South Side, Heinz's glow returned again as he saw a co-worker at the dry-cleaning plant walk in with a girl. They were laughing and had their arms around each other's waist.

"Harry," said Heinz, hurrying toward them. "Guess what, Harry. Guess what just happened." He grinned broadly.

Harry, a tall, dapper, snub-nosed young man, looked down at Heinz with mild surprise. "Oh—hello, Heinz. What's up, boy?"

The girl looked on in perplexity, as though asking why they should be accosted at such an odd hour by such an odd person. Heinz avoided her slightly derisive eyes.

"A baby, Harry. My wife just had a boy."

"Oh," said Harry. He extended his hand. "Well, congratulations." The hand was limp. "I think that's swell, Heinz, perfectly swell." He withdrew his hand and waited for Heinz to say something else.

"Yes, yes—just about an hour ago," said Heinz. "Five pounds nine ounces. I've never been happier in my life."

"Well, I think it's perfectly swell, Heinz. You should be happy."

"Yes, indeed," said the girl.

There was a long silence, with all three shifting from one foot to the other.

"Really good news," said Harry at last.

"Yes, well," said Heinz quickly, "well, that's all I had to tell you."

"Thanks," said Harry. "Glad to hear about it."

There was another uneasy silence.

"See you at work," said Heinz, and strode jauntily back to his bench, but with his reddened neck betraying how foolish he felt.

The girl giggled.

Back home in his small apartment, at two in the morning, Heinz talked to himself, to the empty bassinet, and to the bed. He talked in German, a language he had sworn never to use again.

"They don't care," said Heinz. "They're all too busy, busy, busy to notice life, to feel anything about it. A baby is born." He shrugged. "What could be duller? Who would be so stupid as to talk about it, to think there was anything important or interesting about it?"

He opened a window on the summer night, and looked out at the moonlit canyon of gray wooden porches and garbage cans. "There are too many of us, and we are all too far apart," said Heinz. "Another Knechtmann is born, another O'Leary, another Sousa. Who cares? Why should anyone care? What difference does it make? None."

He lay down in his clothes on the unmade bed, and, with a rattling sigh, went to sleep.

He awoke at six, as always. He drank a cup of coffee, and with a wry sense of anonymity, he jostled and was jostled aboard the downtown train. His face showed no emotion. It was like all the other faces, seemingly incapable of surprise or wonder, joy or anger.

He walked across town to the hospital with the same detachment, a gray, uninteresting man, a part of the city.

In the hospital, he was as purposeful and calm as the doctors and nurses bustling about him. When he was led into the ward where Avchen slept behind white screens, he felt only what he had always felt in her presence—love and aching awe and gratitude for her.

"You go ahead and wake her gently, Mr. Netman," said the nurse.

"Avchen—" He touched her on her white-gowned shoulder. "Avchen. Are you all right, Avchen?"

"Mmmmmmmmmmm?" murmured Avchen. Her eyes opened to narrow slits. "Heinz. Hello, Heinz."

"Sweetheart, are you all right?"

"Yes, yes," she whispered. "I'm fine. How is the baby, Heinz?"

"Perfect. Perfect, Avchen."

"They couldn't kill us, could they, Heinz?"

"No."

"And here we are, alive as we can be."

"Yes."

"The baby, Heinz—" She opened her dark eyes wide. "It's the most wonderful thing that ever happened, isn't it?"

"Yes," said Heinz.

TO BE

From WHITE MULE

William Carlos Williams

William Carlos Williams was one of that small group of great writers who combined a career in literature with another vocation. But unlike Wallace Stevens, whose poetry had little in common with insurance, Williams' works were closely bound to his experiences as a baby doctor. Surely no one but a doctor could have written the following description of the birth of a baby.

She entered, as Venus from the sea, dripping. The air enclosed her, she felt it all over her, touching, waking her. If Venus did not cry aloud after release from the pressures of that sea-womb, feeling the new and lighter flood springing in her chest, flinging out her arms—this one did. Screwing up her tiny smeared face, she let out three convulsive yells—and lay still.

Stop that crying, said Mrs. D, you should be glad to get outa that hole.

It's a girl. What? A girl. But I wanted a boy. Look again. It's a girl, Mam. No! Take it away. I don't want it. All this trouble for another girl.

What is it? said Joe, at the door. A little girl. That's too bad. Is it all right? Yes, a bit small though. That's all right then. Don't you think you'd better cover it up so it won't catch cold? Ah, you go on out of here now and let me manage, said Mrs. D. This appealed to him as proper so he went. Are you all right, Mama? Oh, leave me alone, what kind of a man are you? As he didn't exactly know what she meant he thought it better to close the door. So he did.

In prehistoric ooze it lay while Mrs. D wound the white twine about its pale blue stem with kindly clumsy knuckles and blunt fingers with black nails and with the wiped-off scissors from the cord at her waist, cut it—while it was twisting and flinging up its toes and fingers into the way—free.

Alone it lay upon its back on the bed, sagging down in the middle, by the smeared triple mountain of its mother's disgusted thighs and toppled belly.

The clotted rags were gathered. Struggling blindly against the squeezing touches of the puffing Mrs. D, it was lifted into a nice woolen blanket and covered. It sucked its under lip and then let out two more yells.

Ah, the little love. Hear it, Mam, it's trying to talk.

La, la, la, la, la, la, la! it said with its tongue—in the black softness of the new pressures—and jerking up its hand, shoved its right thumb into its eye, starting with surprise and pain and yelling and rolling in its new agony. But finding the thumb again at random it sobbingly subsided into stillness.

Mrs. D lifted the cover and looked at it. It lay still. Her heart stopped. It's dead! She shook the . . .

With a violent start the little arms and legs flew up into a tightened knot, the face convulsed again—then as the nurse sighed, slowly the tautened limbs relaxed. It did not seem to breathe.

And now if you're all right I'll wash the baby. All right, said the new mother drowsily.

In that two ridges lap with wind cut off at the bend of the neck it lay, half dropping, regrasped—it was rubbed with warm oil that rested in a saucer on the stove while Mrs. D with her feet on the step of the oven rubbed and looked it all over, from the top of its head to the shiny soles of its little feet.

About five pounds is my guess. You poor little mite, to come into a world like this one. Roll over here and stop wriggling or you'll be on the floor. Open your legs now till I rub some of this oil in there. You'll open them glad enough one of these days—if you're not sorry for it. So, in all of them creases. How it sticks. It's like lard. I wonder what they have that on them for. It's a hard thing to be born a girl. There you are now. Soon you'll be in your little bed and I wish I was in the same this minute.

She rubbed the oil under the arm pits and carefully round the scrawny folds of its little neck pushing the wobbly head back and front. In behind the ears there was still that white grease of pre-birth. The matted hair, larded to the head, on the brow it lay buttered heavily while the whole back was caked with it, a yellow-white curd.

In the folds of the groin, the crotch where the genitals all bulging and angry red seemed presages of some future growth, she rubbed the warm oil, carefully—for she was a good woman—and thoroughly, cleaning her fingers on her apron. She parted the little parts looking and wondering at their smallness and perfection and shaking her head forebodingly.

The baby lay back at ease with closed eyes—lolling about as it was, lifted by a leg, an arm, and turned.

Mrs. D looked at the toes, counted them, admired the little perfect nails—and then taking each little hand, clenched tight at her approach, she smoothed it out and carefully anointed its small folds.

Into the little sleeping face she stared. The nose was flattened and askew, the mouth was still, the slits of the eyes were swollen closed—it seemed.

You're a homely little runt, God pardon you, she said—rubbing the spot in the top of the head. Better to leave that—I've heard you'd kill them if you pressed on that too hard. They say a bad nurse will stop a baby crying by pressing there—a cruel thing to do.

She looked again where further back upon the head a soft round lump was sticking up like a jockey cap askew. That'll all go down, she said to herself wisely because it was not the first baby Mrs. D had tended, nor the fifth nor the tenth nor the twentieth even.

She got out the wash boiler and put warm water in it. In that she carefully laid the new-born child. It half floated, half asleep—opening its eyes a moment then closing them and resting on Mrs. D's left hand, spread out behind its neck.

She soaped it thoroughly. The father came into the kitchen where they were and asked if she thought he could have a cup of coffee before he left for work—or should he go and get it at the corner. He shouldn't have asked her—suddenly it flashed upon his mind. It's getting close to six o'clock, he said. How is it? Is it all right?

He leaned to look. The little thing opened its eyes, blinked and closed them in the flare of the kerosene oil lamp close by in the gilded bracket on the wall. Then it smiled a crooked little smile—or so it seemed to him.

It's the light that hurts its eyes, he thought, and taking a dish towel he hung it on the cord that ran across the kitchen so as to cast a shadow on the baby's face.

Hold it, said Mrs. D, getting up to fill the kettle.

He held it gingerly in his two hands, looking curiously, shyly at that ancient little face of a baby. He sat down, resting it on his knees, and covered its still wet body. That little female body. The baby rested. Squirming in the tender grip of his guarding hands, it sighed and opened its eyes wide.

He stared. The left eye was rolled deep in toward the nose; the other seemed to look straight at his own. There seemed to be a spot of blood upon it. He looked and a cold dread started through his arms. Cross eyed! Maybe blind. But as he looked—the eyes seemed straight. He was glad when Mrs. D relieved him—but he kept his peace. Somehow this bit of moving, unwelcome life had won him to itself forever. It was so ugly and so lost.

The pains he had seemed to feel in his own body while the child was being born, now relieved—it seemed almost as if it had been he that had been the mother. It was his baby girl. That's a funny feeling, he thought.

He merely shook his head.

Coffee was cooking on the back of the stove. The room was hot. He went into the front room. He looked through the crack of the door into their bedroom where she lay. Then he sat on the edge of the disheveled sofa where, in a blanket, he had slept that night—and waited. He was a good waiter. Almost time to go to work.

Mrs. D got the cornstarch from a box in the pantry. She had to hunt for it among a disarray of pots and cooking things and made a mental note to put some order into the place before she left. Ah, these women with good husbands, they have no sense at all. They should thank God and get to work.

Now she took the baby once more on her lap, unwrapped it where it lay and powdered the shrivelling, gummy two inch stem of the gummy cord, fished a roll of Canton flannel from the basket at her feet and putting one end upon the little pad of cotton on the baby's middle wrapped the binder round it tightly, round and round, pinning the end in place across the back. The child was hard there as a board now—but did not wake.

She looked and saw a red spot grow upon the fabric. Tie it

again. Once more she unwrapped the belly band. Out she took the stump of the cord and this time she wound it twenty times about with twine while the tiny creature heaved and vermiculated with joy at its relief from the too tight belly band.

Wrapping an end of cotton rag about her little finger, Mrs. D forced that in between the little lips and scrubbed those tender gums. The baby made a grimace and drew back from this assault, working its whole body to draw back.

Hold still, said Mrs. D, bruising the tiny mouth with sedulous care—until the mite began to cough and strain to vomit. She stopped at last.

Dried, diapered and dressed in elephantine clothes that hid it crinkily; stockinged, booted and capped, tied under the chin—now Mrs. D walked with her new creation from the sweaty kitchen into the double light of dawn and lamps, through the hallway to the front room where the father sat, to show him.

Where are you going? For a walk?, he said.

Look at it in its first clothes, she answered him.

Yes, he said, it looks fine. But he wondered why they put the cap and shoes on it.

Turning back again, Mrs. D held the baby in her left arm and with her right hand turned the knob and came once more into the smells of the birth chamber. There it was dark and the lamp burned low. The mother was asleep.

She put out the lamp, opened the inner shutters. There was a dim light in the room.

Waking with a start—What is it? the mother said. Where am I? Is it over? Is the baby here?

It is, said Mrs. D, and dressed and ready to be sucked. Are you flooding any?

Is it a boy? said the mother.

It's a girl, I told you before. You're half asleep.

Another girl. Agh, I don't want girls. Take it away and let me rest. God pardon you for saying that. Where is it? Let me see it, said the mother, sitting up so that her great breasts hung outside her undershirt. Lay down, said Mrs. D. I'm all right. I could get up and do a washing. Where is it?

She took the little thing and turned it around to look at it. Where is its face? Take off that cap. What are these shoes on for? She took them off with a jerk. You miserable scrawny little brat, she thought, and disgust and anger fought inside her chest, she was not one to cry—except in a fury.

The baby lay still, its mouth stinging from its scrub, its belly half strangled, its legs forced apart by the great diaper—and slept, grunting now and then.

Take it away and let me sleep. Look at your breasts, said Mrs. D. And with that they began to put the baby to the breast. It wouldn't wake.

The poor miserable thing, repeated the mother. This will fix it. It's its own mother's milk it needs to make a fine baby of it, said Mrs. D. Maybe it does, said the mother, but I don't believe it. You'll see, said Mrs. D.

As they forced the great nipple into its little mouth, the baby yawned. They waited. It slept again. They tried again. It squirmed its head away. Hold your breast back from its nose. They did.

Mrs. D squeezed the baby's cheeks together between her thumb and index finger. It drew back, opened its jaws and in they shoved the dripping nipple. The baby drew back. Then for a moment it sucked.

There she goes, said Mrs. D, and straightened up with a sigh, pressing her two hands against her hips and leaning back to ease the pain in her loins.

The mother stroked the silky hair, looked at the gently pulsing fontanelle, and holding her breast with the left hand to bring it to a point, straightened back upon the pillows and frowned.

The baby ceased to suck, squirming and twisting. The nipple lay idle in its mouth. It slept. Looking down, the mother noticed what had happened. It won't nurse, Mrs. D. Take it away. Mrs. D come here at once and take this thing, I'm in a dripping perspiration.

Mrs. D came. She insisted it should nurse. They tried. The baby waked with a start, gagging on the huge nipple. It pushed with its tongue. Mrs. D had it by the back of the neck pushing. She flattened out the nipple and pushed it in the mouth. Milk ran down the little throat, a watery kind of milk. The baby gagged purple and vomited.

Take it. Take it away. What's the matter with it? You're too rough with it.

If you'd hold it up properly, facing you and not away off at an angle as if—Mrs. D's professional pride was hurt. They tried again, earnestly, tense, uncomfortable, one cramped over where she sat with knees spread out, the other half kneeling, half on her elbows—till anger against the little rebellious spitting imp, anger and fatigue, overcame them.

Take it away, that's all, said the mother finally.

Reluctantly, red in the face, Mrs. D had no choice but to do what she was told. I'd like to spank it, she said, flicking its fingers with her own.

What! said the mother in such menacing tones that Mrs. D caught a fright and realized whom she was dealing with. She said no more.

But now, the baby began to rebel. First its face got red, its whole head suffused, it caught its breath and yelled in sobs and long shrill waves. It sobbed and forced its piercing little voice so small yet so disturbing in its penetrating puniness, mastering its whole surroundings till it seemed to madden them. It caught its breath and yelled in sobs and long shrill waves. It sobbed and squeezed its yell into their ears.

That's awful, said the mother, I can't have it in this room. I don't think it's any good. And she lay down upon her back exhausted.

Mrs. D with two red spots in her two cheeks and serious jaw and a headache took the yelling brat into the kitchen. Dose it up. What else?

She got the rancid castor oil and gave the baby some. It fought and spit. Letting it catch its breath, she fetched the fennel tea, already made upon the range, and sweetening it poured a portion into a bottle, sat down and rather roughly told the mite to take a drink. There, drat you. Sweet to unsweeten that unhappy belly. The baby sucked the fermentative warm stuff and liked it—and wet its diaper after.

Feeling the wet through her skirt and petticoat and drawers right on her thighs, Mrs. D leaped up and holding the thing out at arm's length, got fresh clothes and changed it.

Feeling the nice fresh diaper, cool and enticing, now the baby grew red all over. Its face swelled, suffused with color. Gripping its tiny strength together, it tightened its belly band even more.

The little devil, said Mrs. D, to wait till it's a new diaper on.

And with this final effort, the blessed little thing freed itself as best it could—and it did very well—of a quarter pound of tarrish, prenatal slime—some of which ran down one leg and got upon its stocking.

That's right, said Mrs. D.

A GARGANTUAN APPETITE

From GARGANTUA AND PANTAGRUEL

Farnçois Rabelais

> *For mothers who boast of their babies' gargantuan appetites, here are some statistics about the eating habits of the original Gargantua, as well as an uninhibited description of his particular way of expressing delight in his food and drink.*

That excellent man Grangousier was drinking and making merry with the others, when he heard a horrible tumult. It was his son emerging into the light of this world, bellowing, "Drink, drink, drink!"

At once Grangousier exclaimed: "*Que grand tu as le gousier*" or "What a great gullet you have!" Hearing this, the company declared that the child should indeed be named "*grand tu as*": Gargantua or Greatgullet. Were these not the first sounds the father had uttered after the child's birth? And was this not an ancient Hebrew custom well worth following? Grangousier assented; Gargamelle was delighted with the idea.

Next, to quiet the babe, they made him drink till his throat almost burst. Then, carrying him to the font, they baptized him, as is the custom among all good Christians.

Shortly after, they appointed seventeen thousand nine hundred and thirteen cows from Pontille and Bréhémont to furnish him with milk in ordinary, for, considering his enormous needs, it was impossible to find a satisfactory nurse in all the country. Nevertheless, certain learned doctors, disciples of Duns Scotus, have affirmed that his own mother suckled him. She could, they say, draw from her breasts two thousand one hundred and three hogsheads and eighteen pints at one time. This seems scarcely probable. Indeed, this point has been condemned by the Sorbonne as mammarily scandalous and reeking with heresy.

Gargantua was thus looked after until he was twenty-two months old. Then, on the advice of the physicians, they began to carry him, and Jean Denyau built a special ox-drawn cart for him. They drove him about in it here, there and everywhere with the greatest pleasure; and a fine sight he was, too, with a great, open face and almost eighteen chins! He cried very little but he beshitted himself at all times. For he was wondrously phlegmatic of bum, as much by natural complexion as from an accidental predisposition, due to exaggerated quaffing of the juices of Septembral mash. Yet he never touched a drop without good reason; for whenever he happened to be out of sorts, vexed, angry or melancholy, if he stamped, wept or shouted, they brought him a drink. This invariably restored his native good humor and at once made him as quiet and happy as before.

One of his governesses told me on oath what a rooted habit this tippling had become. Indeed, the mere clinking of pints and flagons sent him off into the ecstasy of one who takes the joys of Paradise. Accordingly, in view of his divine character, they used to delight him every morning by making music on glasses with knives, on bottles with their stoppers, and on pots with their lids. At this he would turn gay, thrill with joy, wag his head and rock from side to side, monochording with his fingers and barytoning through his tail.

HE'LL NEVER COME TO MUCH

From ABRAHAM LINCOLN: THE PRAIRIE YEARS,
Volume I

Carl Sandburg

"Its skin looks just like red cherry pulp squeezed dry, in wrinkles," was the first description of a future great American in an excerpt from Wilderness Beginnings, *the first volume of* Abraham Lincoln: The Prairie Years, *Carl Sandburg's prize-winning biography.*

One morning in February 1809, Tom Lincoln came out of his cabin to the road, stopped a neighbor and asked him to tell "the granny woman," Aunt Peggy Walters, that Nancy would need help soon. On the morning of February 12, a Sunday, the granny woman was at the cabin. And she and Tom Lincoln and the moaning Nancy Hanks welcomed into a world of battle and blood, of whispering dreams and wistful dust, a new child, a boy.

A little later that morning Tom Lincoln threw extra wood on the fire, an extra bearskin over the mother, and walked two miles up the road to where the Sparrows, Tom and Betsy, lived. Dennis Hanks, the nine-year-old boy adopted by the Sparrows, met Tom at the door. In his slow way of talking Tom Lincoln told them, "Nancy's got a baby boy." A half-sheepish look was in his eyes, as though maybe more babies were not wanted in Kentucky just then.

Dennis Hanks took to his feet down the road to the Lincoln cabin. There he saw Nancy Hanks on a bed of poles cleated to a corner of the cabin, under warm bearskins. She turned her dark head from looking at the baby to look at Dennis and threw him a tired, white smile from her mouth and gray eyes. He stood watching the even, quiet breaths of this fresh, soft red baby. "What you goin' to name him, Nancy?" the boy asked. "Abraham," was the answer, "after his grandfather."

Soon came Betsy Sparrow. She washed the baby, put a yellow petticoat and a linsey shirt on him, cooked dried berries with wild honey for Nancy, put the one-room cabin in better order, kissed Nancy and comforted her, and went home, saying she would come again in the morning.

Dennis rolled up in a bearskin and slept by the fireplace that night. He listened to the crying of the newborn child once in the night and the feet of the father moving on the dirt floor to help the mother and the little one. In the morning he took a long look at the baby and said to himself, "Its skin looks just like red cherry pulp squeezed dry, in wrinkles."

He asked if he could hold the baby. Nancy, as she passed the little one into Dennis' arms, said, "Be keerful, Dennis, fur you air the fust boy he's ever seen." Dennis swung the baby back and forth, keeping up a chatter about how tickled he was to have a new cousin to play with. The baby screwed up its face and began crying with no letup. Dennis turned to Betsy Sparrow, handed her the baby and said, "Aunt, take him! He'll never come to much."

Thus the birthday scene reported years later by Dennis Hanks whose nimble mind sometimes invented more than he saw or heard. Peggy Walters, too, years later, gave the scene as her memory served: "I was twenty years old, then, and helping to bring a baby into the world was more of an event to me than it became afterward. But I was married young, and had a baby of my own, and I had helped mother who was quite famous as a granny woman. It was Saturday afternoon when Tom Lincoln sent over and asked me to come. They sent for Nancy's two aunts, Mis' Betsy Sparrow and Mis' Polly Friend. I was there before them, and we all had quite a spell to wait, and we got everything ready. Nancy had a good feather-bed under her, it wasn't a goose-feather bed, hardly anyone had that kind then, but good hen feathers. And she had blankets enough. A little girl there, two years old, Sarah, went to sleep before much of anything happened.

"Nancy had about as hard a time as most women, I reckon,

easier than some and maybe harder than a few. The baby was born just about sunup, on Sunday morning. Nancy's two aunts took the baby and washed him and dressed him, and I looked after Nancy. And I remember after the baby was born, Tom came and stood beside the bed and looked down at Nancy lying there, so pale and so tired, and he stood there with that sort of hang-dog look that a man has, sort of guilty like, but mighty proud, and he says to me, 'Are you sure she's all right, Mis' Walters?' And Nancy kind of stuck out her hand and reached for his, and said, 'Yes, Tom, I'm all right.' And then she said, 'You're glad it's a boy, Tom, aren't you? So am I.' "

Whatever the exact particulars, the definite event on that 12th of February, 1809, was the birth of a boy they named Abraham after his grandfather who had been killed by Indians—born in silence and pain from a wilderness mother on a bed of perhaps cornhusks and perhaps hen feathers—with perhaps a laughing child prophecy later that he would "never come to much."

INFANT JOY AND INFANT SORROW

From SONGS OF INNOCENCE and SONGS OF EXPERIENCE

William Blake

The joys and sorrows of new parents are perfectly epitomized in two brief lyrics, the first, clearly, a Song of Innocence, and the second, also clearly, a Song of Experience.

INFANT JOY

I have no name
I am but two days old—
What shall I call thee?
I happy am
Joy is my name,—
Sweet joy befall thee!

Pretty joy!
Sweet joy but two days old.
Sweet joy I call thee:
Thou dost smile.
I sing the while
Sweet joy befall thee.

INFANT SORROW

My mother groan'd! My father wept.
Into the dangerous world I leapt:

101

Helpless, naked, piping loud:
Like a fiend hid in a cloud.

Struggling in my father's hands:
Striving against my swaddling bands:
Bound and weary I thought best
To sulk upon my mother's breast.

A MAN IS BORN

From THE SELECTED SHORT STORIES OF
MAXIM GORKY

Maxim Gorky

In a day of childbirth courses and prenatal check-ups, a story of a peasant woman interrupting her journey to give birth by the side of the road may be hard to believe. Gorky's story becomes credible through his perception of a new mother's feeling for her baby, a relief and joy and gratitude that is the same for a peasant woman in nineteenth-century Russia and a mother in a modern maternity hospital.

It was in '92 the famine year, between Sukhum and Ochemchiry, on the river Kodor, not far from the coast—hollow sounding above the merry ripple of the glittering mountain stream I heard the rolling sea.

Autumn. Small, yellowed bay leaves were darting hither and thither in the white surf of the Kodor like nimble salmon-trout. I was sitting on the high stony bank overlooking the river and thinking that the gulls and cormorants were also, probably, taking the leaves for fish and being fooled—and that was why they were screaming so plaintively over there, on the right, beyond the trees, where the waves were lapping the shore.

The chestnut trees spreading above me were decorated with gold—at my feet lay numerous leaves that looked like hands severed from human wrists. The branches of the hornbeam on the opposite bank were already bare and hung in the air like a torn net. Inside the net, as if caught in it, hopped a yellow and red mountain woodpecker, tapping at the bark of the trunk with its black beak, driving out the insects, which were at once gobbled up by those guests from the north—the agile tomtits and gray nut-hatches.

On my left, smoky clouds hung low over the mountain tops, threatening rain, and causing shadows to glide across the green slopes on which the boxwood trees grew, and where, in the hollows of the ancient beeches and lindens, one can find the "grog honey" which in the days of old nearly sealed the fate of the troops of Pompeius the Great. It knocked a whole legion of the Roman ironsides off their feet with its inebriating sweetness. The wild bees made this honey from the pollen of bay and azalea blossoms, and "wayfarers" scoop it from the hollows and eat it, spreading it on their *lavash*—flat cakes made from wheat flour.

This is what I was doing, sitting on the stones under a chestnut tree, frightfully stung by an angry bee—I dipped my bread into my tea can, filled with honey, and ate, meanwhile admiring the idle play of the tired autumn sun.

The Caucasus in the autumn is like the interior of a magnificent cathedral which the great sages—being also great sinners—built to hide their shame for their past from prying eyes. They built a vast temple of gold, turquoise and emerald, and hung the mountain sides with the finest carpets embroidered in silk by the Turkmen in Samarkand and Shemaha; they plundered the whole world and brought all their loot here as a gift to the sun, as much as to say:

"Thine—from Thine—to Thee!"

. . . I saw a vision of long-bearded, hoary giants, large-eyed like merry children, descending from the mountains, beautifying the earth, scattering their multi-colored treasures with a lavish hand, covering the mountain tops with thick layers of silver and the terraces with the living fabric of a vast variety of trees—and under their hands this patch of heaven-blessed earth was endowed with enchanting beauty.

It's a fine job—being a man in this world! What wonderful things one sees! How the heart is stirred by pleasure almost akin to pain in one's calm contemplation of beauty!

Yes, it's true, sometimes you find it hard. Your breast is filled with burning hatred, and grief greedily sucks the blood from your heart—but this cannot last for ever. Even the sun often looks down on men in infinite sadness: it has labored so hard for them, and what wretched manikins they have turned out to be! . . .

Of course, there's a lot of good ones—but they need repair, or better still, to be made all over again.

. . . Above the bushes on my left I saw dark heads bobbing; barely perceptible above the murmur of the waves and the rippling sounds of the river. I heard human voices—those were the "starving" on their way from Sukhum, where they had been building a road, to Ochemchiry, in the hope of getting another job.

I knew them—they were from Orel. I had worked with them in Sukhum and we had been paid off together the day before. I had left before them, at night, so as to reach the seashore in time to see the sunrise.

They were four muzhiks and a young peasant woman with high cheekbones; she was pregnant, her huge abdomen protruded upward; she had bluish-gray eyes, seemingly bulging with fright. I could see her head above the bushes too, covered with a yellow kerchief, nodding like a sunflower in full bloom swaying in the wind. Her husband had died in Sukhum from overeating fruit. I had lived in the same hutment with these people: from the good old Russian habit they had complained about their misfortunes so much, and so loudly, that their lamentations must have been heard a good five versts away.

They were dull people, crushed by sorrow, which had torn them from their native, worn out, barren soil and had swept them like autumn leaves to this place, where the strange, luxuriant clime amazed and dazzled them, and where the hard conditions of labor had finally broken them. They gazed at everything about them, blinking their sad, faded eyes in perplexity, smiling pitifully to each other and saying in low voices:

"Ai-e-e . . . what a soil!"

"The stuff just shoots up!"

"Ye-e-es . . . but still . . . it's very stony."

"It's not so good, you have to admit."

And then they recalled Kobili Lozhok, Sukhoi Gon, Mokrenki —their native villages, where every handful of earth contained the ashes of their forefathers; they remembered it, it was familiar and dear to them, they had watered it with the sweat of their brows.

There was another woman with them—tall, upright, with a

chest as flat as a board, a heavy jaw and dull, squinting eyes as black as coal.

In the evening she, together with the woman in the yellow kerchief, would go a little distance behind the hutment, squat down on a heap of stones, and resting her chin in the palm of her hand and inclining her head to the side, would sing in a high-pitched angry voice:

Beyond the village churchyard,
Among the bushes green,
On the yellow sand I'll spread
My shawl so white and clean
And there I'll wait. . . .
Until my darling comes. . . .
And when he comes. . . .
I'll greet him heartily. . . .

Usually the one in the yellow kerchief would sit silently looking down at her abdomen; but sometimes she would suddenly join in and in a deep, drawling, masculine voice would sing the words of that sad refrain:

Oh my darling. . . .
My dear darling. . . .
I am not fated. . . .
To see thee more. . . .

In the black, suffocating darkness of the southern night, these wailing voices awakened in me the memory of the snowy wilderness of the north, of the shrieking blizzard, and the howling of the wolves. . . .

Later the cross-eyed woman was struck down by fever and she was carried to the town on a canvas stretcher—on the way she shivered and moaned, and the moaning sounded as if she was continuing her song about the churchyard and the sand.

. . . The head in the yellow kerchief dived below the bush and vanished.

I finished my breakfast, covered the honey in my tea can with leaves, tied up my knapsack and leisurely followed in the track of the other people, tapping the firm ground with my cornel-wood walking stick.

And so, there I was on the narrow, gray strip of road. On my right heaved the deep blue sea. It looked as though thousands of invisible carpenters were planing it with their planes, and the white shavings rustled on the beach, blown there by the wind, which was moist, warm and fragrant, like the breath of a robust woman. A Turkish felucca, listing heavily to port, was gliding towards Sukhum, its sails puffed out like the fat cheeks of the pompous road engineer in Sukhum—a most important fellow. For some reason he always said "shoot oop" for "shut up," and "mebbe" for "may be."

"Shoot oop! Mebbe you think you can fight, but in two ticks I'll have you hauled off to the police station!"

He used to take a delight in having people dragged off to the police station, and it is good to think that by now the worms in his grave must have eaten his body right down to the bones.

. . . How easy it was to walk! Like treading on air. Pleasant thoughts, brightly-clad reminiscences, sang in soft chorus in my memory. These voices in my soul were like the white-crested waves of the sea—on the surface; deep down, however, my soul was calm. The bright and joyous hopes of youth swam leisurely, like silvery fish in the depths of the sea.

The road led to the seashore, winding its way nearer and nearer to the sandy strip that was lapped by the waves—the bushes too seemed to be striving to get a glimpse of the sea and swayed over the ribbon of road as if nodding greetings to the blue expanse.

The wind was blowing from the mountains—threatening rain.

. . . A low moan in the bushes—a human moan, which always goes to the heart.

Pushing the bushes apart I saw the woman in the yellow kerchief sitting with her back against the trunk of a walnut tree; her head was dropped on one shoulder, her mouth was contorted, her eyes bulged with a look of insanity. She was supporting her huge abdomen with her hands and breathing with such unnatural effort that her abdomen positively leapt convulsively. The woman moaned faintly, exposing her yellow wolfish teeth.

"What's the matter? Did somebody hit you?" I asked, bending over her. She rubbed one bare foot against the other in the gray dust like a fly cleansing itself and, rolling her heavy head, she gasped:

"Go away! . . . Ain't you got no shame? . . . Go away! . . ."

I realized what was the matter—I had seen something like this before—of course I was scared and skipped back into the road, but the woman uttered a loud prolonged shriek, her bulging eyes seemed to burst and tears rolled down her flushed and swollen cheeks.

This compelled me to go back to her. I threw my knapsack, kettle and tea can to the ground, lay the woman flat on her back and was about to bend her legs at the knees when she pushed me away, punched me in the face and chest and turning over, she crept off on all fours deep into the bushes, grunting and growling like a she-bear:

"Devil! . . . Beast!"

Her arms gave way and she dropped, striking her face on the ground. She shrieked again, convulsively stretching her legs.

In the heat of the excitement I suddenly remembered all I had known about this business. I turned the woman over on her back and bent up her legs—the chorion was already visible.

"Lie still, it's coming!" I said to her.

I ran to the beach, rolled up my sleeves, washed my hands and returned, ready to act as midwife.

The woman writhed like birch-bark in the flames. She tapped the ground around her with the palms of her hands and tearing up handfuls of faded grass she wanted to stuff it into her mouth; and in doing so she dropped earth on to her frightful, inhumanly contorted face and into her wild, bloodshot eyes—and now the chorion burst and the child's head appeared. I had to restrain the convulsive jerking of her legs, help the child emerge, and see that she did not stuff grass into her distorted mouth. . . .

We swore at each other a bit—she through clenched teeth, and I in a low voice; she from pain and, perhaps, from shame. I from embarrassment and heartrending pity for her. . . .

"Oh Lord! Oh Lord!" she cried hoarsely. Her livid lips were bitten through, there was foam at the corners of her mouth, and from her eyes, which seemed suddenly to have faded in the sun, flowed those abundant tears of a mother's unbearable pain. Her whole body was taut, as if it were being torn in two.

"Go . . . away . . . you . . . devil!"

She kept pushing me away with her feeble, seemingly dislocated arms. I said to her appealingly:

"Don't be a fool! Try, try hard. It'll be over soon."

My heart was torn with pity for her, it seemed to me that her tears had splashed into my eyes. I felt as if my heart would burst. I wanted to shout, and I did shout:

"Come on! Hurry up!"

And lo—a tiny human being lay in my arms—as red as a beet-root. Tears streamed from my eyes, but through the tears I saw that this tiny red creature was already discontented with the world, kicking, struggling and yelling, although it was still tied to its mother. It had blue eyes, its funny little nose looked squashed on its red, crumpled face, and its lips were moving as it bawled:

"Ya-a-a-ah . . . Ya-a-a-ah."

Its body was so slimy that I was afraid it would slip out of my arms. I was on my knees looking into its face and laughing—laughing with joy at the sight of him . . . and I forgot what had to be done next. . . .

"Cut the cord . . ." the mother whispered. Her eyes were closed. Her face was haggard and gray, like that of a corpse, her livid lips barely moved as she said:

"Cut it . . . with your knife. . . ."

But somebody in the hut had stolen my knife—so I bit the navel cord through with my teeth. The child yelled in a real, Orel bass voice. The mother smiled. I saw her eyes miraculously revive, and a blue flame burned in their bottomless depths. Her dark hand groped in her skirt, searching for her pocket, and her blood-stained, bitten lips moved.

"I've . . . no . . . strength. . . . Bit of tape . . . in my pocket . . . tie up . . . navel," she said.

I found the piece of tape and tied up the child's navel. The mother smiled still more happily; that smile was so bright that it almost dazzled me.

"Put yourself straight while I go and wash him," I said.

"Take care. Do it gently now. Take care," she muttered anxiously.

But this red manikin didn't need gentle handling. He waved his fists and yelled as if challenging me to fight:

"Ya-a-a-ah . . . ya-a-a-ah."

"That's it! That's it, little brother! Assert yourself. The neighbors will pull your head off if you don't," I warned him.

He emitted a particularly savage yell at the first impact of the surf which splashed us both, but when I began to slap his chest and back he screwed up his eyes, and he struggled and shrieked as wave after wave washed his body.

"Go on, yell! Yell at the top of your lungs! Show 'em you come from Orel!" I shouted encouragingly.

When I brought him back to his mother she was lying on the ground with her eyes closed again, biting her lips from the fits of after-pain; but amidst her groaning and moaning I heard her whisper:

"Give . . . give him . . . to me."

"He can wait!"

"No! Give . . . him . . . to . . . me!"

She unbuttoned her blouse with trembling uncertain hands. I helped her to uncover her breast, which nature had made fit to feed twenty children, and put the struggling Orelian to her warm body. The Orelian understood at once what was coming and stopped yelling.

"Holy Virgin, Mother of God," the mother muttered with a sigh, rolling her disheveled head from side to side on the knapsack.

Suddenly she uttered a low shriek, fell silent again, and then opened her inexpressively beautiful eyes—the sacred eyes of a mother who has just given birth to a child. They were blue, and they gazed into the blue sky. A grateful, joyful smile gleamed and melted in them. Raising her weary arm the mother slowly crossed herself and her child. . . .

"Bless you, Holy Virgin, Mother of God. . . . Oh . . . bless you. . . ."

The light in her eyes died out again. Her face again assumed that haggard hue. She remained silent for a long time, scarcely breathing. But suddenly she said in a firm, matter-of-fact tone:

"Laddie, untie my bag."

I untied the bag. She looked hard at me, smiled faintly, and I thought I saw a blush, ever so faint, pass over her hollow cheeks and perspiring brow.

"Go off a little way," she said.

"Take care, don't disturb yourself too much," I warned her.

"All right. . . . All right. . . . Go away!"

I retired into the bushes nearby. I felt very tired, and it seemed as though beautiful birds were singing softly in my heart—and together with the unceasing murmur of the sea this singing sounded so good that I thought I could listen to it for a whole year. . . .

Somewhere, not far away, a brook was bubbling—it sounded like the voice of a girl telling her friend about her lover. . . .

A head rose above the bushes, covered with a yellow kerchief, already tied, in the regular way.

"Hey! What's this? You've got up rather soon, haven't you?" I cried in amazement.

The woman sat down on the ground, holding on to the branches for support; she looked as if all the strength had been drained from her. There was not a hint of color in her ashen-gray face, except for her eyes, which looked like large, blue pools. She smiled a tender smile and whispered:

"Look—he's asleep."

Yes, he was sleeping all right, but no different from any other kid as far as I could see; if there was any difference it was only in the surroundings. He was lying on a heap of bright autumn leaves, under a bush, of the kind that don't grow in the Orel Province.

"You ought to lie down for a bit, mother," I said.

"No-o-o," she answered, shaking her head weakly. "I've got to collect my things and go on to that place . . . what do they call it?"

"Ochemchiry?"

"Yes, that's right! I suppose my folks are a good few versts from here now."

"But will you be able to walk?"

"What about the Virgin Mary? Won't she help me?"

Well, since she was going with the Virgin Mary—I had nothing more to say!

She gazed down at the tiny, puckered, discontented face, warm rays of kindly light radiating from her eyes. She licked her lips and slowly stroked her breast.

I lit a fire and heaped some stones near it on which to place the kettle.

"I'll give you some tea in a minute, mother," I said.

"Oh! That will be fine. . . . My breasts feel dried up," she answered.

"Have your folks deserted you?"

"No! Why should they? I dropped behind. They had had a drink or two. . . . And a good thing, too. I don't know what I'd have done if they were around. . . ."

She glanced at me, covered her face with her arm, spat out blood and then smiled shamefacedly.

"Is he your first?" I asked.

"Yes, my first. . . . Who are you?"

"It looks like I'm a man. . . ."

"You're a man all right! Are you married?"

"I haven't had the honor."

"You are fibbing, aren't you?"

"No, why should I?"

She cast down her eyes in reflection. Then she asked:

"How is it you know about this women's business?"

Now I did tell a fib. I said:

"I learned about it. I'm a student. Do you know what that is?"

"Of course, I do! Our priest's eldest son is a student. He's learning to be a priest. . . ."

"Well, I'm one of those. . . . I had better go and fill the kettle."

The woman inclined her head towards her baby to hear whether he was breathing. Then she looked at the direction of the sea and said:

"I'd like to have a wash, but I don't know what the water's like. . . . What kind of water is it? It's both salty and bitter."

"Well, you go and wash in it. It's healthy water!"

"What!"

"I'm telling you the truth. And it's warmer than the water in the brook. The brook here is as cold as ice."

"You ought to know."

An Abkhazian, wearing a shaggy sheepskin hat, rode past at a walking pace, his head drooped on his chest. He was dozing. His little wiry horse, twitching its ears, looked at us askance with its round black eyes and snorted. The rider raised his head with a jerk, also glanced in our direction, and then allowed his head to droop again.

"They're funny people here. And they look so fierce too," the Orel woman said softly.

I went to the brook. The water, as bright and volatile as quicksilver, bubbled and gurgled over the stones, and the autumn leaves were merrily tumbling over and over in it. It was wonderful! I washed my hands and face and filled the kettle. Through the bushes, on my way back, I saw the woman on her hands and knees crawling over the ground, over the stones, looking back anxiously.

"What's the matter?" I inquired.

The woman stopped short as if she were scared, her face became ashen gray, and she tried to conceal something under her body. I guessed what it was.

"Give it to me, I'll bury it," I said.

"Oh, my dear! What are you talking about? It's got to be taken to a bathhouse and buried under the floor. . . ."

"Do you think they'll build a bathhouse here soon?"

"You are joking, but I am afraid! Suppose a wild beast eats it. . . . Still, it's got to be buried. . . ."

And with that she turned her face away and handing me a moist, heavy bundle, she said shamefacedly, in a soft imploring voice:

"You'll do it thoroughly, won't you? Bury it as deep as you can for the sake of Christ . . . and my little one. You will, won't you?"

. . . When I returned I saw her walking from the seashore with faltering steps and outstretched arms. Her skirt was wet to the waist. Her face had a touch of color in it and seemed to be shining with an inner light. I helped her to the fire, thinking to myself in amazement:

"She has the strength of an ox!"

Later, as we were drinking tea with honey, she asked me quietly:

"Have you stopped your book learning?"

"Yes."

"Why? Did you take to drink?"

"Yes, mother. I went to the dogs!"

"That was a nice thing to do! I remember you, though. I noticed you in Sukhum when you had a row with the boss over the food. I said to myself then: He must be a drunkard. He's not afraid of anything. . . ."

Licking the honey from her swollen lips she kept turning her blue eyes to the bush where the latest Orelian was sleeping peacefully.

"How's he going to live?" she said with a sigh, looking into my face. "You helped me. For that I thank you. . . . But whether it will be good for him . . . I don't know."

When she had finished her meal she crossed herself, and while I was collecting my things she sat drowsily swaying her body and gazing at the ground with eyes that seemed to have faded again, evidently engrossed in thought. A little later she got up.

"Are you really going?" I asked.

"Yes."

"Take care of yourself, mother."

"What about the Virgin Mary? . . . Pick him up and give him to me!"

"I'll carry him."

We argued about it for a bit and then she yielded, and we set out, walking side by side, shoulder to shoulder.

"I hope I won't stumble," she said, laughing guiltily and placing her arm on my shoulder.

The new inhabitant of the land of Russia, the man of unknown destiny, was lying in my arms, snoring heavily. The sea, all covered with white lace trimmings, splashed and surged on the shore. The bushes whispered to each other. The sun shone as it passed the meridian.

We walked on slowly. Now and again the mother halted, heaved a deep sigh, and throwing her head back she looked around, at the sea, at the woods, at the mountains, and then into the face of her son—and her eyes, thoroughly washed with the tears of suffering, were again wonderfully clear, again they shone with the blue light of inexhaustible love.

Once she halted and said:

"Lord! Dear, good God! How good it is. How good! Oh, if I could go on like this, all the time, to the very end of the world, and he, my little one, would grow, would keep on growing in freedom, near his mother's breast, my darling little boy...."

... The sea murmured and murmured. ...

Part IV

THE BABY SITTER

THE NURSEMAID

From NERVOUS PEOPLE AND OTHER SATIRES

Mikhail Zoshchenko

How many working mothers wonder and worry about what the nursemaid does with their babies the whole day? The Farforovs thought their nursemaid was a treasure . . . until they learned the secret of her daily outings with their baby in this satirical Soviet short story.

A shocking thing happened here in Leningrad recently.

A certain couple, the Farforovs, had a nursemaid. They hired her even before their baby was born. They could not provide their baby with care and tenderness themselves because the two of them had jobs in industry.

Seryoga Farforov himself worked, and his wife worked. He earned a respectable salary. And she earned quite a bit.

In such circumstances their baby was born.

They had a real, honest-to-goodness baby and, of course, were obliged to hire a nursemaid for him. Otherwise, of course, they wouldn't have hired one. The more so that they had never been in the habit of hiring nursemaids. They didn't understand such aristocratic customs. But now it was more economical to have a nursemaid than for Madame Farforov herself to quit her job in industry.

And so, of course, a nursemaid offered them her services.

She was neither so very old nor so very young. In a word, she was middle-aged and fairly terrifying to look at. But beneath her ugly exterior the Farforovs soon espied a kind heart. And they

117

could not have dreamed what a viper they had taken to their bosom.

They, of course, had purposely hired such an ugly woman, one who would have no personal happiness and would have eyes for no one but their baby.

They had hired her with good recommendations. They were told that she was a completely sober, elderly, ugly old lady. And that she loved children and could hardly keep her hands off them. And that though she was an old woman, she was an old woman completely worthy of entering the new, classless society.

That's what they were told. But they still hadn't arrived at their own opinion.

So they hired this nursemaid and realized that it was true—she was a treasure, not a nursemaid. Especially as she fell in love with the child at once. She walked with him all the time, hardly put him down, and kept him outdoors until nightfall.

And the Farforovs, being advanced people, did nothing to prevent this. They knew that fresh air and outings would strengthen their baby's organism, and they thought, Go right ahead. Let her walk with him. Besides, we won't have to look at her so much.

Then the following incident took place.

In the morning the parents would be off to the factory, and the nursemaid would take the baby and a bottle of cow's milk and go walking about the streets of Leningrad.

But one day a member of the administration named Tsaplin was walking along the street. He was on the house committee.

He was walking along the street thinking, perhaps, about his own personal affairs, when suddenly he saw a rather bedraggled citizeness standing on the corner. She was standing there, just like that, and holding a baby. And she was begging money for the baby.

Semyon Mikhailovich Tsaplin didn't want to give her anything —he simply took a look at her. And he realized that the face was familiar: it was none other than the nursemaid with the Farforov baby.

S. M. Tsaplin, member of the house committee, didn't say anything to her about it and didn't give her anything, but turned around and went back home.

We don't know how he spent the rest of the day, but in the evening he said to Farforov himself: "I am exceedingly astonished, esteemed comrade, that either you're not paying your domestic anything, or I don't know what's the matter with her. But I'll tell you right now: if you're sending her out to beg with the baby on purpose, then you constitute a definitely alien stratum in our proletarian house."

Farforov, of course, said, "Excuse me, but what are you talking about?"

Then the member of the administration told him what he had seen and what he had felt on witnessing a street spectacle of that sort.

At this point various scenes took place. There were shouts and smiles, and everything became clear.

Then they called the nursemaid. They said to her, "How could you behave like that? Have you lost your wits? Maybe not everyone's home upstairs."

The nursemaid said, "There's nothing wrong with it. What's the difference whether I just stand there, or whether sympathetic passers-by give me a handout. I," she said, "just can't understand why you're offended. It doesn't hurt the baby. And maybe it even amuses him to see so many people bustling around him."

Farforov said, "Yes, but I don't want my child to be exposed to such attitudes from his earliest years. I will not permit you to do such things. I won't allow you to go begging with my child. Besides, we pay you a decent salary, you have everything, you're perfectly well fed and shod."

The nursemaid said, "Yes, but I want to make a little extra."

Madame Farforov, pressing her child to her breast, said, "This is offensive to us in the highest degree. You are discharged from your position."

Tsaplin said, "As a member of the administration I shall say this: you are completely right to fire this crazy nursemaid, inasmuch as she, and not you, is the alien stratum in our proletarian house."

The old woman said, "Goodness, how you do frighten me! Nursemaids are scarce now. I'll probably be snapped up right away. I hardly made three rubles begging with your brat, and got showered with reproaches into the bargain. I'll leave of my own free will, since you're heartless scoundrels and not employers."

On hearing these words Farforov got angry and yelled at her. He even wanted to shake her aged soul out of her frail body, but the member of the administration did not let him do this, and even made a brief speech on the subject. He told Farforov and his spouse the following: "Take a look at this nursemaid of yours. With all her roots she goes back to the distant past when gentry and subordinate slaves got along together. She became reconciled to that life and doesn't see anything shameful in being a beggar or taking handouts. That is the reason why she did the disgusting thing that offended you. However, don't touch her physically but simply dismiss her from her job."

The Farforovs did just that—they dismissed the nursemaid in disgrace.

The latter left without asking for references and no one knew where she went. But she's probably looking after a child somewhere and using him to beg herself a pretty good income.

EMMA VISITS THE WET NURSE

From MADAME BOVARY

Gustave Flaubert

As recently as the latter part of the nineteenth century, the wet nurse provided the most common type of substitute feeding for mothers of the middle and upper classes. In many cases the infant was "put out to nurse" and spent his early months (sometimes years) in the peasant home of his wet nurse.

An idea of what life was like for such an infant in the middle of the last century is given in the following passage from Madame Bovary, *in which Emma Bovary, accompanied by her admirer Léon, visits her baby at the wet nurse's home.*

One day Emma suddenly felt that she had to see her little daughter, who had been put out to nurse with the cabinetmaker's wife; and without looking at the almanac to see whether the six weeks of the Virgin had elapsed, she made her way toward the house occupied by Rollet, at the end of the village at the foot of the hills, between the main road and the meadows.

It was noon: the houses had their shutters closed, and under the harsh light of the blue sky the ridges of the glittering slate roofs seemed to be shooting sparks. A sultry wind was blowing. Emma felt weak as she walked; the stones of the footpath hurt her feet, and she wondered whether she shouldn't return home or stop in somewhere to rest.

At that moment Monsieur Léon emerged from a nearby door, a sheaf of papers under his arm. He advanced to greet her and stood in the shade in front of Lheureux's store, under the gray awning.

Madame Bovary said that she was on her way to see her child but was beginning to feel tired.

"If . . ." Léon began, and then dared go no further.

"Have you an appointment somewhere?" she asked him.

And when he replied that he hadn't she asked him to accompany her. By evening the news of this had spread throughout Yonville, and Madame Tuvache, the wife of the mayor, said in her maid's presence that Madame Bovary was risking her reputation.

To reach the wet nurse's house they had to turn left at the end of the village street, as though going to the cemetery, and follow a narrow path that led them past cottages and yards between privet hedges. These were in bloom; and blooming, too, were veronicas and wild roses and nettles and the wild blackberries that thrust out their slender sprays from the thickets. Through holes in the hedges they could see, in the farmyards, a pig on a manure pile or cows in wooden collars rubbing their horns against tree trunks. The two of them walked on slowly side by side, she leaning on his arm and he shortening his step to match hers; in front of them hovered a swarm of flies, buzzing in the warm air.

They recognized the house by an old walnut tree that shaded it. It was low, roofed with brown tiles, and from the attic window hung a string of onions. Brushwood propped up against a thorn hedge formed a fence around a bit of garden given over to lettuce, a few plants of lavender, and sweet peas trained on poles. A trickle of dirty water ran off into the grass, and all around were odds and ends of rags, knitted stockings, a red calico wrapper, a large coarsely woven sheet spread out on the hedge. At the sound of the gate the wet nurse appeared, carrying an infant at her breast. With her other hand she was pulling along a frail, unhappy-looking little boy, his face covered with scrofulous sores—the son of a Rouen knit-goods dealer whom his parents were too busy in their shop to bother with.

"Come in," she said. "Your little girl's asleep inside."

The ground-floor bedroom—the only bedroom in the house—had a wide uncurtained bed standing against its rear wall; the window wall (one pane was mended with a bit of wrapping paper) was taken up by the kneading-trough. In the corner behind the door was a raised slab for washing, and under it stood a row of heavy boots with shiny hobnails and a bottle of oil with a feather in its mouth. A Mathieu Laensberg almanac lay on the dusty mantelpiece among gun flints, candle ends and bits of tinder. And as a final bit of clutter there was a figure of Fame blowing her trumpets—a picture probably cut out of a perfume advertisement and now fastened to the wall with six shoe tacks.

Emma's baby was asleep in a wicker cradle on the floor, and she took it up in its little blanket and began to sing softly to it and rock it in her arms.

Léon walked around the room: it seemed to him a strange sight, this elegant lady in her nankeen gown here among all this squalor. Madame Bovary blushed; he turned away, fearing that his glance might have been indiscreet; and she put the baby back in its cradle—it had just thrown up over the collar of her dress. The wet nurse quickly wiped off the mess, assuring her it wouldn't show.

"It isn't the first time, you know," she said. "I do nothing but wipe up after her all day long. Would you mind leaving word with Camus the grocer to let me pick up a little soap when I need it? That would be the easiest for you—I wouldn't have to trouble you."

"I will, I will," said Emma. "Good-bye, Madame Rollet."

And she left the house, wiping her feet on the doorsill.

The wet nurse walked with her as far as the gate, talking about how hard it was to have to get up during the night.

"I'm so worn out sometimes I fall asleep in my chair. So couldn't you at least let me have just a pound of ground coffee? It would last me a month; I'd drink it with milk in the morning."

After undergoing a deluge of thanks, Madame Bovary moved on; and then when she had gone a little way down the path there was the sound of sabots and she turned around: it was the wet nurse again.

"What is it now?"

And the peasant woman drew her aside behind an elm and began to talk to her about her husband. He "had only his trade and the six francs a year the captain gave him, so . . ."

"Come to the point!" said Emma brusquely.

"Well, what I mean is," the wet nurse said, sighing after every word, "I'm afraid he wouldn't like it, seeing me sitting there drinking coffee by myself; you know how men are, they . . ."

"But you'll both have coffee!" Emma cried. "I just told you I'd give you some! Leave me alone!"

"Ah, Madame, you see he's had terrible cramps in his chest ever since he was wounded, and he says cider makes him feel worse, and . . ."

"Won't you please let me go?"

"So," she went on, making a curtsy, "if it isn't too much to ask"—she curtsied again—"if you would"—and she gave a beseeching glance—"just a little jug of brandy," she finally got out, "and I'll rub your little girl's feet with it—they're as tender as your tongue."

THE TRIUMPH OF NANNY

From "BLISS," The Short Stories of Katherine Mansfield

Katherine Mansfield

"Why have a baby," thought Bertha, "if it has to be kept—not in a case like a rare, rare fiddle—but in another woman's arms?"

Nurse sat at a low table giving Little B her supper after her bath. The baby had on a white flannel gown and a blue woolen jacket, and her dark, fine hair was brushed up into a funny little peak. She looked up when she saw her mother and began to jump.

"Now, my lovey, eat it up like a good girl," said Nurse, setting her lips in a way that Bertha knew, and that meant she had come into the nursery at another wrong moment.

"Has she been good, Nanny?"

"She's been a little sweet all the afternoon," whispered Nanny. "We went to the park and I sat down on a chair and took her out of the pram and a big dog came along and put its head on my knee and she clutched its ear, tugged it. Oh, you should have seen her."

Bertha wanted to ask if it wasn't rather dangerous to let her clutch at a strange dog's ear. But she did not dare to. She stood watching them, her hands by her side, like the poor little girl in front of the rich little girl with the doll.

The baby looked up at her again, stared, and then smiled so charmingly that Bertha couldn't help crying:

"Oh, Nanny, do let me finish giving her her supper while you put the bath things away."

"Well, M'm, she oughtn't to be changed hands while she's eating," said Nanny, still whispering. "It unsettles her; it's very likely to upset her."

How absurd it was. Why have a baby if it has to be kept—not in a case like a rare, rare fiddle—but in another woman's arms?

"Oh, I must!" said she.

Very offended, Nanny handed her over.

"Now, don't excite her after her supper. You know you do, M'm. And I have such a time with her after!"

Thank heaven! Nanny went out of the room with the bath towels.

"Now I've got you to myself, my little precious," said Bertha, as the baby leaned against her.

She ate delightfully, holding up her lips for the spoon and then waving her hands. Sometimes she wouldn't let the spoon go; and sometimes, just as Bertha had filled it, she waved it away to the four winds.

When the soup was finished Bertha turned round to the fire.

"You're nice—you're very nice!" said she, kissing her warm baby. "I'm fond of you. I like you."

And, indeed, she loved Little B so much—her neck as she bent forward, her exquisite toes as they shone transparent in the firelight—that all her feeling of bliss came back again, and again she didn't know how to express it—what to do with it.

"You're wanted on the telephone," said Nanny, coming back in triumph and seizing *her* Little B.

BABY BOARDMAN

From ULYSSES

James Joyce

At a time when babies in fiction were invariably devices to advance a plot or develop a character, James Joyce included in Ulysses *a real baby, a chubby, laughing, crying, diaper-wetting little individual, perhaps the first believable baby in modern literature.*

The summer evening had begun to fold the world in its mysterious embrace. Far away in the west the sun was setting and the last glow of all too fleeting day lingered lovingly on sea and strand, on the proud promontory of dear old Howth guarding as ever the waters of the bay, on the weedgrown rocks along Sandymount shore and, last but not least, on the quiet church whence there streamed forth at times upon the stillness the voice of prayer to her who is in her pure radiance a beacon ever to the storm-tossed heart of man, Mary, star of the sea.

The three girl friends were seated on the rocks, enjoying the evening scene and the air which was fresh but not too chilly. Many a time and oft were they wont to come there to that favourite nook to have a cosy chat beside the sparkling waves and discuss matters feminine, Cissy Caffrey and Edy Boardman with the baby in the pushcar and Tommy and Jacky Caffrey, two little curlyheaded boys, dressed in sailor suits with caps to match and the name H.M.S. Belleisle printed on both. For Tommy and Jacky Caffrey were twins, scarce four years old and very noisy and spoiled twins sometimes but for all that darling little fellows with bright merry faces and endearing ways about them. They were dabbling in the sand with their spades and buckets, building castles as children do, or playing with their big coloured ball, happy as the day was long. And Edy Boardman was rocking the chubby baby to and fro in the pushcar while that young gentleman fairly chuckled with delight. He was but eleven months and nine days old and, though still a tiny toddler, was just beginning to lisp his first babyish words. Cissy Caffrey bent over him to tease his fat little plucks and the dainty dimple in his chin.

—Now, baby, Cissy Caffrey said. Say out big, big. I want a drink of water.

And baby prattled after her:

—A jink a jink a jawbo.

Cissy Caffrey cuddled the wee chap for she was awfully fond of children, so patient with little sufferers and Tommy Caffrey could never be got to take his castor oil unless it was Cissy Caffrey that held his nose and promised him the scatty heel of the loaf of brown bread with golden syrup on. What a persuasive power that girl had! But to be sure baby was as good as gold, a perfect little dote in his new fancy bib. None of your spoilt beauties, Flora MacFlimsy sort, was Cissy Caffrey. A truer-hearted lass never drew the breath of life, always with a laugh in her gipsylike eyes and a frolicsome word on her cherryripe red lips, a girl lovable in the extreme. And Edy Boardman laughed too at the quaint language of little brother.

But just then there was a slight altercation between Master Tommy and Master Jacky. Boys will be boys and our two twins were no exception to this golden rule. The apple of discord was a certain castle of sand which Master Jacky had built and Master Tommy would have it right go wrong that it was to be architecturally improved by a frontdoor like the Martello tower had. But if Master Tommy was headstrong Master Jacky was selfwilled too and, true to the maxim that every little Irishman's house is his castle, he fell upon his hated rival and to such purpose that the wouldbe assailant came to grief and (alas to relate!) the coveted castle too. Needless to say the cries of discomfited Master Tommy drew the attention of the girl friends.

—Come here, Tommy, his sister called imperatively, at once!

And you, Jacky, for shame to throw poor Tommy in the dirty sand. Wait till I catch you for that.

His eyes misty with unshed tears Master Tommy came at her call for their big sister's word was law with the twins. And in a sad plight he was after his misadventure. His little man-o'-war top and unmentionables were full of sand but Cissy was a past mistress in the art of smoothing over life's tiny troubles and very quickly not one speck of sand was to be seen on his smart little suit. Still the blue eyes were glistening with hot tears that would well up so she kissed away the hurtness and shook her hand at Master Jacky the culprit and said if she was near him she wouldn't be far from him, her eyes dancing in admonition.

—Nasty bold Jacky! she cried.

She put an arm round the little mariner and coaxed winningly:

—What's your name? Butter and cream?

—Tell us who is your sweetheart, spoke Edy Boardman. Is Cissy your sweetheart?

—Nao, tearful Tommy said.

—Is Edy Boardman your sweetheart? Cissy queried.

—Nao, Tommy said.

—I know, Edy Boardman said none too amiably with an arch glance from her shortsighted eyes. I know who is Tommy's sweetheart, Gerty is Tommy's sweetheart.

—Nao, Tommy said on the verge of tears.

Cissy's quick motherwit guessed what was amiss and she whispered to Edy Boardman to take him there behind the pushcar where the gentlemen couldn't see and to mind he didn't wet his new tan shoes. . . .

Edy Boardman asked Tommy Caffrey was he done and he said yes, so then she buttoned up his little knickerbockers for him and told him to run off and play with Jacky and to be good now and not to fight. But Tommy said he wanted the ball and Edy told him no that baby was playing with the ball and if he took it there'd be wigs on the green but Tommy said it was his ball and he wanted his ball and he pranced on the ground, if you please. The temper of him! O, he was a man already was little Tommy Caffrey since he was out of pinnies. Edy told him no, no and to be off now with him and she told Cissy Caffrey not to give in to him.

—You're not my sister, naughty Tommy said. It's my ball.

But Cissy Caffrey told baby Boardman to look up, look up high at her finger and she snatched the ball quickly and threw it along the sand and Tommy after it in full career, having won the day.

—Anything for a quiet life, laughed Ciss.

And she tickled tiny tot's two cheeks to make him forget and played here's the lord mayor, here's his two horses, here's his gingerbread carriage and here he walks in, chinchopper, chinchopper, chinchopper chin. But Edy got as cross as two sticks about him getting his own way like that from everyone always petting him.

—I'd like to give him something, she said, so I would, where I won't say.

—On the beetoteetom, laughed Cissy merrily.

Gerty MacDowell bent down her head and crimsoned at the idea of Cissy saying an unladylike thing like that out loud she'd be ashamed of her life to say, flushing a deep rosy red, and Edy Boardman said she was sure the gentleman opposite heard what she said. But not a pin cared Ciss.

—Let him! she said with a pert toss of her head and a piquant tilt of her nose. Give it to him too on the same place as quick as I'd look at him. . . .

The twins were now playing again right merrily for the troubles of childhood are but as fleeting summer showers. Cissy played with baby Boardman till he crowed with glee, clapping baby hands in air. Peep she cried behind the hood of the pushcar and Edy asked where was Cissy gone and then Cissy popped up her head and cried ah! and, my word, didn't the little chap enjoy that! And then she told him to say papa.

—Say papa, baby. Say pa pa pa pa pa pa pa.

And baby did his level best to say it for he was very intelligent for eleven months everyone said and big for his age and the picture of health, a perfect little bunch of love, and he would certainly turn out to be something great, they said.

—Haja ja ja haja.

Cissy wiped his little mouth with the dribbling bib and wanted him to sit up properly, and say pa pa pa but when she undid the strap she cried out, holy saint Denis, that he was possing wet and to double the half blanket the other way under him. Of course his infant majesty was most obstreperous at such toilet formalities and he let everyone know it:

—Habaa baaaahabaaa baaaa.

And two great big lovely big tears coursing down his cheeks. It was all no use soothering him with no, nono, baby, no and telling him about the geegee and where was the puffpuff but Ciss, always readywitted, gave him in his mouth the teat of the suckingbottle and the young heathen was quickly appeased.

THE HIGH-BORN BABE

From THE WOULD-BE GOODS

E. Nesbit

The books of E. Nesbit have their place in that small collection of stories loved by children and grown-ups equally. Especially beloved are the books about the Bastable children, whose everyday activities are as transformed by their readings of romantic adventure books as Don Quixote's were by his exposure to Moorish romances.

In this chapter from The Would-be Goods, *Oswald Bastable, aged twelve, narrates an adventure the Bastable children had with a very real baby—a story that young readers find amusing, and a new mother might find somewhat chilling.*

It really was not such a bad baby—for a baby. Its face was round and quite clean, which babies' faces are not always, as I daresay you know by your own youthful relatives; and Dora said its cape was trimmed with real lace, whatever that may be—I don't see myself how one kind of lace can be realler than another. It was in a very swagger sort of perambulator when we saw it; and the perambulator was standing quite by itself in the lane that leads to the mill.

"I wonder whose baby it is," Dora said. "Isn't it a darling, Alice?"

Alice agreed to its being one, and said she thought it was most likely the child of noble parents stolen by gipsies.

"These two, as likely as not," Noël said. "Can't you see something crime-like in the very way they're lying?"

They were two tramps, and they were lying on the grass at the edge of the lane on the shady side fast asleep, only a very little further on than where the Baby was. They were very ragged, and their snores did have a sinister sound.

"I expect they stole the titled heir at dead of night, and they've been travelling hot-foot ever since, so now they're sleeping the sleep of exhaustedness," Alice said. "What a heart-rending scene when the patrician mother wakes in the morning and finds the infant aristocrat isn't in bed with his mamma."

The Baby was fast asleep or else the girls would have kissed it. They are strangely fond of kissing. The author never could see anything in it himself.

"If the gipsies *did* steal it," Dora said, "perhaps they'd sell it to us. I wonder what they'd take for it."

"What could you do with it if you'd got it?" H. O. asked.

"Why, adopt it, of course," Dora said. "I've often thought I should enjoy adopting a baby. It would be a golden deed, too. We've hardly got any in the book yet."

"I should have thought there were enough of us," Dicky said.

"Ah, but you're none of you babies," said Dora.

"Unless you count H. O. as a baby: he behaves jolly like one sometimes."

This was because of what had happened that morning when Dicky found H. O. going fishing with a box of worms, and the box was the one Dicky keeps his silver studs in, and the medal he got at school, and what is left of his watch and chain. The box is lined with red velvet and it was not nice afterwards. And then H. O. said Dicky had hurt him, and he was a beastly bully, and he cried. We thought all this had been made up, and were sorry to see it threatened to break out again. So Oswald said—

"Oh, bother the Baby! Come along, do!"

And the others came.

We were going to the miller's with a message about some flour that hadn't come, and about a sack of sharps for the pigs.

After you go down the lane you come to a cloverfield, and then a cornfield, and then another lane, and then it is the mill. It is a jolly fine mill: in fact it is two—water and wind ones—one of each kind—with a house and farm buildings as well. I never saw a mill like it, and I don't believe you have either.

If we had been in a story-book the miller's wife would have taken us into the neat sanded kitchen where the old oak settle was black with time and rubbing, and dusted chairs for us—old brown Windsor chairs—and given us each a glass of sweet-scented cowslip wine and a thick slice of rich home-made cake. And there would have been fresh roses in an old china bowl on the table. As it was, she asked us all into the parlour and gave us Eiffel Tower lemonade and Marie biscuits. The chairs in her parlour were "bent wood," and no flowers, except some wax ones under a glass shade, but she was very kind, and we were very much obliged to her. We got out to the miller, though, as soon as we could; only Dora and Daisy stayed with her, and she talked to them about her lodgers and about her relations in London.

The miller is a MAN. He showed us all over the mills—both kinds—and let us go right up into the very top of the wind-mill, and showed us how the top moved round so that the sails could catch the wind, and the great heaps of corn, some red and some yellow (the red is English wheat), and the heaps slide down a little bit at a time into a square hole and go down to the millstones. The corn makes a rustling soft noise that is very jolly—something like the noise of the sea—and you can hear it through all the other mill noises.

Then the miller let us go all over the water-mill. It is fairy palaces inside a mill. Everything is powdered over white, like sugar on pancakes when you are allowed to help yourself. And he opened a door and showed us the great water-wheel working on slow and sure, like some great, round, dripping giant, Noël said, and then he asked us if we fished.

"Yes," was our immediate reply.

"Then why not try the mill-pool?" he said, and we replied politely; and when he was gone to tell his man something we owned to each other that he was a trump.

He did the thing thoroughly. He took us out and cut us ash saplings for rods; he found us lines and hooks, and several different sorts of bait, including a handsome handful of meal-worms, which Oswald put loose in his pocket.

When it came to bait, Alice said she was going home with Dora and Daisy. Girls are strange, mysterious, silly things. Alice always enjoys a rat hunt until the rat is caught, but she hates fishing from beginning to end. We boys have got to like it. We don't feel now as we did when we turned off the water and stopped the competition of the competing anglers. We had a grand day's fishing that day. I can't think what made the miller so kind to us. Perhaps he felt a thrill of fellow-feeling in his manly breast for his fellow-sportsmen, for he was a noble fisherman himself.

We had glorious sport—eight roach, six dace, three eels, seven perch, and a young pike, but he was so very young the miller asked us to put him back, and of course we did.

"He'll live to bite another day," said the miller.

The miller's wife gave us bread and cheese and more Eiffel Tower lemonade, and we went home at last, a little damp, but full of successful ambition, with our fish on a string.

It had been a strikingly good time—one of those times that happen in the country quite by themselves. Country people are much more friendly than town people. I suppose they don't have to spread their friendly feelings out over so many persons, so it's thicker, like a pound of butter on one loaf is thicker than on a dozen. Friendliness in the country is not scrape, like it is in London. Even Dicky and H. O. forgot the affair of honour that had taken place in the morning. H. O. changed rods with Dicky because H. O.'s was the best rod, and Dicky baited H. O.'s hook for him just like loving, unselfish brothers in Sunday School magazines.

We were talking fishlikely as we went along down the lane and through the cornfield and the cloverfield, and then we came to the other lane where we had seen the Baby. The tramps were gone, and the perambulator was gone, and, of course, the Baby was gone too.

"I wonder if those gipsies *had* stolen the Baby?" Noël said dreamily. He had not fished much, but he had made a piece of poetry. It was this:

> *How I wish*
> *I was a fish.*
> *I would not look*
> *At your hook,*
> *But lie still and be cool*
> *At the bottom of the pool*
> *And when you went to look*
> *At your cruel hook,*
> *You would not find me there,*
> *So there!*

"If they did steal the Baby," Noël went on, "they will be tracked by the lordly perambulator. You can disguise a baby in rags and walnut juice, but there isn't any disguise dark enough to conceal a perambulator's person."

"You might disguise it as a wheel-barrow," said Dicky.

"Or cover it with leaves," said H. O., "like the robins."

We told him to shut up and not gibber, but afterwards we had to own that even a young brother may sometimes talk sense by accident.

For we took the short cut home from the lane—it begins with a large gap in the hedge and the grass and weeds trodden down by the hasty feet of persons who were late for church and in too great a hurry to go round by the road. Our house is next to the church, as I think I have said before, some time.

The short cut leads to a stile at the edge of a bit of wood (the Parson's Shave, they call it, because it belongs to him). The wood has not been shaved for some time, and it has grown out beyond the stile; and here, among the hazels and chestnuts and young dogwood bushes, we saw something white. We felt it was our duty to investigate, even if the white was only the under side of the tail of a dead rabbit caught in a trap. It was not—it was part of the perambulator. I forget whether I said that the perambulator was enamelled white—not the kind of enamelling you do at home with Aspinall's and the hairs of the brush come out and it is gritty-looking, but smooth, like the handles of ladies' very best lace parasols. And whoever had abandoned the helpless perambulator in that lonely spot had done exactly as H. O. said, and covered it with leaves, only they were green and some of them had dropped off.

The others were wild with excitement. Now or never, they thought, was a chance to be real detectives. Oswald alone retained a calm exterior. It was he who would not go straight to the police station.

He said: "Let's try and ferret out something for ourselves before we tell the police. They always have a clue directly they hear about the finding of the body. And besides, we might as well let Alice be in anything there is going. And besides, we haven't had our dinners yet."

This argument of Oswald's was so strong and powerful—his arguments are often that, as I daresay you have noticed—that the others agreed. It was Oswald, too, who showed his artless brothers why they had much better not take the deserted perambulator home with them.

"The dead body, or whatever the clue is, is always left exactly as it is found," he said, "till the police have seen it, and the coroner, and the inquest, and the doctor, and the sorrowing relations. Besides, suppose someone saw us with the beastly thing, and thought we had stolen it; then they would say, '*What have you done with the Baby?*' and then where should we be?"

Oswald's brothers could not answer this question, but once more Oswald's native eloquence and far-seeing discerningness conquered.

"Anyway," Dicky said, "let's shove the derelict a little further under cover."

So we did.

Then we went on home. Dinner was ready and so were Alice and Daisy, but Dora was not there.

"She's got a—well, she's not coming to dinner anyway," Alice said when we asked. "She can tell you herself afterwards what it is she's got."

Oswald thought it was headache, or pain in the temper, or in the pinafore, so he said no more, but as soon as Mrs. Pettigrew had helped us and left the room he began the thrilling tale of the foresaken perambulator. He told it with the greatest thrillingness anyone could have, but Daisy and Alice seemed almost unmoved. Alice said—

"Yes, very strange," and things like that, but both the girls seemed to be thinking of something else. They kept looking at each other and trying not to laugh, so Oswald saw they had got some silly secret and he said—

"Oh, all right! I don't care about telling you. I only thought you'd like to be in it. It's going to be a real big thing, with policemen in it, and perhaps a judge."

"In what?" H. O. said; "the perambulator?"

Daisy choked and then tried to drink, and spluttered and got purple, and had to be thumped on the back. But Oswald was not appeased. When Alice said, "Do go on, Oswald. I'm sure we all like it very much," he said—

"Oh, no, thank you," very politely. "As it happens," he went on, "I'd just as soon go through with this thing without having any girls in it."

"In the perambulator?" said H. O. again.

"It's a man's job," Oswald went on, without taking any notice of H. O.

"Do you really think so," said Alice, "when there's a baby in it?"

"But there isn't," said H. O., "if you mean in the perambulator."

"Blow you and your perambulator," said Oswald, with gloomy forbearance.

Alice kicked Oswald under the table and said—

"Don't be waxy, Oswald. Really and truly Daisy and I *have* got a secret, only it's Dora's secret, and she wants to tell you herself. If it was mine or Daisy's we'd tell you this minute, wouldn't we, Mouse?"

"This very second," said the White Mouse.

And Oswald consented to take their apologies.

Then the pudding came in, and no more was said except asking for things to be passed—sugar and water, and bread and things.

Then when the pudding was all gone, Alice said—

"Come on."

And we came on. We did not want to be disagreeable, though really we were keen on being detectives and sifting that perambulator to the very dregs. But boys have to try to take an interest in their sisters' secrets, however silly. This is part of being a good brother.

Alice led us across the field where the sheep once fell into the brook, and across the brook by the plank. At the other end of the next field there was a sort of wooden house on wheels, that the shepherd sleeps in at the time of year when lambs are being born, so that he can see that they are not stolen by gipsies before the owners have counted them.

To this hut Alice now led her kind brothers and Daisy's kind brother.

"Dora is inside," she said, "with the Secret. We were afraid to have it in the house in case it made a noise."

The next moment the Secret was a secret no longer, for we all beheld Dora, sitting on a sack on the floor of the hut, with the Secret in her lap.

It was the High-born Babe!

Oswald was so overcome that he sat down suddenly, just like Betsy Trotwood did in *David Copperfield*, which just shows what a true author Dickens is.

"You've done it this time," he said. "I suppose you know you're a baby-stealer?"

"I'm not," Dora said. "I've adopted him."

"Then it was you," Dicky said, "who scuttled the perambulator in the wood?"

"Yes," Alice said; "we couldn't get it over the stile unless Dora put down the Baby, and we were afraid of the nettles for his legs. His name is to be Lord Edward."

"But, Dora—really, don't you think—"

"If you'd been there you'd have done the same," said Dora firmly. "The gipsies had gone. Of course something had frightened them and they fled from justice. And the little darling was awake and held out his arms to me. No, he hasn't cried a bit, and I know all about babies; I've often nursed Mrs. Simpkins's daughter's baby when she brings it up on Sundays. They have bread and milk to eat. You take him, Alice, and I'll go and get some bread and milk for him."

Alice took the noble brat. It was horribly lively, and squirmed about in her arms, and wanted to crawl on the floor. She could only keep it quiet by saying things to it a boy would be ashamed even to think of saying, such as "Goo goo," and "Did ums was," and "Ickle ducksums then."

When Alice used these expressions the Baby laughed and chuckled and replied—

"Daddadda," "Bababa," or "Glueglue."

But if Alice stopped her remarks for an instant the thing screwed its face up as if it was going to cry, but she never gave it time to begin.

It was a rummy little animal.

Then Dora came back with the bread and milk, and they fed the noble infant. It was greedy and slobbery, but all three girls seemed unable to keep their eyes and hands off it. They looked at it exactly as if it was pretty.

We boys stayed watching them. There was no amusement left for us now, for Oswald saw that Dora's Secret knocked the bottom out of the perambulator.

When the infant aristocrat had eaten a hearty meal it sat on Alice's lap and played with the amber heart she wears that Albert's uncle brought her from Hastings after the business of the bad sixpence and the nobleness of Oswald.

"Now," said Dora, "this is a council, so I want to be business-like. The Duckums Darling has been stolen away; its wicked steal-ers have deserted the Precious. We've got it. Perhaps its ancestral halls are miles and miles away. I vote we keep the little Lovey Duck till it's advertised for."

"If Albert's uncle lets you," said Dicky, darkly.

"Oh, don't say 'you' like that," Dora said; "I want it to be all of our baby. It will have five fathers and three mothers, and a grand-father and a great Albert's uncle, and a great grand-uncle. I'm sure Albert's uncle will let us keep it—at any rate till it's advertised for."

"And suppose it never is," Noël said.

"Then so much the better," said Dora, "the little Duckywux."

She began kissing the baby again. Oswald, ever thoughtful, said—

"Well, what about your dinner?"

"Bother dinner!" Dora said—so like a girl. "Will you all agree to be his fathers and mothers?"

"Anything for a quiet life," said Dicky, and Oswald said—

"Oh, yes, if you like. But you'll see we shan't be allowed to keep it."

"You talk as if he was rabbits or white rats," said Dora, "and he's not—he's a little man, he is."

"All right, he's no rabbit, but a man. Come on and get some grub, Dora," rejoined the kind-hearted Oswald, and Dora did, with Oswald and the other boys. Only Noël stayed with Alice. He really seemed to like the baby. When I looked back he was stand-ing on his head to amuse it, but the baby did not seem to like him any better whichever end of him was up.

Dora went back to the shepherd's house on wheels directly she had had her dinner. Mrs. Pettigrew was very cross about her not being in to it, but she had kept her some mutton hot all the same. She is a decent sort. And there were stewed prunes. We had some to keep Dora company. Then we boys went fishing again in the moat, but we caught nothing.

Just before tea-time we all went back to the hut, and before we got half across the last field we could hear the howling of the Secret.

"Poor little beggar," said Oswald, with manly tenderness. "They must be sticking pins in it."

We found the girls and Noël looking quite pale and breathless. Daisy was walking up and down with the Secret in her arms. It looked like Alice in Wonderland nursing the baby that turned into a pig. Oswald said so, and added that its screams were like it too.

"What on earth is the matter with it?" he said.

"*I* don't know," said Alice. "Daisy's tired, and Dora and I are quite worn out. He's been crying for hours and hours. *You* take him a bit."

"Not me," replied Oswald, firmly, withdrawing a pace from the Secret.

Dora was fumbling with her waistband in the furthest corner of the hut.

"I think he's cold," she said. "I thought I'd take off my flannelette petticoat, only the horrid strings got into a hard knot. Here, Oswald, let's have your knife."

With the word she plunged her hand into Oswald's jacket pocket, and next moment she was rubbing her hand like mad on her dress, and screaming almost as loud as the Baby. Then she began to laugh and to cry at the same time. This is called hysterics.

Oswald was sorry, but he was annoyed too. He had forgotten that his pocket was half full of the meal-worms the miller had kindly given him. And, anyway, Dora ought to have known that a man always carries his knife in his trousers pocket and not in his jacket one.

Alice and Daisy rushed to Dora. She had thrown herself down on the pile of sacks in the corner. The titled infant delayed its screams for a moment to listen to Dora's, but almost at once it went on again.

"Oh, get some water!" said Alice. "Daisy, run!"

The White Mouse, ever docile and obedient, shoved the baby into the arms of the nearest person, who had to take it or it would have fallen a wreck to the ground. This nearest person was Oswald. He tried to pass it on to the others, but they wouldn't. Noël would have, but he was busy kissing Dora and begging her not to.

So our hero, for such I may perhaps term him, found himself the degraded nursemaid of a small but furious kid.

He was afraid to lay it down, for fear in its rage it should beat its brains out against the hard earth, and he did not wish, however innocently, to be the cause of its hurting itself at all. So he walked earnestly up and down with it, thumping it unceasingly on the back, while the others attended to Dora, who presently ceased to yell.

Suddenly it struck Oswald that the High-born also had ceased to yell. He looked at it, and could hardly believe the glad tidings of his faithful eyes. With bated breath he hastened back to the sheep-house.

The others turned on him, full of reproaches about the meal-worms and Dora, but he answered without anger.

"Shut up," he said in a whisper of imperial command. "Can't you see it's *gone to sleep?*"

As exhausted as if they had all taken part in all the events of a very long Athletic Sports, the youthful Bastables and their friends dragged their weary limbs back across the fields. Oswald was compelled to go on holding the titled infant, for fear it should wake up if it changed hands, and begin to yell again. Dora's flannelette petticoat had been got off somehow—how I do not seek to inquire—and the Secret was covered with it. The others surrounded Oswald as much as possible, with a view to concealment if we met Mrs. Pettigrew. But the coast was clear. Oswald took the Secret up into his bedroom. Mrs. Pettigrew doesn't come there much, it's too many stairs.

With breathless precaution Oswald laid it down on his bed. It sighed, but did not wake. Then we took it in turns to sit by it and see that it did not get up and fling itself out of bed, which, in one of its furious fits, it would just as soon have done as not.

We expected Albert's uncle every minute.

At last we heard the gate, but he did not come in, so we looked out and saw that there he was talking to a distracted-looking man on a piebald horse—one of the miller's horses.

A shiver of doubt coursed through our veins. We could not remember having done anything wrong at the miller's. But you never know. And it seemed strange his sending a man up on his own horse. But when we had looked a bit longer our fears went down and our curiosity got up. For we saw that the distracted one was a gentleman.

Presently he rode off, and Albert's uncle came in. A deputation met him at the door—all the boys and Dora, because the baby was her idea.

"We've found something," Dora said, "and we want to know whether we may keep it."

The rest of us said nothing. We were not so very extra anxious to keep it after we had heard how much and how long it could howl. Even Noël had said he had no idea a baby could yell like it. Dora said it only cried because it was sleepy, but we reflected that it would certainly be sleepy once a day, if not oftener.

"What is it?" said Albert's uncle. "Let's see this treasure-trove. Is it a wild beast?"

"Come and see," said Dora, and we led him to our room.

Alice turned down the pink flannelette petticoat with silly pride, and showed the youthful heir fatly and pinkly sleeping.

"A baby!" said Albert's uncle. "*The* Baby! Oh, my cat's alive!"

That is an expression which he uses to express despair unmixed with anger.

"Where did you—but that doesn't matter. We'll talk of this later."

He rushed from the room, and in a moment or two we saw him mount his bicycle and ride off.

Quite shortly he returned with the distracted horseman.

It was *his* baby, and not titled at all. The horseman and his wife were the lodgers at the mill. The nursemaid was a girl from the village.

She *said* she only left the Baby five minutes while she went to speak to her sweetheart who was gardener at the Red House. But *we* knew she left it over an hour, and nearly two.

I never saw anyone so pleased as the distracted horseman.

When we were asked we explained about having thought the Baby was the prey of gipsies, and the distracted horseman stood hugging the Baby, and actually thanked us.

But when he had gone we had a brief lecture on minding our own business. But Dora still thinks she was right. As for Oswald and most of the others, they agreed that they would rather mind their own business all their lives than mind a baby for a single hour.

If you have never had to do with a baby in the frenzied throes of sleepiness you can have no idea what its screams are like.

If you have been through such a scene you will understand how we managed to bear up under having no baby to adopt.

Oswald insisted on having the whole thing written in the

Golden Deed book. Of course his share could not be put in without telling about Dora's generous adopting of the forlorn infant outcast, and Oswald could not and cannot forget that he was the one who did get that baby to sleep.

What a time Mr. and Mrs. Distracted Horseman must have of it, though—especially now they've sacked the nursemaid.

If Oswald is ever married—I suppose he must be some day—he will have ten nurses to each baby. Eight is not enough. We know that because we tried, and the whole eight of us were not enough for the needs of that deserted infant who was not so extra high-born after all.

SONGS OF EDUCATION: III. FOR THE CRÈCHE

From THE COLLECTED POEMS OF G. K. CHESTERTON

G. K. Chesterton

A baby (a male baby, by the sound of him) gives his rueful opinion of working mothers who believe in Progress and Freedom, in this early poem by the British novelist, essayist, critic and poet, G. K. Chesterton.

I remember my mother, the day that we met,
A thing I shall never entirely forget;
And I toy with the fancy that, young as I am,
I should know her again if we met in a tram.
  But mother is happy in turning a crank
  That increases the balance at somebody's bank;
  And I feel satisfaction that mother is free
  From the sinister task of attending to me.

They have brightened our room, that is spacious and
    cool,
With diagrams used in the Idiot School,
And Books for the Blind that will teach us to see;
But mother is happy, for mother is free.
  For mother is dancing up forty-eight floors,
  For love of the Leeds International Stores,
  And the flame of that faith might perhaps have
    grown cold,
  With the care of a baby seven weeks old.

145

For mother is happy in greasing a wheel
For somebody else, who is cornering Steel;
And though our one meeting was not very long,
She took the occasion to sing me this song:
    "O, hush thee, my baby, the time will soon come
    When thy sleep will be broken with hooting and hum;
    There are handles want turning and turning all day,
    And knobs to be pressed in the usual way;

"O, hush thee, my baby, take rest while I croon,
For Progress comes early, and Freedom too soon."

Part V

LIFE WITH BABY

BLUES

From SPECIAL DELIVERY

Shirley Jackson

An eminent writer and mother of seven offers sympathy and sound advice for that time, usually somewhere between Baby's second and fourth month, when the knowledge comes home acutely and miserably that nothing is ever going to be the same again.

There is no really adequate preparation for a first baby. Any prospective mother, of course, can recite almost endless lists of *facts* about the baby she is going to have, she can describe the neat piles of shirts and nightgowns and sweaters and diapers, she can point out the neat crib, made up with sheets and blankets since the seventh month of her pregnancy, she can show off the bottle sterilizer and the little blue dish and the carriage and the bathinette and the cotton and the swabs and the baby towels and washcloths and powder and she can even remark amusedly that if anyone else arrived at her house with this quantity of baggage she would expect them to be planning on a lengthy stay. In spite of all the arranging, however, and the wonderful joy of folding and refolding the little pink sweaters and the wealth of blankets, and the excitement of arranging the baby furniture—so immaculate, so new and fresh—none of it really brings home the fact that when the baby does come, he comes to stay. Twenty-four hours a day. Twenty-four hours a day for years and years and years. From the minute they first hand him to you in the hospital and you finally

149

get a chance to count his arms and legs to make sure they are all there, you are never going to be without him again. When you get into this Mommy racket, you're in it for good.

Mercifully, the realization of this does not come all at once. At first it is enough just to get through one day at a time without bothering about the years to come, and of course the excitement of folding and refolding the little clothes is nothing compared with the excitement of actually putting them on the baby, and nothing is ever as real as the sight of that small creature settling down at last in his very own crib. *His* crib, mind you. None of these things had any slightest reason for existing until there was going to be a baby; chances are good that you never even *heard* of some of these things until there was going to be a baby (oleum percomorph? dextro-maltose 1? soakers?) but one thing is certain. Nothing is ever going to be the same again.

Your relationship to the entire world has been hopelessly altered. Life without a baby and life with a baby are simply two different kinds of lives. You will never, for instance, be able to walk down the street again, the way you did before the baby came. For one thing, you will be pushing a baby carriage, and for another, your whole view of things will be different. Instead of noticing what other women are wearing, you will be noticing what their babies are wearing. If you stop to talk to someone you will not chat lightly about what good movies you have seen lately. You will never be able to pass a toy shop without wondering, fleetingly, if that fuzzy bear would enchant Baby. Your grocery order will change its character, leaning more heavily toward strained bananas and away from wild rice and chocolate-covered ants. The weekly laundry, the dishwashing, the house cleaning, will be different. (The laundry, by the way, never really begins to hurt until Baby gets to be about sixteen and starts sending out his shirts; a sixteen-year-old boy, particularly one who is falling in love for the second or third time, somehow manages to wear as many as nine shirts a week.) The faces of old and dear friends will be subtly changed, even a little dimmer, and see what happens to the close friendship you have cherished since childhood, when your friend remarks critically that she thinks Baby is slow in learning to turn over.

The whole foundation of the world has shifted. The center of the universe is certainly asleep there in the crib and, all unconscious, he has even managed to change the shape of time. Up until now years went along by themselves, moving reasonably in weeks and months, turning up fresh every January. Holidays were pleasant, but minor; even Christmas and wedding anniversaries were one-day affairs, marked by no particular hysteria. That is going to be different. Time now is not going to be reckoned by years, it is going to be in terms of teeth, and sitting up, and going on solid food, and taking a first step. The baby is going to be six weeks old, and four months old, and the new year is not going to begin on January first any more, but on that odd new holiday which has taken what always used to be a perfectly ordinary day and turned it into a permanent occasion for celebration. By the time the child is old enough to know that he has a birthday you are going to have to be able to tell, at any time of the year, exactly how many weeks and months and days will have to pass before the birthday arrives again. Christmas and Valentine's Day and Thanksgiving Day will all take on aspects you never dreamed of before. Mother's Day will stop being the day you remember to send flowers to your mother; someday the little creature in the crib will come home from kindergarten with enormous pride bringing you a grimy tattered drawing of a flower or a bird or a rabbit on which is written in erratic print: I LOVE MOTHER. That's when you find out why it's called Mother's Day.

By then, of course, the year will have somehow been cut down to the period of time between September and June, with the summer months thrown in as one long glorious sunny day with no school. The school year will be neatly divided up into seasons of marbles, sleds, still-warm-enough-to-swim, and cold-enough-to-put-on-a-jacket.

No, nothing is ever going to be the same again. There is a time, somewhere between Baby's second and fourth month usually, when this knowledge comes home acutely, miserably. It is the point when the difficulties of schedule and planning are no longer insurmountable, when life has achieved a kind of daily pattern, things are cooling off a little, and the mother has her first real chance to take a deep breath and stand and look around her a little. The first thing she sees is the future, stretching interminably on and on, a limitless space of days in which one obligation to her baby succeeds another, her whole life to come irretrievably committed to her child. Other people are free, people without babies;

other people do not have horizons so entirely limited, other people can come and go as they please, can enjoy themselves without their weight of responsibility, other people do not have to slave and drudge at degrading monotonous work. Other people, indeed— what about the father of this child? No one expects *him* to stay home every day and do the same things over and over again. He goes off every morning and stays away all day, he meets other people and talks to them about business and news and anything in the world except babies, he sees the outside world, he has a reason for dressing well and he almost certainly lunches every day with clever, interesting people—those career women who always have a manicure. When Dr. Johnson was asked what he would do if he was shut up in a castle with a newborn baby he said, "Sir, I should not much like my company." Well, Dr. Johnson knew what he was talking about. It takes a little longer for the baby's own mother, but the truth is there—after a while, you can simply get *bored* with a little baby.

This state of mind goes on simmering for two or three days, and then one evening the baby's mother meets her husband at the front door when he comes home. She has made no attempt to hide the fact that she is feeling very sorry for herself. She has probably attempted to set her hair and botched it. The husband, with no inkling of the rebellion breeding on his fireside, asks at once, "What's wrong? Is the baby all right?"

The wife will almost certainly answer, "Is *that* all that matters to you?" or "Of course he's all right, but what about *me*?" or "You *used* to say hello to me *first*."

None of this is going to make things any clearer to her husband, who will make matters worse by saying, "But I *did* say hello to you, I asked was the baby all right?"

The wife's next remark (and it is very odd to hear yourself saying it) is, inevitably, "You never even *talk* to me any more."

"Of course I talk to you," he says, still groping. "I talk to you all the time."

"And you never take me out any more and you never say anything except 'How's the baby' and 'Is dinner ready' and you have lunch in restaurants with all kinds of people and women every day and I sit here all alone with nothing to do but take care of the baby and do you know how long it's been since I even saw a *movie* and I suppose you think I can go just anywhere all day long but how would *you* like having to push a carriage everywhere you go?"

"Well, listen," the husband says helpfully, "sure I'll take you to a movie—we can call up your mother and she'll come over and take care of the baby and we can go to the movies. What picture did you want to see so much?"

This is disastrous, and the husband is extremely lucky if he does not get belted one. The only possible worse thing he could say is "Well, look, honey, you go along to the movies if you want to— you call up one of your girl friends and run along, and I'll take care of the baby."

(There is actually one *worse* thing he could say, but if he has been married long enough to have a baby he knows enough to let it alone; he *could* say, "I don't have lunch with women every day.")

It would be quite fair to say that it is not in the makeup of husbands to understand a state of mind like this, any more than they can understand why a wife will get up out of a sickbed to dust the room before the doctor comes, or exactly what the good-looking woman in the black dress could have said to make her so mad. (It was the *way* she said it; she said it the way those good-looking women in black dresses always manage to say those little slighting things men never understand.) At any rate, this inexplicable temper tantrum in his wife is going to leave the husband bewildered and concerned and he is not going to be any better off a week later, when he suggests timidly and after a good deal of hesitation that they get a baby-sitter and go to the theater and his wife smiles at him happily and tolerantly and says, "Oh, *that*? Don't be silly—I don't really want to go anywhere."

Naturally, while he has been going around all this time trying to figure out what he did that was so terrible, she has been busy altering an unbearable pattern of her days into a more tolerable one; no one knows better than a female creature caught up in a round of house and baby care that a pattern of days must not be allowed to descend into monotony, and even a relatively minor change in the pattern is going to leave her feeling better. Wives are always doing this, anyway; consider the millions of jokes about wives changing the furniture around, buying new hats to cheer themselves up, throwing themselves into an orgy of spring cleaning, switching seemingly at random from one hairdresser or butcher to another. Consequently, once this mother has blown off steam and had her tantrum, she has taken the traditional female method of adjusting her life more satisfactorily, and has probably bought herself a new set of dishes, or dressed the baby in blue jeans, or changed the kitchen curtains, or dyed her hair.

Babies are supposed to be fun, after all, and they might as well start out being fun right from the beginning, because they're going to stay a long, long time.

ON THE SHELF

From LITTLE WOMEN

Louisa May Alcott

The following chapter from Little Women *has a particularly modern ring to it, especially in its portrait of infant tyranny at its worst, long before permissiveness came into fashion (and then went out of fashion again).*

In France the young girls have a dull time of it till they are married, when *"Vive la liberté"* becomes their motto. In America, as everyone knows, girls early sign the declaration of independence, and enjoy their freedom with republican zest; but the young matrons usually abdicate with the first heir to the throne, and go into a seclusion almost as close as a French nunnery, though by no means as quiet. Whether they like it or not, they are virtually put upon the shelf as soon as the wedding excitement is over, and most of them might exclaim, as did a very pretty woman the other day, "I'm as handsome as ever, but no one takes any notice of me because I'm married."

Not being a belle or even a fashionable lady, Meg did not experience this affliction till her babies were a year old, for in her little world primitive customs prevailed, and she found herself more admired and beloved than ever.

As she was a womanly little woman, the maternal instinct was very strong, and she was entirely absorbed in her children, to the utter exclusion of everything and everybody else. Day and night she brooded over them with tireless devotion and anxiety, leaving

John to the tender mercies of the help, for an Irish lady now presided over the kitchen department. Being a domestic man, John decidedly missed the wifely attentions he had been accustomed to receive; but, as he adored his babies, he cheerfully relinquished his comfort for a time, supposing, with masculine ignorance, that peace would soon be restored. But three months passed, and there was no return or repose; Meg looked worn and nervous, the babies absorbed every minute of her time, the house was neglected, and Kitty, the cook, who took life "aisy," kept him on short commons. When he went out in the morning he was bewildered by small commissions for the captive mamma; if he came gaily in at night, eager to embrace his family, he was quenched by a "Hush! They are just asleep after worrying all day." If he proposed a little amusement at home, "No, it would disturb the babies." If he hinted at a lecture or concert, he was answered with a reproachful look, and a decided "Leave my children for pleasure, never!" His sleep was broken by infant wails and visions of a phantom figure pacing noiselessly to and fro in the watches of the night; his meals were interrupted by the frequent flight of the presiding genius, who deserted him, half helped, if a muffled chirp sounded from the nest above; and when he read his paper of an evening, Demi's colic got into the shipping list, and Daisy's fall affected the price of stocks, for Mrs. Brooke was only interested in domestic news.

The poor man was very uncomfortable, for the children had bereft him of his wife; home was merely a nursery, and the perpetual "hushing" made him feel like a brutal intruder whenever he entered the sacred precincts of Babyland. He bore it very patiently for six months, and, when no signs of amendment appeared, he did what other paternal exiles do—tried to get a little comfort elsewhere. Scott had married and gone to housekeeping not far off, and John fell into the way of running over for an hour or two of an evening, when his own parlor was empty and his own wife singing lullabies that seemed to have no end. Mrs. Scott was a lively, pretty girl, with nothing to do but be agreeable, and she performed her mission most successfully. The parlor was always bright and attractive, the chessboard ready, the piano in tune, plenty of gay gossip, and a nice little supper set forth in tempting style.

John would have preferred his own fireside if it had not been so lonely; but as it was, he gratefully took the next best thing, and enjoyed his neighbor's society.

Meg rather approved of the new arrangement at first, and found it a relief to know that John was having a good time instead of dozing in the parlor or tramping about the house and waking the children. But by and by, when the teething worry was over, and the idols went to sleep at proper hours, leaving mamma time to rest, she began to miss John, and find her workbasket dull company, when he was not sitting opposite in his old dressing gown, comfortably scorching his slippers on the fender. She would not ask him to stay at home, but felt injured because he did not know that she wanted him without being told, entirely forgetting the many evenings he had waited for her in vain. She was nervous and worn out with watching and worry, and in that unreasonable frame of mind which the best of mothers occasionally experience when domestic cares oppress them. Want of exercise robs them of cheerfulness, and too much devotion to that idol of American women, the teapot, makes them feel as if they were all nerve and no muscle.

"Yes," she would say, looking in the glass, "I'm getting old and ugly; John doesn't find me interesting any longer, so he leaves his faded wife and goes to see his pretty neighbor, who has no incumbrances. Well, the babies love me; they don't care if I am thin and pale, and haven't time to crimp my hair; they are my comfort, and someday John will see what I've gladly sacrificed for them, won't he, my precious?"

To which pathetic appeal Daisy would answer with a coo, or Demi with a crow, and Meg would put by her lamentations for a maternal revel, which soothed her solitude for the time being. But the pain increased as politics absorbed John, who was always running over to discuss interesting points with Scott, quite unconscious that Meg missed him. Not a word did she say, however, till her mother found her in tears one day, and insisted on knowing what the matter was, for Meg's drooping spirits had not escaped her observation.

"I wouldn't tell anyone except you, mother; but I really do need advice, for if John goes on so much longer I might as well be widowed," replied Mrs. Brooke, drying her tears on Daisy's bib, with an injured air.

"Goes on how, my dear?" asked her mother anxiously.

"He's away all day, and at night, when I want to see him, he is continually going over to the Scotts'. It isn't fair that I should have the hardest work, and never any amusement. Men are very selfish, even the best of them."

"So are women; don't blame John till you see where you are wrong yourself."

"But it can't be right for him to neglect me."

"Don't you neglect him?"

"Why, mother, I thought you'd take my part!"

"So I do, as far as sympathizing goes; but I think the fault is yours, Meg."

"I don't see how."

"Let me show you. Did John ever neglect you, as you call it, while you made it a point to give him your society of an evening, his only leisure time?"

"No; but I can't do it now, with two babies to tend."

"I think you could, dear; and I think you ought. May I speak quite freely, and will you remember that it's mother who blames as well as mother who sympathizes?"

"Indeed I will! Speak to me as if I were little Meg again. I often feel as if I needed teaching more than ever since these babies look to me for everything."

Meg drew her low chair beside her mother's, and, with a little interruption in either lap, the two women rocked and talked lovingly together, feeling that the tie of motherhood made them more one than ever.

"You have only made the mistake that most young wives make—forgotten your duty to your husband in your love for your children. A very natural and forgivable mistake, Meg, but one that had better be remedied before you take to different ways; for children should draw you nearer than ever, not separate you, as if they were all yours and John had nothing to do but support them. I've seen it for some weeks, but have not spoken, feeling sure it would come right in time."

"I'm afraid it won't. If I ask him to stay, he'll think I'm jealous; and I wouldn't insult him by such an idea. He doesn't see that I want him, and I don't know how to tell him without words."

"Make it so pleasant he won't want to go away. My dear, he's longing for his little home; but it isn't home without you, and you are always in the nursery."

"Oughtn't I to be there?"

"Not all the time; too much confinement makes you nervous, and then you are unfitted for everything. Besides, you owe something to John as well as to the babies; don't neglect husband for children, don't shut him out of the nursery, but teach him how to help in it. His place is there as well as yours, and the children need him; let him feel that he has his part to do, and he will do it gladly and faithfully, and it will be better for you all."

"You really think so, mother?"

"I know it, Meg, for I've tried it; and I seldom give advice unless I've proved its practicability. When you and Jo were little, I went on just as you are, feeling as if I didn't do my duty unless I devoted myself wholly to you. Poor father took to his books, after I had refused all offers of help, and left me to try my experiment alone. I struggled along as well as I could, but Jo was too much for me. I nearly spoilt her by indulgence. You were poorly, and I worried about you till I fell sick myself. Then father came to the rescue, quietly managed everything, and made himself so helpful that I saw my mistake, and never have been able to get on without him since. That is the secret of our home happiness: he does not let business wean him from the little cares and duties that affect us all, and I try not to let domestic worries destroy my interest in his pursuits. We each do our part alone in many things, but at home we work together, always."

"It is so, mother; and my great wish is to be to my husband and children what you have been to yours. Show me how; I'll do anything you say."

"You always were my docile daughter. Well, dear, if I were you, I'd let John have more to do with the management of Demi, for the boy needs training, and it's none too soon to begin. Then I'd do what I have often proposed, let Hannah come and help you; she is a capital nurse, and you may trust the precious babies to her while you do more housework. You need exercise, Hannah would enjoy the rest, and John would find his wife again. Get out more; keep cheerful as well as busy, for you are the sunshine-maker of the family, and if you get dismal there is no fair weather. Then I'd try to take an interest in whatever John likes—talk with him, let him read to you, exchange ideas, and help each other in that way. Don't shut yourself up in a bandbox because you are a woman, but understand what is going on, and educate yourself to take your part in the world's work, for it all affects you and yours."

"John is so sensible, I'm afraid he will think I'm stupid if I ask questions about politics and things."

"I don't believe he would; love covers a multitude of sins, and of whom could you ask more freely than of him? Try it, and see if he doesn't find your society far more agreeable than Mrs. Scott's suppers."

"I will. Poor John! I'm afraid I *have* neglected him sadly, but I thought I was right, and he never said anything."

"He tried not to be selfish, but he *has* felt rather forlorn, I fancy. This is just the time, Meg, when young married people are apt to grow apart, and the very time when they ought to be most together; for the first tenderness soon wears off, unless care is taken to preserve it; and no time is so beautiful and precious to parents as the first years of the little lives given them to train. Don't let John be a stranger to the babies, for they will do more to keep him safe and happy in this world of trial and temptation than anything else, and through them you will learn to know and love one another as you should. Now, dear, good-by; think over mother's preachment, act upon it if it seems good, and God bless you all!"

Meg did think it over, found it good, and acted upon it, though the first attempt was not made exactly as she planned to have it. Of course the children tyrannized over her, and ruled the house as soon as they found out that kicking and squalling brought them whatever they wanted. Mamma was an abject slave to their caprices, but papa was not so easily subjugated, and occasionally afflicted his tender spouse by an attempt at paternal discipline with his obstreperous son. For Demi inherited a trifle of his sire's firmness of character—we won't call it obstinacy—and when he made up his little mind to have or to do anything, all the king's horses and all the king's men could not change that pertinacious little mind. Mamma thought the dear too young to be taught to conquer his prejudices, but papa believed that it never was too soon to learn obedience; so Master Demi early discovered that when he undertook to "wrastle" with "parpar," he always got the worst of it; yet, like the Englishman, Baby respected the man who conquered him, and loved the father whose grave "No, no," was more impressive than all mamma's love pats.

A few days after the talk with her mother, Meg resolved to try a social evening with John; so she ordered a nice supper, set the parlor in order, dressed herself prettily, and put the children to bed early, that nothing should interfere with her experiment. But, unfortunately, Demi's most unconquerable prejudice was against going to bed, and that night he decided to go on a rampage; so poor Meg sung and rocked, told stories and tried every sleep-provoking wile she could devise, but all in vain, the big eyes wouldn't shut; and long after Daisy had gone to bye-low, like the chubby little bunch of good nature she was, naughty Demi lay staring at the light, with the most discouragingly wide-awake expression of countenance.

"Will Demi lie still like a good boy, while mamma runs down and gives poor papa his tea?" asked Meg, as the hall door softly closed, and the well-known step went tiptoeing into the dining room.

"Me has tea!" said Demi, preparing to join in the revel.

"No; but I'll save you some little cakies for breakfast, if you'll go bye-bye like Daisy. Will you, lovey?"

"Iss!" and Demi shut his eyes tight, as if to catch sleep and hurry the desired day.

Taking advantage of the propitious moment, Meg slipped away, and ran down to greet her husband with a smiling face, and the little blue bow in her hair which was his especial admiration. He saw it at once, and said, with pleased surprise:

"Why, little mother, how gay we are tonight. Do you expect company? Is it a birthday, anniversary, or anything?"

"No; I'm tired of being a dowdy, so I dressed up as a change. You always make yourself nice for table, no matter how tired you are; so why shouldn't I when I have the time?"

"I do it out of respect to you, my dear," said the old-fashioned John.

"Ditto, ditto, Mr. Brooke," laughed Meg, looking young and pretty again, as she nodded to him over the teapot.

"Well, it's altogether delightful, and like old times. This tastes right. I drink your health, dear." And John sipped his tea with an air of reposeful rapture, which was of very short duration, however; for, as he put down his cup, the door handle rattled mysteriously, and a little voice was heard, saying impatiently:

"Opy doy; me's tummin!"

"It's that naughty boy. I told him to go to sleep alone, and here he is, downstairs getting his death a-cold pattering over that canvas," said Meg, answering the call.

"Mornin' now," announced Demi, in a joyful tone, as he entered, with his long nightgown gracefully festooned over his arm, and every curl bobbing gaily as he pranced about the table, eying the "cakies" with loving glances.

"No, it isn't morning yet. You must go to bed, and not trouble poor mamma; then you can have the little cake with sugar on it."

"Me loves parpar," said the artful one, preparing to climb the paternal knee, and revel in forbidden joys. But John shook his head, and said to Meg:

"If you told him to stay up there, and go to sleep alone, make him do it, or he will never learn to mind you."

"Yes, of course. Come, Demi," and Meg led her son away, feeling a strong desire to spank the little marplot who hopped beside her, laboring under the delusion that the bribe was to be administered as soon as they reached the nursery.

Nor was he disappointed; for that shortsighted woman actually gave him a lump of sugar, tucked him into his bed, and forbade any more promenades till morning.

"Iss!" said Demi the perjurer, blissfully sucking his sugar and regarding his first attempt as eminently successful.

Meg returned to her place, and supper was progressing pleasantly, when the little ghost walked again, and exposed the maternal delinquencies by boldly demanding:

"More sudar, marmar."

"Now this won't do," said John, hardening his heart against the engaging little sinner. "We shall never know any peace till that child learns to go to bed properly. You have made a slave of yourself long enough; give him one lesson, and then there will be an end of it. Put him in his bed and leave him, Meg."

"He won't stay there; he never does, unless I sit by him."

"I'll manage him. Demi, go upstairs, and get into your bed, as mamma bids you."

"S'ant!" replied the young rebel, helping himself to the coveted cakie, and beginning to eat the same with calm audacity.

"You must never say that to papa; I shall carry you if you don't go by yourself."

"Go 'way; me don't love parpar," and Demi retired to his mother's skirts for protection.

But even that refuge proved unavailing, for he was delivered over to the enemy, with a "Be gentle with him, John," which struck the culprit with dismay; for when mamma deserted him, then the judgment day was at hand. Bereft of his cake, defrauded of his frolic, and borne away by a strong hand to that detested bed, poor Demi could not restrain his wrath, but openly defied papa, and kicked and screamed lustily all the way upstairs. The minute he was put into bed on one side, he rolled out on the other, and made for the door, only to be ignominiously caught up by the tail of his little toga, and put back again, which lively performance was kept up till the young man's strength gave out, when he devoted himself to roaring at the top of his voice. The vocal exercise usually conquered Meg; but John sat as unmoved as the post which is popularly believed to be deaf. No coaxing, no sugar, no lullaby, no story, even the light was put out, and only the red glow of the fire enlivened the "big dark" which Demi regarded with curiosity rather than fear. This new order of things disgusted him, and he howled dismally for "marmar," as his angry passions subsided, and recollections of his tender bond-woman returned to the captive autocrat. The plaintive wail which succeeded the passionate roar went to Meg's heart, and she ran up to say beseechingly:

"Let me stay with him; he'll be good now, John."

"No, my dear, I've told him he must go to sleep, as you bid him; and he must, if I stay here all night."

"But he'll cry himself sick," pleaded Meg, reproaching herself for deserting the boy.

"No, he won't, he's so tired he will soon drop off, and then the matter is settled; for he will understand that he has got to mind. Don't interfere; I'll manage him."

"He's my child, and I can't have his spirit broken by harshness."

"He's my child, and I won't have his temper spoilt by indulgence. Go down, my dear, and leave the boy to me."

When John spoke in that masterful tone, Meg always obeyed, and never regretted her docility.

"Please let me kiss him once, John?"

"Certainly. Demi, say good night to mamma, and let her go and rest, for she is very tired with taking care of you all day."

Meg always insisted upon it that the kiss won the victory; for after it was given, Demi sobbed more quietly, and lay quite still at the bottom of the bed, whither he had wriggled in his anguish of mind.

"Poor little man, he's worn out with sleep and crying. I'll cover him up, and then go and set Meg's heart at rest," thought John, creeping to the bedside, hoping to find his rebellious heir asleep.

But he wasn't; for the moment his father peeped at him, Demi's eyes opened, his little chin began to quiver, and he put up his arms, saying, with a penitent hiccough, "Me's dood, now."

Sitting on the stairs, outside, Meg wondered at the long silence which followed the uproar; and, after imagining all sorts of impossible accidents, she slipped into the room, to set her fears at rest. Demi lay fast asleep; not in his usual spread-eagle attitude, but in a subdued bunch, cuddled close in the circle of his father's arm and holding his father's finger, as if he felt that justice was tempered with mercy, and had gone to sleep a sadder and wiser baby. So held, John had waited with womanly patience till the little hand relaxed its hold; and, while waiting, had fallen asleep, more tired by that tussle with his son than with his whole day's work.

As Meg stood watching the two faces on the pillow, she smiled to herself, and then slipped away again, saying, in a satisfied tone:

"I never need fear that John will be too harsh with my babies: he *does* know how to manage them, and will be a great help, for Demi *is* getting too much for me."

When John came down at last, expecting to find a pensive or reproachful wife, he was agreeably surprised to find Meg placidly trimming a bonnet, and to be greeted with the request to read something about the election, if he was not too tired. John saw in a minute that a revolution of some kind was going on, but wisely asked no questions, knowing that Meg was such a transparent little person, she couldn't keep a secret to save her life, and therefore the clew would soon appear. He read a long debate with the most amiable readiness and then explained in his most lucid manner, while Meg tried to look deeply interested, to ask intelligent questions, and keep her thoughts from wandering from the state of the nation to the state of her bonnet. In her secret soul, however, she decided that politics were as bad as mathematics, and that the mission of politicians seemed to be calling each other names; but she kept these feminine ideas to herself, and when John paused shook her head, and said with what she thought diplomatic ambiguity:

"Well, I really don't see what we are coming to."

John laughed and watched her for a minute, as she poised a pretty little preparation of lace and flowers on her hand, and regarded it with the genuine interest which his harangue had failed to waken.

"She is trying to like politics for my sake, so I'll try and like millinery for hers, that's only fair," thought John the Just, adding aloud:

"That's very pretty; is it what you call a breakfast cap?"

"My dear man, it's a bonnet! My very best go-to-concert-and-theater bonnet."

"I beg your pardon; it was so small, I naturally mistook it for one of the flyaway things you sometimes wear. How do you keep it on?"

"These bits of lace are fastened under the chin with a rosebud, so," and Meg illustrated by putting on the bonnet and regarding him with an air of calm satisfaction that was irresistible.

"It's a love of a bonnet, but I prefer the face inside, for it looks young and happy again," and John kissed the smiling face, to the great detriment of the rosebud under the chin.

"I'm glad you like it, for I want you to take me to one of the new concerts some night; I really need some music to put me in tune. Will you, please?"

"Of course I will, with all my heart, or anywhere else you like. You have been shut up so long, it will do you no end of good, and I shall enjoy it, of all things. What put it into your head, little mother?"

"Well, I had a talk with Marmee the other day, and told her how nervous and cross and out of sorts I felt, and she said I needed change and less care: so Hannah is to help me with the children, and I'm to see to things about the house more, and now and then have a little fun, just to keep me from getting to be a fidgety, broken-down old woman before my time. It's only an experiment, John, and I want to try it for your sake as much as for mine, because I've neglected you shamefully lately, and I'm going to make home what it used to be, if I can. You don't object, I hope?"

Never mind what John said, or what a very narrow escape the little bonnet had from utter ruin; all that we have any business to know is that John did *not* appear to object, judging from the changes which gradually took place in the house and its inmates. It was not all Paradise by any means, but everyone was better for the division of labor system; the children throve under the paternal rule, for accurate, steadfast John brought order and obedience into Babydom, while Meg recovered her spirits and composed her nerves by plenty of wholesome exercise, a little pleasure, and much confidential conversation with her sensible husband. Home grew homelike again, and John had no wish to leave it, unless he took Meg with him. The Scotts came to the Brookes' now, and everyone found the little house a cheerful place, full of happiness, content, and family love. Even gay Sallie Moffat liked to go there. "It is always so quiet and pleasant here; it does me good, Meg," she used to say, looking about with wistful eyes, as if trying to discover the charm, that she might use it in her great house, full of splendid loneliness; for there were no riotous, sunny-faced babies there, and Ned lived in a world of his own, where there was no place for her.

This household happiness did not come all at once, but John and Meg had found the key to it, and each year of married life taught them how to use it, unlocking the treasuries of real home love and mutual helpfulness, which the poorest may possess, and the richest cannot buy. This is the sort of shelf on which young wives and mothers may consent to be laid, safe from the restless fret and fever of the world, finding loyal lovers in the little sons and daughters who cling to them, undaunted by sorrow, poverty, or age; walking side by side, through fair and stormy weather, with a faithful friend, who is, in the true sense of the good old Saxon word, the "houseband," and learning, as Meg learned, that a woman's happiest kingdom is home, her highest honor the art of ruling it not as a queen, but as a wise wife and mother.

AN EXEMPLARY WIFE
AND MOTHER

From WAR AND PEACE

Leo Tolstoy

In the course of War and Peace, *Tolstoy's heroine, Natásha Rostova, undergoes a transformation from child to young girl to young woman. The transformation is completed at the end of the book as Natásha, now married to Pierre Bezúkhov, is shown in her role as wife and mother.*

To some readers this final picture of Natásha comes as a disappointment after that enchanting creature who appeared earlier in the novel. Others, new mothers perhaps most of all, find this happy and fulfilled (albeit slightly overweight) young matron no less glorious than the delightful child whose singing cast a mystical spell on the listener, or the glowing girl who danced all night at her first ball.

Natásha had married in the early spring of 1813, and in 1820 already had three daughters, besides a son for whom she had longed and whom she was now nursing. She had grown stouter and broader, so that it was difficult to recognize the slim lively Natásha of former days in this robust motherly woman. Her features were more defined and had a calm, soft and serene expression. In her face there was none of the ever-glowing animation that had formerly burned there and constituted its charm. Now her face and

167

body were often all that one saw, and her soul was not visible at all. All that struck the eye was a strong, handsome and fertile woman. The old fire very rarely kindled in her face now. That happened only when, as was the case that day, her husband returned home, or a sick child was convalescent, or when she and Countess Mary spoke of Prince Andrew (she never mentioned him to her husband, who she imagined was jealous of Prince Andrew's memory), or on the rare occasions when something happened to induce her to sing, a practice she had quite abandoned since her marriage. At the rare moments when the old fire kindled in her handsome fully-developed body she was even more attractive than in former days.

Since their marriage Natásha and her husband had lived in Moscow, in Petersburg, on their estate near Moscow, or with her mother, that is to say, in Nicholas's house. The young Countess Bezúkhova was not often seen in society, and those who met her there were not pleased with her and found her neither attractive nor amiable. Not that Natásha liked solitude—she did not know whether she liked it or not, she even thought that she did not—but with her pregnancies, her confinements, the nursing of her children, and sharing every moment of her husband's life, she had demands on her time which could only be satisfied by renouncing society. All who had known Natásha before her marriage wondered at the change in her as at something extraordinary. Only the old countess, with her maternal instinct, had realized that all Natásha's outbursts had been due to her need of children and a husband—as she herself had once exclaimed at Otrádnoe not so much in fun as in earnest—and her mother was now surprised by the surprise expressed by those who had never understood Natásha, and kept saying that she had always known that Natásha would make an exemplary wife and mother.

"Only she lets her love of her husband and children overflow all bounds," said the countess, "so that it even becomes absurd."

Natásha did not follow the golden rule advocated by clever folk, especially the French, which says that a girl should not let herself go when she marries, should not neglect her accomplishments, should be even more careful of her appearance than when she was unmarried, and should fascinate her husband as much as she did before he became her husband. Natásha, on the contrary, had at once abandoned all her witchery, of which her singing had been an unusually powerful part. She gave it up just because it was so powerfully seductive. She took no pains with her manners, or with delicacy of speech, or with her toilet, or to show herself to her husband in her most becoming attitudes, or to avoid inconveniencing him by being too exacting. She acted in contradiction to all those rules. She felt that the allurements instinct had formerly taught her to use would now be merely ridiculous in the eyes of her husband, to whom she had from the first moment given herself up entirely—that is, with her whole soul, leaving no corner of it hidden from him. She felt that her unity with her husband was not maintained by the poetic feelings that had attracted him to her, but by something else—indefinite but firm as the bond between her own body and soul.

To fluff out her curls, put on fashionable dresses, and sing romantic songs to fascinate her husband, would have seemed as strange as to adorn herself to attract herself. To adorn herself for others might perhaps have been agreeable—she did not know—but she had no time at all for it. The chief reason for devoting no time either to singing, to dress, or to choosing her words, was that she really had not time to spare for these things.

It is known that man has the faculty of becoming completely absorbed in a subject however trivial it may be. And it is known that there is no subject so trivial that it will not grow to infinite proportions if one's entire attention is devoted ot it.

The subject which wholly engrossed Natásha's attention was her family, that is, her husband whom she had to keep so that he should belong entirely to her and to the home—and the children whom she had to bear, bring into the world, nurse, and bring up.

And the deeper she penetrated, not with her mind only but with her whole soul, her whole being, into the subject that absorbed her, the larger did that subject grow and the weaker and more inadequate her own powers appeared, so that she concentrated them all on that one thing and yet was unable to accomplish all that she considered necessary.

There were then, as there are now, conversations and discussions about women's rights, the relations of husband and wife, and their freedom and rights, though these themes were not yet termed *questions* as they are now; but these topics were not uninteresting to Natásha, she positively did not understand them.

Those questions, then as now, existed only for those who see nothing in marriage but the pleasure married people get from one another, that is, only the beginnings of marriage and not its whole significance, which lies in the family.

Discussions and questions of that kind, which are like the question of how to get the greatest gratification from one's dinner, did not then, and do not now, exist for those for whom the purpose of a dinner is the nourishment it affords, and the purpose of marriage is the family.

If the purpose of dinner is to nourish the body, a man who eats two dinners at once may perhaps get more enjoyment, but will not attain his purpose, for his stomach will not digest the two dinners.

" If the purpose of marriage is the family, the person who wishes to have many wives or husbands may perhaps obtain much pleasure, but in that case will not have a family.

If the purpose of food is nourishment, and the purpose of marriage is the family, the whole question resolves itself into not eating more than one can digest, and not having more wives or husbands than are needed for the family—that is, one wife or one husband. Natásha needed a husband. A husband was given her, and he gave her a family. And she not only saw no need of any other or better husband, but as all the powers of her soul were intent on serving that husband and family she could not imagine, and saw no interest in imagining, how it would be if things were different.

Natásha did not care for society in general, but prized the more the society of her relatives—Countess Mary and her brother, her mother, and Sónya. She valued the company of those to whom she could come striding disheveled from the nursery in her dressing-gown, and with joyful face show a yellow instead of a green stain on baby's napkin, and from whom she could hear reassuring words to the effect that baby was much better.

To such an extent had Natásha let herself go, that the way she dressed and did her hair, her ill-chosen words, and her jealousy—she was jealous of Sónya, of the governess, and of every woman, pretty or plain—were habitual subjects of jest to those about her. The general opinion was that Pierre was under his wife's thumb, which was really true. From the very first days of their married life Natásha had announced her demands. Pierre was greatly surprised by his wife's view, to him a perfectly novel one, that every moment of his life belonged to her and to the family. His wife's demands astonished him, but they also flattered him, and he submitted to them.

Pierre's subjection consisted in the fact that he not only dared not flirt with, but dared not even speak smilingly to, any other woman; did not dare to dine at the Club as a pastime, did not dare to spend money on a whim, and did not dare absent himself for any length of time, except on business—in which his wife included his intellectual pursuits, which she did not in the least understand but to which she attributed great importance. To make up for this, Pierre had the right of completely regulating his life at home as he chose, as well as that of the whole family. At home Natásha placed herself in the position of a slave to her husband, and the whole household went on tiptoe when he was occupied—that is, was reading or writing in his study. Pierre had but to show a partiality for anything, to get just what he liked done always. He had only to express a wish and Natásha would jump up and run to fulfill it.

The entire household was governed according to Pierre's supposed orders, that is, by his wishes which Natásha tried to guess. Their way of life and place of residence, their acquaintances and ties, Natásha's occupations, the children's upbringing, were all selected not merely with regard to Pierre's expressed wishes, but to what Natásha supposed his wishes to be from the thoughts he expressed in conversation. And she deduced the essentials of his wishes quite correctly, and having once arrived at them clung to them tenaciously. When Pierre himself wanted to change his mind she would fight him with his own weapons.

Thus in a time of trouble ever memorable to him, after the birth of their first child who was delicate, when they had to change the wet nurse three times and Natásha fell ill from despair, Pierre one day told her of Rousseau's view, with which he quite agreed, that to have a wet nurse is unnatural and harmful. When her next baby was born, despite the opposition of her mother, the doctors, and even of her husband himself—who were all vigorously opposed to her nursing her baby herself, a thing then unheard of and considered injurious—she insisted on having her own way, and after that nursed all her babies herself.

It very often happened that in a moment of irritation husband and wife would have a dispute, but long afterwards Pierre, to his surprise and delight, would find in his wife's ideas and actions the very thought against which she had argued, but divested of everything superfluous that in the excitement of the dispute he had added when expressing his opinion.

After seven years of marriage Pierre had the joyous and firm consciousness that he was not a bad man, and he felt this because he saw himself reflected in his wife. He felt the good and bad within himself inextricably mingled and overlapping. But only what was really good in him was reflected in his wife, all that was not quite good was rejected. And this was not the result of logical reasoning but was a direct and mysterious reflection.

Two months previously, when Pierre was already staying with the Rostóvs, he had received a letter from Prince Theodore asking him to come to Petersburg to confer on some important questions that were being discussed there by a Society of which Pierre was one of the principal founders.

On reading that letter (she always read her husband's letters) Natásha herself suggested that he should go to Petersburg, though she would feel his absence very acutely. She attributed immense importance to all her husband's intellectual and abstract interests though she did not understand them, and she always dreaded being a hindrance to him in such matters. To Pierre's timid look of inquiry after reading the letter, she replied by asking him to go, but to fix a definite date for his return. He was given four weeks' leave of absence.

Ever since that leave of absence had expired, more than a fortnight before, Natásha had been in a constant state of alarm, depression, and irritability.

Denísov, now a general on the retired list and much dissatisfied with the present state of affairs, had arrived during that fortnight. He looked at Natásha with sorrow and surprise, as at a bad likeness of someone once dear. A dull dejected look, random replies, and talk about the nursery was all he saw and heard from his former enchantress.

Natásha was sad and irritable all that time, especially when her mother, her brother, Sónya, or Countess Mary, in their efforts to console her, tried to excuse Pierre and suggested reasons for his delay in returning.

"It's all nonsense, all rubbish—those discussions which lead to nothing, and all those idiotic Societies!" Natásha declared of the very affairs in the immense importance of which she firmly believed.

And she would go to the nursery to nurse Pétya, her only boy.

No one else could tell her anything so comforting or so reasonable as this little three-months-old creature when he lay at her breast and she was conscious of the movement of his lips and the snuffling of his little nose. That creature said: "You are angry, you are jealous, you would like to pay him out, you are afraid—but here am I! And I am he . . ." and that was unanswerable. It was more than true.

During that fortnight of anxiety Natásha resorted to the infant for comfort so often, and fussed over him so much, that she over-fed him and he fell ill. She was terrified by his illness, and yet that was just what she needed. While attending to him she bore the anxiety about her husband more easily.

She was nursing her baby when the sound of Pierre's sledge was heard at the front door, and the old nurse—knowing how to please her mistress—entered the room inaudibly but hurriedly and with a beaming face.

"Has he come?" Natásha asked quickly in a whisper, afraid to move lest she should rouse the dozing baby.

"He's come, ma'am," whispered the nurse.

The blood rushed to Natásha's face and her feet involuntarily moved, but she could not jump up and run out. The baby again opened his eyes and looked at her. "You are here?" he seemed to be saying, and again lazily smacked his lips.

Cautiously withdrawing her breast, Natásha rocked him a little, handed him to the nurse and went with rapid steps towards the door. But at the door she stopped as if her conscience reproached her for having in her joy left the child too soon, and she glanced round. The nurse, with raised elbows, was lifting the infant over the rail of his cot.

"Go, ma'am! Don't worry, go!" she whispered, smiling, with the kind of familiarity that grows up between a nurse and her mistress.

Natásha ran with light footsteps to the ante-room.

Denísov, who with his pipe had come out of the study into the dancing-room, now recognized the old Natásha for the first time. A flood of brilliant, joyful light poured from her transfigured face.

"He's come!" she exclaimed as she ran past, and Denísov felt that he was delighted that Pierre, whom he did not much care for, had returned.

On reaching the vestibule Natásha saw a tall figure in a fur coat unwinding his scarf. "It's he! It's really he! He has come!" she said to herself, and rushing at him, embraced him, pressed his head to her breast, and then pushed him back and gazed at his ruddy, happy face, covered with hoar-frost. "Yes, it is he, happy and contented . . ."

Then all at once she remembered the tortures of suspense she had experienced for the last fortnight: the joy that had lit up her face vanished, she frowned, and overwhelmed Pierre with a torrent of reproaches and angry words.

"Yes, it's all very well for you. You are pleased, you've had a good time . . . but what about me? You might at least have shown consideration for the children. I am nursing, and my milk was spoilt . . . Pétya was at death's door. But you were enjoying yourself. Yes, enjoying . . ."

Pierre knew he was not to blame, for he could not have come sooner; he knew this outburst was unseemly and would blow over in a minute or two; above all, he knew that he himself was bright and happy. He wanted to smile but dared not even think of doing so. He made a piteous, frightened face and stooped down.

"I could not, on my honor. But how is Pétya?"

"All right now. Come along! I wonder you're not ashamed! If only you could see what I was like without you, how I suffered!"

"You are well?"

"Come, come!" she said, not letting go of his arm. And they went to their rooms.

When Nicholas and his wife came to look for Pierre he was in the nursery holding his baby son, who was again awake, on his huge right palm and dandling him. A blissful bright smile was fixed on the baby's broad face, with its toothless open mouth. The storm was long since over and there was bright, joyous sunshine on Natásha's face as she gazed tenderly at her husband and child.

"And have you talked everything well over with Prince Theodore?" she asked.

"Yes, capitally."

"You see, he holds it up." (She meant the baby's head.) "But how he did frighten me . . . You've seen the princess? Is it true she's in love with that . . ."

"Yes, just fancy . . ."

At that moment Nicholas and Countess Mary came in. Pierre, with the baby on his hand, stooped down, kissed them, and replied to their inquiries. But in spite of much that was interesting and had to be discussed, the baby with the little cap on its unsteady head evidently absorbed all his attention.

"How sweet!" said Countess Mary, looking at and playing with the baby. "Now, Nicholas," she added turning to her husband, "I can't understand how it is you don't see the charm of these delicious marvels."

"I don't and can't," replied Nicholas, looking coldly at the baby. "A lump of flesh. Come along, Pierre!"

"And yet he's such an affectionate father," said Countess Mary, vindicating her husband, "but only after they are a year old or so . . ."

"Now Pierre nurses them splendidly," said Natásha. "He says his hand is just made for a baby's seat. Just look!"

"Only not for this . . ." Pierre suddenly exclaimed with a laugh, and shifting the baby he gave him to the nurse.

THE WAY IT REALLY WAS

From TOLSTOY

Henri Troyat

In the preceding section from War and Peace *Tolstoy portrays an ideal picture of contented motherhood: Natásha nursing her own baby. It comes as somewhat of a surprise to discover that the situation was different (perhaps more believable, however) in Tolstoy's own household, when his wife Sonya tried to nurse her first baby.*

On June 27, in the dead of night, the first pains came. Tolstoy ran to fetch the midwife from Tula. When he returned, Sonya was pacing up and down in her bedroom, "in a peignoir open over her lace-inset gown, her black hair in disorder, her face afire, her dark eyes shining with extraordinary intensity." How beautiful she was, with her expression of suffering, shy reserve and majesty! He helped her to stretch out on the leather couch on which he himself had been born. Touching her half-naked body gave him a feeling completely unlike any he had ever known in other circumstances: not desire, but compassion, and incisive attention to every detail, the curiosity of a professional writer eager to learn something new. But when the pains began to come more quickly, he lost his self-possession. He could not recognize Sonya in this "screaming and writhing" female. She pressed his hand weakly between contractions. The midwife, the Polish doctor sitting in the corner smoking cigarettes, the candles burning in their sockets, the smell of vinegar and eau-de-Cologne, the twisted sheets, rags, basins, it was all part

176

of a nightmare. Suddenly there was a terrible heaving and thrashing around the leather couch. The midwife and doctor were bending over a slaughter. A sharp cry cut through the jerking gasps of the mother. The doctor said, "It's a boy!" Tolstoy saw a tiny creature, "strange and reddish," with a big soft head. Remembering the scene, he wrote in *Anna Karenina*, "Levin had to make an enormous effort to believe that his wife was still alive, that she was all right, that this wailing baby was his son. . . . Why this child? Who was he? Where did he come from? He had great difficulty in accepting the idea. It took him a long time to get used to it."

When Tanya Behrs was allowed into the room, she saw Tolstoy "white-faced and red-eyed with weeping," and Sonya "appeared tired, but happy and proud." Champagne was drunk. They decided to call the child Sergey, after his uncle. Receiving his family's congratulations, Tolstoy was surprised to find that he felt neither joy nor pride but a sort of apprehension, as though from that day on there were "another area of vulnerability" in his life. Wouldn't this added source of care drive him still farther away from himself and his work? The only good thing about the birth, he thought, was that Sonya, filled with the new joy of motherhood, would become even-tempered and cheerful once more. He was prepared to worship her, if only she would behave like a proper wife again.

It was he, however, who started their first quarrel. As befits a true disciple of Rousseau, he believed that all mothers should nurse their babies. Sonya herself agreed, although paid wet nurses were more the custom in her circle. But from the beginning, she suffered excruciating pain. Her breasts were soon fissured and the doctors ordered her to stop. Tolstoy protested vehemently, in the name of nature, against "official pretexts" that allowed a young mother to shirk her obligations; he asserted that his wife was spoiled and soft, her mind perverted by civilization, and he demanded that she fulfill her role as giver-of-life to the bitter end. When Sonya, exhausted, engaged a nurse, he refused to enter the nursery because he could not bear to see the heir to his name suspended from the breast of a strange woman. Why must a common girl be able to perform what Countess Tolstoy considered beyond her strength?

Exasperated by his son-in-law's irrational obstinacy, Dr. Behrs wrote to the couple: "I see you have both lost your wits. . . . Be reasonable, dear Sonya, calm yourself, don't make a mountain out of a molehill. . . . As for you, dear Leo Nikolayevich, rest assured that you will never be transformed into a real muzhik, any more than your wife will be able to endure what a Pelagya can endure. . . . And you, Tanya, do not let your mad sister out of your sight for one moment, scold her as often as possible for her crazy notions that are enough to try the patience of the Lord, and pitch the first object that comes to hand straight at Leo's head, to knock some sense into it. He is a great master at speechifying and literature, but life is another matter. Let him write a story about a husband who tortures his sick wife by forcing her to nurse her baby. He will be stoned by every woman alive."

Neither Dr. Behrs' letter nor Sonya's tears nor the gentle remonstrances of Tanya made any dent in Tolstoy's dogged disapproval. He could not look at his wife without finding fault with her. In his diary—which she read—he sarcastically called her "the countess":

"I arrive in the morning, full of joy and gladness, and I find the countess in a tantrum while Dunyasha, the chambermaid, is combing her hair; seeing her thus I mistake her for Mashenka* on one of her bad days, everything collapses, and I stand there as though I had been scalded. I am afraid of everything and I see that there can be no happiness or poetry for me except when I am alone. I am kissed tenderly, out of habit, but then the quarrels resume immediately, with Dunyasha, Auntie, Tanya, me. . . . One o'clock in the morning already, and I can't sleep at all, much less in her room with her, when I have such a weight on my heart; she will begin to whine and moan as soon as she knows there is someone to listen; just now she is snoring peacefully away. She will wake up absolutely convinced that I am wrong and she is the most unfortunate woman alive. . . . And the worst of it is that I must hold my tongue and sulk, however much I execrate and despise such a situation."

And, pen in hand, Sonya exhaled her despair:

"It is monstrous not to nurse one's child! Well, who says it isn't? But what can I do in the face of a physical impossibility? . . . He would banish me from the earth because I am suffering and not doing my duty, and I cannot bear him because he is not suffering and he is writing. . . . How can one love a fly that will not stop

* Marya, Tolstoy's sister.

tormenting one? . . . I shall take care of my son and do everything I can, but not for Lyova, certainly, because he deserves to get evil in return for evil."

After letting off steam, she melted, and ended: "It's starting to rain. I am afraid he will catch cold. My irritation has vanished. I love him. God protect him." Sincere statement or subtle maneuver? As soon as he had read these lines Tolstoy, deeply touched, wanted to retract what he had written and added, below her entry: "Sonya, forgive me . . . I was cruel and crude. And to whom? To the person who has given me the greatest joy in my life and the only one who loves me. . . . Sonya, my darling, I am guilty, but I am wretched too. There is an excellent man in me, but sometimes he is asleep. Love him, Sonya, and do not criticize him." A fresh quarrel broke out immediately afterward, he snatched up the notebook and furiously crossed out what he had just written. And at the bottom of the desecrated page Sonya, the tears welling in her eyes, added: "I had deserved those few lines of tenderness and repentance, but in a moment of anger he took them away from me before I had even read them."

THE BABIES

Mark Twain

Mark Twain was the fifteenth and final speaker at a banquet honoring General Ulysses S. Grant and the Army of the Tennessee. Speech after impassioned speech had been delivered with ever-mounting intensity, again and again bringing the audience to its feet, cheering and stamping; only the great "Man of Destiny," General Grant, sat unmoved and impassive. But by the third sentence of Twain's speech, which had an unexpected subject for a military banquet, babies, Grant was laughing and cheering with the rest, even as the speech seemed to be heading for a monumental insult at the end.

MR. CHAIRMAN AND GENTLEMEN:—"The Babies!" Now, that's something like. We haven't all had the good fortune to be ladies; we have not all been generals, or poets, or statesmen; but when the toast works down to the babies, we stand on common ground—for we've all been babies. (*Laughter.*) It is a shame that for a thousand years the world's banquets have utterly ignored the baby, as if he didn't amount to anything! If you, gentlemen, will stop and think a minute—if you will go back fifty or a hundred years, to your early married life, and recontemplate your first baby—you will remember that he amounted to a good deal—and even something over. (*Laughter.*)

You soldiers all know that when the little fellow arrived at family headquarters you had to hand in your resignation. He took entire command. You become his lackey, his mere bodyguard; and

180

you had to stand around, too. He was not a commander who made allowances for the time, distance, weather, or anything else; you had to execute his order whether it was possible or not. And there was only one form of marching in his manual of tactics, and that was the double-quick. (*Laughter.*) He treated you with every sort of insolence and disrespect, and the bravest of you did not dare to say a word. You could face the death-storm of Donelson and Vicksburg, and give back blow for blow; but when he clawed your whiskers and pulled your hair, and twisted your nose you had to take it. (*Laughter.*) When the thunders of war sounded in your ears, you set your faces toward the batteries and advanced with steady tread; but when he turned on the terrors of his war-whoop (*laughter*), you advanced in—the other direction, and mighty glad of the chance, too. When he called for soothing syrup, did you venture to throw out any remarks about certain services unbecoming to an officer and a gentleman? No; you got up and got it! If he ordered his pap-bottle and it wasn't warm, did you talk back? Not you; you went to work and warmed it! You even descended so far in your menial office as to take a suck at that warm, insipid stuff yourself to see if it was right!—three parts water to one of milk, a touch of sugar to midify the colic, and a drop of peppermint to kill those immortal hiccoughs. I can taste that stuff yet! (*Uproarious laughter.*)

And how many things you learned as you went along! Sentimental young folks still take stock in that beautiful old saying, that when the baby smiles in his sleep it is because the angels are whispering to him. Very pretty, but "too thin"—simply wind on the stomach, my friend. (*Laughter.*)

If the baby proposed to take a walk at his usual hour—half past three in the morning—didn't you rise up promptly and remark (with a mental addition which wouldn't improve a Sunday-school much) that that was the very thing you were about to propose yourself? Oh, you were under good discipline. And as you went fluttering up and down the room in your "undress uniform" (*laughter*), you not only prattled undignified baby-talk, but even tuned up your martial voice, and tried to sing "Rock-a-bye-baby on the tree top," for instance. What a spectacle for an Army of the Tennessee! And what an affliction for the neighbors, too, for it isn't everybody within a mile around that likes military music at three o'clock in the morning. (*Laughter.*) And when you had been keeping that sort of thing up two or three hours, and your little velvet head intimated that nothing suited him like exercise and noise, and proposed to fight it out on that line if it took all night— Go on! What did you do? You simply went on till you dropped in the last ditch. (*Laughter.*)

I like the idea that a baby doesn't amount to anything! Why, one baby is just a house and a front yard full by itself; one baby can furnish more business than you and your whole interior department can attend to; he is enterprising, irrepressible, brimful of lawless activities; do what you please you can't make him stay on the reservation. Sufficient unto the day is one baby. As long as you are in your right mind don't you ever pray for twins. Twins amount to a permanent riot; and there aint any difference between triplets and insurrection. (*Great laughter.*)

Among the three or four million cradles now rocking in the land, are some which this nation would preserve for ages as sacred things if we knew which ones they are. For in one of these cradles the unconscious Farragut of the future is at this moment teething. Think of it! and putting a word of dead earnest, unarticulated, but justifiable, profanity over it, too; in another, the future renowned astronomer is blinking at the shining Milky Way with but a languid interest, poor little chap, and wondering what has become of that other one they call the wet nurse; in another the future great historian is lying, and doubtless he will continue to lie until his earthly mission is ended; in another, the future President is busying himself with no profounder problem of State than what mischief has become of his hair so early (*laughter*); and in a mighty array of other cradles there are now some sixty thousand future office-seekers getting ready to furnish him occasion to grapple with the same problem a second time! And in still one more cradle, somewhere under the flag, the future illustrious commander-in-chief of the American armies is so little burdened with his approaching grandeurs and responsibilities as to be giving his whole strategic mind, at this moment, to trying to find out some way to get his own big toe into his mouth, an achievement which (meaning no disrespect) the illustrious guest of this evening turned his attention to some fifty-six years ago! And if the child is but a prophecy of the man there are mighty few will doubt that he succeeded. (*Laughter and prolonged applause.*)

Part VI

THE NATURE OF THE BEAST

FOUR WEEKS OLD

From THE FIRST FIVE YEARS OF LIFE

Arnold Gesell, M.D., et al.

Mothers have always compared their children to other children of the same age to find reassuring similarities in their behavior and development. Dr. Arnold Gesell and his associates at the Yale Clinic of Child Development spent fifteen years observing and comparing hundreds of preschool children in order to study these similarities in a scientific way and discover the typical growth and behavior patterns for normal children at various stages of development. The following excerpt is a normative summary of a four-week-old infant.

The developmental transformations which occur in the first year of life far exceed those of any other period excepting only the period of gestation. "The poor, new-born babe like a seaman wrecked, thrown from the waves, lies naked o'er the ground." But in the brief space of a year this helpless creature is on his two feet, cruising, prying, exploring. He becomes a complex individual capable of varied emotions, of flashes of insight, and of persevering stretches of effort. His personality and his diversified abilities at one year of age are the product of an extremely swift season of growth.

So multiform are these mental transformations that it is difficult to see them in proportion and perspective. Although the rate of development in infancy is extremely rapid, the process itself is no

185

different from that which prevails in later years. In terms of process, the infant advances psychologically by the same steps which carry him forward in childhood and youth. The infant displays essentially the same kind of drive, the same fumbling power to profit by experience, the same proclivity to abstraction and generalization, in his progress from the known to the unknown, from the familiar to the novel.

The more minutely his behavior is examined, the more completely does it resemble in its dynamics the operations of the mature mind. Behavior development entails continuous interweaving of patterns and components of patterns. The organism is forever doing new things, but "learning" to do them in an old way—reincorporating at a higher level what it has already approximated at a lower one. The structure of the mind is built up by a spiral kind of cross-stitching. This process of reincorporation is mental growth. The methods of growth of the infant therefore anticipate and simulate those of later years. The infant is predictive of his later self. The characteristics of mental growth in the nursery school and kindergarten child are those of infancy. . . .

These normative summaries are factual, but they are intended to be more than mere inventories. They are characterizations of maturity. It is hoped that they will enable the reader to conjure up an organic image of a child as a living whole even though this child must be portrayed as a somewhat generalized type. As the mind grows it changes in shape rather than in size; it is always personalistic and organic in make-up. In the following series of sketches we must not look for linear increases in a single intellectual function, but for progressive patterns of maturity. Nor must we look for static absolutes. In mental growth nothing *is*; everything is *becoming*.

FOUR WEEKS OLD

Of all infants, the human infant is at birth the most helpless. In a sense, he is not fully born until he is about 4 weeks of age. It takes him that long to attain a working physiological adjustment to his postnatal environment. Even so he may still show a certain precariousness of organizatation in fitful waking, in startle reactions, and in irregular respiration, also in sneezing, choking, regurgitation or vomiting on slight provocation. Such "instability" is relatively normal at this tender age, because the primary vegetative network of the nervous system is still only incompletely organized.

Frequently the neonate seems to be in a twilight zone between sleeping and waking. He is quasi-dormant. It seems as though sleep itself were an extremely complicated pattern of behavior and that it takes time for the rhythms of sleep and of open-eyed attention to define themselves. He is indeed growing so rapidly in all fields of behavior that he shows variations and fluctuations from day to day. He does not follow a rigid schedule in his spontaneous activities and cravings. He is ill-suited to an over-rigid routine.

The behavior characteristics of the 4-week-old infant, however, are in no sense chaotic or formless. They fall into their proper position in a genetic sequence. The following summary will suggest how certain 4-week-old patterns are developmentally related to those of the fetal period on the one hand, and to those of the 16-week-old infant on the other.

Motor Characteristics The 4-week-old infant when awake lies on his back with head averted, usually to a preferred side. Only momentarily does he bring his head to a mid position. Almost invariably his arm is extended on the side toward which his head is turned. The opposite arm is flexed with the hand resting near or in the head-chest region. This combination of averted head, extended arm, and flexed arm is the so-called tonic-neck-reflex attitude (t.n.r.) which dominates the waking life of the infant for some twelve weeks.

Occasionally the 4-week-old infant bursts into startle responses, his head coming momentarily to the mid-line and all his extremities extending abruptly. Occasionally he lashes the air with more or less symmetric windmill movements of the arms. But the asymmetric t.n.r. attitude underlies most of his postural behavior. Indeed, the t.n.r. is part of the ground plan of the total reaction system. In partial form it was present prenatally, helping the fetus to accommodate to the outlines of the uterine cavity. At 16 weeks it gives way to more symmetric patterns of behavior, but it is a precondition for the growth of these later patterns.

Adaptive Behavior The most active and adept muscles of the 4-week-old are those of mouth and eyes. A light touch in the mouth region causes the lips to close and then to purse; the head will also make seeking movements, particularly if the infant is hungry. Whether reflexive, deliberate, or conscious, this represents a form of adaptive behavior. Sucking and swallowing were within the infant's capacity even before birth.

The twelve tiny muscles which move and immobilize the eye balls are brought under increasing control in the neonatal period. The 4-week-old infant indulges in long spells of ocular immobilization and fixation. He stares vacantly and detachedly at large masses like windows, ceilings, and adults.

His visual field is delimited by the postural set of the t.n.r. attitude. He disregards a ring dangled in the mid plane; but if the ring is slowly moved into the field of vision, he will pursue it with combined eye and head movements, through a small arc of less than 90°. At *16* weeks he "picks up" the ring with his eye muscles, more promptly, and they operate more independently of the head in pursuit of a moving object.

However, at 4 weeks the picking up capacity of the eyes really exceeds that of the hands. Ocular apprehension precedes manual prehension. Both hands are predominantly closed (even when the eyes are open). There is no reaching out to grasp objects. Yet the patterning of prehension is well under way, for if one touches the child's hand (with the handle of a rattle) the activity of the arm is increased, and the hand either clenches or opens.

Language   The 4-week-old infant is heedful of sounds. If, while he is busy with postural activity, a hand bell is tinkled, the activity ceases. This is a significant pattern of behavior, a kind of auditory fixation or "staring" at sound. At later ages the sound perception will become discriminating for things. He will listen to and understand the sound of footsteps. Yet later he will listen to and comprehend the sound of words.

Except for crying he is almost inarticulate. The intensity and manner of his cry vary with cause and circumstance. His vocalizations are meager and non-expressive, but he mews and makes small throaty noises, precursors of babbling.

Personal-Social   The 4-week-old infant fixates transiently on a face that bends over into his field of vision. His own facial activity may subdue or slightly brighten on social approach, but a brief intent regard is the chief token of his "social" reaction. He may make a comparable response to the human voice. He tends to soothe when he is picked up and when he is snugly and warmly wrapped. He probably feels a dim sense of security from calm and assured handling. This tactile responsiveness and sense of protectedness must be set down as early genetic items which have social import.

THE GOLDEN RULE OF RAISING BABIES

From THE COMPLETE BOOK OF ABSOLUTELY PERFECT BABY AND CHILD CARE

Elinor Goulding Smith

For parents who are terrorized by the Gesell charts, here is some very practical advice.

This brings us to the primary rule of baby raising, which is the solution to this and all subsequent problems. This rule must be followed faithfully, and practiced regularly, and you should make it a habit to repeat it to yourself ten times a day. It is the *Golden Rule* of raising babies. *LIE.* Lie to your mother, lie to your sisters and aunts, and above all, lie to all the other mothers you meet on the street. When a newer mother than you asks for your help, tell her you never had the least trouble. *Your* baby just *loved* his mashed banana on the first try.

A crisis sometimes arises during the early months when you discover that Gesell's babies all hold up their right hand and look at it. Yours hasn't done this yet. The important thing now is not to mention this awful fact to your relatives and neighbors. Should any of them bring up the subject, remember the RULE. Meanwhile, call the pediatrician, never mind what time it is. However, he is often unsympathetic. Here you are with this baby that has something terrible the matter with it, and the pediatrician *doesn't care.* You can now find a new pediatrician who is less hard boiled, and you can also take the baby to a neurologist, an orthopedist and an ophthalmologist. Unfortunately, after you've made all the ap-

190

pointments, and told that first pediatrician just what you think of him, the sly and traitorous baby will now, out of sheer contrariness, immediately hold up his right hand and look at it. I could tell he was a trouble maker from the start. As a matter of fact, he has been holding up his right hand and looking at it for weeks now, but he only did it while he was alone.

The age at which a baby walks varies greatly with the individual, some managing it by a year while others may wait till they are eighteen months old. Some babies creep or crawl first at varying ages, some stand up first. I myself had a child who learned to sit when he was six months old and then never did another thing till he was eighteen months old. He never crawled, or crept, or stood up or moved around, and what's worse, he didn't even *care*. He sat there with his two parents standing over him imploring him to move around just a little bit, and he went right on playing with his little pegs and blocks and *laughed*. He didn't care that every other child in the park was galloping around pushing little push toys and pulling little pull toys. He just sat and smiled. After a time, we got into the hands of a capable neurologist who treated us with sedatives until the child got up and started pulling the lamps off the tables. It was during this period that I was first working on THE RULE.

Of course for a time you can face this sort of situation out bravely by remarking from time to time that it's funny how a child will run around at home but just not want to move when he gets to the park. You can hint that these other babies are so *rough* that yours is a little afraid of them. You can point out that yours really talked terribly young. You can observe that these other babies get awfully *dirty* from playing in the gravel. But when the word finally gets out that that Smith baby hasn't *walked* yet, there's nothing for it but to go to another park for a while.

We then proceeded to have a second child who crept around at five months and was pulling the lamps off the tables by a year. However, in spite of all this activity he didn't walk till he was eighteen months old either. This absolutely proves my point, which, in the face of the entire medical profession I still believe to be true: LAMP TABLES SHOULD BE STEADIER.

Some babies have considerable trouble with teething. They may cry a lot and be fretful, and wake during the night for no apparent reason and in general make more fuss than you do for the extraction of an impacted lower third molar. The extraction of an impacted lower third molar, sometimes wittily called a wisdom tooth, is the most painful dental operation ever discovered. Whoever discovered it should have covered it right up again. So don't let the baby fool you. No matter how much he cries during the appearance of his first little incisors, they can't possibly hurt him all *that* much. He's just making a big fuss over nothing and acting like a *baby*. Sometimes, during this trying period a little paregoric, judiciously used, is helpful. If you drink a lot of it, it will help you to sleep through the baby's crying. Some people rub paregoric on the baby's gums, but after all, let's not be silly.

WHY THE BABY SMILES

From THE MAGIC YEARS

Selma H. Fraiberg

Pages and pages have been written about what makes a baby cry. Here a noted psychoanalyst poses a question that is rarely asked: "Why does the baby smile?"

The response smile which occurs around two months is a significant milestone in the baby's development. Scientists have been much slower to grasp the significance of this event than a baby's parents. This is the occasion for great excitement. The news is transmitted to grandparents and all interested relatives. No trumpets are blown, no formal holidays proclaimed, but everyone concerned seems to understand that this smile is very special.

Now no parent cares in the least *why* the baby smiles, or why the psychologists think he smiles, and you might wish to skip the next few paragraphs except that I hope you don't. Why the baby smiles is a matter of some significance in understanding the early phases of human attachment in the infant.

First of all, let's remember that this response smile has had antecedents. Even in the early weeks we will notice that satisfaction in the course of nursing or at the end of the nursing period will cause the mouth to relax in a little smile of contentment. This early smile of satisfaction is an instinctive reaction and is not yet a response to a human face.

Now let's watch this baby as he nurses. If he is not too sleepy his eyes fix solemnly on the face of his mother. We have learned experimentally that he does not take in the whole face before him, only the upper part of the face, the eyes and forehead. Through repetition of the experience of nursing and its regular accompaniment, the human face, an association between nursing and the human face will be established. But more than this, the pleasure, the satisfactions of nursing become associated with the human face. Repetition of this pleasurable experience gradually traces an image of the face on the surface of the memory apparatus and the foundations of memory are established. When the mental image is firmly established the visual image of the human face is "recognized" (very crudely), that is, the sight of the human face evokes the mental image and it is "remembered." Now comes the turning point. This is not just a memory based on pictures, but a memory derived from image plus pleasure, the association established through nursing. The baby's response to the sight of the human face is now seen as a response of pleasure. He smiles at the sight of the human face. The little smile which had originated as an instinctive reaction to satisfaction in nursing is now produced occasionally, then more and more, at the sight of the face, as if the face evokes the memory of satisfaction and pleasure. The baby has made his first human connections.

We should not be disappointed to learn that the baby does not yet discriminate his mother's face from other human faces. "How can they prove *that?*" we'd like to know. "That smile certainly *looks* very special." We know this from two sets of observations. For many weeks after the response smile has been established, almost any human face that presents itself to the baby can elicit the smile. (Ironically, a mask representing the eyes and forehead of the human face can be presented to the baby of this age and this, too, will bring forth a pleasure response.) We may not find this so convincing a proof. How do we know this isn't just a sociable little guy who likes his mother *and* the rest of the human race? And maybe his response to the mask only proves that he has a sense of humor. Perhaps the second set of observations will be more convincing. Psychologists place the positive identification and differentiation of the mother's face around eight months because of certain responses of the infant which are familiar to all of us. He no longer smiles at any face that swims into view. On the contrary, let your jolliest uncle approach with beaming face and twenty keys on a chain to dangle before his eyes and he may be greeted by a quizzical look, an uncomprehending stare or—worse for family relations—a howl! Now let mother or father come over to offer reassurances to the baby and apologies to the uncle, and upon seeing these two faces, the baby relaxes, wriggles and smiles. He may study these three sets of faces for a few minutes and, finally satisfied that the familiar faces are re-established, he turns to the unfamiliar face and permits his uncle to jingle keys and make comical faces for which he may later be rewarded with a smile. Or let Grandma who is a frequent, but not constant visitor, offer to take over a bottle feeding. He is hungry, shows eagerness for the bottle, but when he takes in the face that is not mother's he looks dismayed, the face puckers and he howls in protest. "He never did *that* before!" says his grandmother. And it is true that several weeks ago when grandma had taken over a feeding he had polished off his bottle with as much zest as when his mother fed him.

This reaction to the strange face, the not-mother face, is the first positive evidence that he differentiates his mother's face from others. (We should not fail to mention that if father has had close contact with the baby and if there are sisters and brothers, these faces will be differentiated, too. We use "mother" as a convenient reference point and with the understanding that for the period of infancy she will be the primary love object.) The reaction to being fed by Grandma shows us, too, that pleasure in eating is no longer simply a matter of biological need and satisfaction, but is bound to the person of his mother. He has finally linked this face, this person, with the satisfaction of his needs and regards her as the source of satisfaction. The pleasure and satisfaction given him through feeding and caring for him are now transferred to her image, and the sight of her face, her presence, will bring forth such crowing and joyful noises, and the disappearance of her face such disappointment that we can say that he loves his mother as a person.

That has a curious sound! "Loves his mother as a person." Obviously, since she is a person how else could he love her? And if we say that we mean "loves her as a person outside himself," that sounds just as foolish to our adult ears. Of course, she is a person outside himself. We know that! But the baby did not. He learned this slowly, awkwardly, in the course of the first months of life. For during the early months the infant doesn't differentiate between his body and other bodies, or between mental images and perceptions, between inner and outer. Everything is undifferentiated oneness, the oneness being centered in the baby himself.

At the time that the baby discovers that his mother is a person outside himself a tremendous amount of learning has taken place. In order to achieve something that seems commonplace to us he had to engage in hundreds of experiments over a period of months. He had to assemble hundreds of pieces in a vast and intricate jigsaw puzzle in order to establish a crude picture of the person-mother and a crude image of his own body. We can reconstruct these experiments largely through observation.

WHY I SMILED

From THE AUTOBIOGRAPHY OF LINCOLN STEFFENS

Lincoln Steffens

While the psychologists analyze the complexities of the mother-child relationship, a writer can sometimes find his way to the heart of the matter in a lighthearted fashion, as in this chapter from the autobiography of a famous American journalist, Lincoln Steffens.

Early in the morning of April 6, 1866, in a small house "over in the Mission" of San Francisco, California, I was born—a remarkable child. This upon the authority of my mother, a remarkable woman, who used to prove her prophetic judgment to all listeners till I was old enough to make my own demonstration. Even then, even though I was there to frown her down, she was ever ready to bring forth her evidence, which opened with the earthquake of 1868. When that shock shook most San Franciscans out of their houses into the streets, she ran upstairs to me and found me pitched out of bed upon the floor but otherwise unmoved. As she said with swimming eyes, I was "not killed, not hurt, and, of course, not crying; I was smiling, as always, good as gold."

My own interpretation of this performance is that it was an exhibit less of goodness than of wisdom. I knew that my mother would not abandon me though the world rocked and the streets yawned. Nor is that remarkable. Every well-born baby is sure he can trust his mother. What strikes me as exceptional and promising in it is that I had already some sense of values; I could take such events as earthquakes all in my stride. That, I think, is why I smiled then; that is why I smile now; and that may be why my story is of a happy life—happier and happier. Looking back over it now for review, it seems to me that each chapter of my adventures is happier than the preceding chapters right down to this, the last one: age, when it comes, comes a-laughing, the best of all. I have a baby boy of my own now; my first—a remarkable child, who—when he tumbles out of bed—laughs; as good as gold.

WHY THE BABY SAYS GOO

Penobscot Indian Legend

An American Indian legend may be assumed to be ancient when it is told to set forth an origin. *This tale of the Penobscot Indians of Maine, featuring Glooskap, the central divinity of their mythology, proposes a wry origin for the universal phenomenon of a baby's crowing.*

Now it came to pass when Glooskap had conquered all his enemies, even the *Kewahqu'*, who were giants and sorcerers, and the *M'téoulin*, who were magicians, and the *Pamola*, who is the evil spirit of the night air, and all manner of ghosts, witches, devils, cannibals, and goblins, that he thought upon what he had done, and wondered if his work was at an end.

And he said this to a certain woman. But she replied, "Not so fast, Master, for there yet remains One whom no one has ever conquered or got the better of in any way, and who will remain unconquered to the end of time."

"And who is he?" inquired the Master.

"It is the mighty *Wasis*," she replied, "and there he sits; and I warn you that if you meddle with him you will be in sore trouble."

Now *Wasis* was the Baby. And he sat on the floor sucking a piece of maple-sugar, greatly contented, troubling no one.

As the Lord of Men and Beasts had never married or had a child, he knew naught of the way of managing children. Therefore he was quite certain, as is the wont of such people, that he knew all about it. So he turned to Baby with a bewitching smile and bade him come to him.

199

Then Baby smiled again, but did not budge. And the Master spake sweetly and made his voice like that of the summer bird, but it was of no avail, for Wasis sat still and sucked his maple-sugar.

Then the Master frowned and spoke terribly, and ordered Wasis to come crawling to him immediately. And Baby burst out into crying and yelling, but did not move for all that.

Then, since he could do but one thing more, the Master had recourse to magic. He used his most awful spells, and sang the songs which raise the dead and scare the devils. And Wasis sat and looked on admiringly, and seemed to find it very interesting, but all the same he never moved an inch.

So Glooskap gave it up in despair, and Wasis, sitting on the floor in the sunshine, went *goo! goo!* and crowed.

And to this day when you see a babe well contented, going *goo! goo!* and crowing, and no one can tell why, know that it is because he remembers the time when he overcame the Master who had conquered all the world. For of all the beings that have ever been since the beginning, Baby is alone the only invincible one.

DEVELOPING A PERSONALITY

From CHILD CARE AND THE GROWTH OF LOVE

John Bowlby

In 1948, under the auspices of the United Nations World Health Organization, Dr. John Bowlby undertook a study of infants and children separated from their parents and cared for in foster-homes or institutions. His report on his findings, published under the title Maternal Care and Mental Health, *presented a mass of evidence underlining the unique importance of mother-love in the development of a child's personality. The following essay, taken from a simplified version of Bowlby's report, presents an explanatoin of why maternal deprivation produces such devastating results.*

Just how we develop as personalities and how this development depends on our being in constant touch with some one person who cares for our nourishment and other needs during the critical time in our early years, whilst our ability to adjust ourselves to the outside world of things and of people is growing, is a very interesting question. The problems raised are very complicated, and as yet by no means clearly understood. Yet our progress in practice will depend very much on our growing insight into theory.

As our personality develops we become less and less at the mercy of our immediate surroundings and the ways in which they affect us, and become more and more able to choose and create our surroundings and to plan ahead, often over long periods of time,

201

for the things we want. Amongst other things, this means that we have to learn to think in an abstract way, to exercise our imagination and to consider things other than just our immediate sensations and desires. Only when he has reached this stage is the individual able to control his wish of the moment in the interests of his own more fundamental long-term needs. One expects the child of three, or even five, to run into the road and seek his ball—at those ages he is still largely at the mercy of the immediate situation. As he grows older, however, he is expected to take more things into account and to think ahead. By ten or eleven he is capable of pursuing goals some months distant in time. At sixteen or eighteen the more developed boy or girl is able to perform great feats of abstraction in time and space. This is the process whereby the individual frees himself from slavery to his instincts and the urge for immediate pleasure, and develops mental processes more adapted to the demands of reality.

In the course of this process we develop within ourselves ways of harmonizing our different, and often conflicting, needs and learn to seek their satisfaction in the world outside ourselves: we begin to judge between the things we want in the future, to consider what things we desire most, to realize that some wishes have to give way to others, so that our actions may have purpose and may not clash in a haphazard way. Because one of our foremost long-term needs is to remain on friendly and co-operative terms with others we must keep their requirements firmly in the front of our minds: from this awareness of the things which please and displease the people round us come the rudiments of conscience.

In infancy and early childhood we are not able to act in this thoughtful way with regard to getting our own ends or to recognizing the claims of other people. During this time his mother has to act for the child in both these ways. She arranges where he shall be, when he shall feed and sleep and be washed, provides for him in every way, allows him to do some things, checks him in others. She is, as it were, his personality and his conscience. Gradually he learns these arts for himself, and, as he does so, the skilled parent transfers the roles to him. This is a slow, subtle, and continuous process, beginning when he first learns to walk and feed himself and not ending completely until maturity is reached. But the unfolding of the child's self and conscience can only go on satisfactorily when his first human relationships are continuous and happy.

Here we are struck by a similarity between this process and the development of the unborn child during the time while tissues, which do not yet show the characters of the different parts of the future baby, take on these characters under the influence of certain chemicals called organizers. If growth is to proceed smoothly, the tissues must be exposed to the influence of the appropriate organizer at certain critical periods. In the same way, if mental development is to proceed smoothly, it would appear to be necessary for the unformed mentality to be exposed, during certain critical periods, to the influence of the psychic organizer—the mother. For this reason, in considering the disorders to which personality and conscience are liable, it is imperative to have regard to the phases of development of the child's capacity for human relationships. These are many and, naturally, merge into one another. In broad outline, the following are the most important:

(a) The phase during which the infant is in course of establishing a relation with a clearly identified person—his mother; this is normally achieved by five or six months of age.

(b) The phase during which he needs her as an ever-present companion; this usually continues until about his third birthday.

(c) The phase during which he is becoming able to maintain a relationship with her in her absence. During the fourth and fifth years such a relationship can only be maintained in favorable circumstances and for a few days or weeks at a time; after seven or eight the relationship can be maintained, though not without strain, for periods of a year or more.

The ages by which these phases are completed no doubt vary greatly from child to child in the same way that the stages of physical maturity vary. For instance, the capacity to walk matures at any time between nine and twenty-four months, and it may well be that psychic growth is equally variable. If this is so, it will be wise in research to reckon age rather by the stage of development reached than by actual length of life, since it seems fairly certain that the kind and degree of psychological disorder following deprivation depends on the phase of development the child is in at the time. In putting forward this theory well-established principles gained from the study of embryos are again followed. We learn that

abnormalities are produced by attacking, at just the right time, a region in which profound growth activity is under way. . . . Possible abnormalities will tend to fall into classes and types corresponding to the most critical stages and regions in development. Injuries inflicted early will in general produce widespread disturbances of growth . . . late injuries will tend on the other hand to produce local defects.

Furthermore,

a given undifferentiated tissue can respond to an organizer only during a limited period. It must have reached a certain stage of differentiation before it can respond; and later its character becomes fixed, so that it can yield only a more limited type of response.

In the same way the mother by her mere presence and tenderness can act as an "organizer" on the mind of the child, still in the quite undeveloped stages of very early growth. But the time when this action can take place is, as in the case of the chemical "organizer," limited to the time whilst the child's personality is quite unformed (this, of course, is quite a different matter from the continuing influence of the mother upon the child later). The evidence is fairly clear that if the first phase of development—that of establishing a relation with one particular person recognized as such—is not satisfactorily completed during the first twelve months or so, there is the greatest difficulty in making it good: the character of the psychic tissue has become fixed. (The limit for many children may well be a good deal earlier.) Similarly, there appears to be a limit by which the second and third phases must be completed if further development is to proceed. Now it is these vital growth processes which are impaired by the experience of deprivation. Observations of severely deprived children show that their personalities and their consciences are not developed—their behavior is impulsive and uncontrolled and they are unable to pursue long-term goals because they are the victims of the momentary whim. For them, all wishes are born equal and equally to be acted upon. Their power of checking themselves is absent or feeble; and without this people cannot find their way efficiently about the world—they are swayed this way and that by every impulse. They are thus ineffective personalities unable to learn from experience, and consequently their own worst enemies. We cannot yet explain exactly how the deprivation of a mother's care produces this result, but two of the observations which have already been noticed may carry us some way towards understanding the problem. These are, first, Dr. Goldfarb's discovery of the difficulty which these patients have in abstract thinking, of dealing with ideas rather than being tied to the objects immediately present to the senses; and second, the observation of doctors trying to help them of their being unable to come out of themselves through affection for other people or interest in things outside themselves.

All the institution children studied by Dr. Goldfarb showed serious and special incapacity for abstract thinking. Now we have just seen that such thinking is necessary to the action of the self and of the conscience—the baby must gradually learn to think before he acts and to give up responding automatically to every happening, a sound, a light, hunger, or pain: only then can he become a full person. So it may well be that where abstract thinking has not developed properly the personality cannot fully unfold. But even so, there remains the puzzle as to why deprivation should injure the power of abstract thinking.

The failure of personality development in deprived children is perhaps more easily understood when it is considered that it is the mother who in the child's earliest years acts as his personality and his conscience. The institution children had never had this experience, and so had never had the opportunity of completing the first phase of development—that of establishing a relationship with a clearly known mother-figure. All they had had was a succession of makeshift agents each helping them in some limited way, but none providing continuity in time, which is of the essence of personality. It may well be that these grossly deprived infants, never having been the continuous objects of care of a single human being, had never had the opportunity to learn the processes of abstraction and of the organization of behavior in time and space. Certainly their grave psychical deformities are clear examples of the principle that injuries inflicted early produce widespread disturbances of growth.

In the institutional setting, moreover, there is less opportunity for the child who has learnt how to think to exercise this art. In the family the young child is within limits encouraged to express himself both socially and in play. A child of eighteen months or two years has already become a character in the family. It is known that he enjoys certain things and dislikes others, and the family has learnt to respect his wishes. Furthermore, he is getting to know how to induce his parents or his brothers and sisters to do what he wants. In this way he is learning to change his social environment to a shape more congenial to him. The same occurs in his play, where in a symbolic way he is creating and recreating new worlds for himself. Here are the exercise grounds for the personality. In any institutional setting much of this is lost; in the less good it may all be lost. The child is not encouraged to individual activity because it is a nuisance; it is easier if he stays put and does what he is told. Even if he strives to change his environment he fails. Toys are lacking: often the children sit inert or rock themselves for hours together. Above all, the brief intimate games which mother and baby invent to amuse themselves as an accompaniment to getting up and washing, dressing, feeding, bathing, and returning to sleep—they are all missing. In these conditions, the child has no opportunity of learning and practicing functions which are as basic to living as walking and talking.

The case of the child who has a good relation with his mother for a year or two and then suffers deprivation may be rather different. He has passed through the first phase of social development, that of establishing a relationship, and the shock affects the second phase in which, though personality development is proceeding apace, the child's awareness of his relative lack of skill in the art of living is reflected in his limpet-like attachment to his mother, to whom he looks constantly for help. Only if she is with him or near at hand can he manage his environment and manage himself. If he is suddenly removed from her, to hospital or institution, he is faced with tasks which he feels to be impossible. In a terrifying situation of this kind it is usual for such skill as has already been learnt to be lost. In these circumstances children often go back to more babyish ways of thinking and behaving and find it very difficult to grow out of them again.

A further principle of the theory of learning is that an individual cannot learn a skill unless he has a friendly feeling towards his teacher, and is ready to identify himself with her. Now this positive attitude towards his mother is either lacking in the deprived child, or, if present, is mixed with keen resentment. How early in a child's life deprivation causes a definitely hostile attitude is debatable, but it is certainly evident for all to see in the second year. No observation is more common than that of the child separated for a few weeks or months during the second, third, or fourth years failing to recognize his mother on reunion. It seems probable that this is sometimes a true failure to recognize, based on a loss of the capacity to abstract and identify. At others, it is certain that it is a refusal to recognize, since the children, instead of treating their parents as though they were strangers, are deliberate in their avoidance of them. The parents have become hated people. This hostility is variously expressed. It may take the form of tempers and violence; in older children it may be expressed in words. All who have treated such children are familiar with the violence of their fantasies against the parents whom they feel to have deserted them. Such an attitude not only is incompatible with their desire for love and security, and results in acute conflict, anxiety, and depression, but is clearly a hindrance to their future social learning. So far from idolizing their parents and wishing to become like them, one side of their nature hates them and wishes to avoid having anything to do with them. This is what brings about aggressively bad or delinquent behavior; it may also lead ultimately to suicide which is a result of the same conflict being fought out between different parts of a person's self.

In other cases the child has suffered so much pain through making relationships and having them interrupted that he is reluctant ever again to give his heart to anyone for fear of its being broken. And not only his own heart: he is afraid, too, to break the heart of new persons whom he might love because he might also vent his anger on them. Older children are sometimes aware of this and will remark to a psychiatrist: "We had better not become too familiar, for I am afraid I shall get hostile with you then." It is feelings such as these which underlie a child's shutting into himself. To withdraw from human contact is to avoid further frustration and to avoid the intense depression which human beings experience as a result of hating the person whom they most dearly love and need. Withdrawal is thus felt to be the better of two bad alternatives. Unfortunately, it proves to be a blind alley, since no further development is then possible. For progress in human relations the individual must take the other road, in which he learns to tolerate his contradictory feelings and to bear the anxiety and depression which go with them. But experience shows that once a person has taken refuge in the relative painlessness of withdrawal he is reluctant to change course and to risk the turmoil of feeling and misery which attempting relationships brings with it. As a result he loses his capacity to make affectionate relationships and to identify himself with loved people, and any treatment offered is resisted. Thenceforward he becomes a lone wolf, pursuing his ends irrespective of others. But his desire for love, repressed though it is, persists, resulting in behavior such as promiscuous sex relations and the stealing of other people's possessions. Feelings of revenge also smoulder on, leading to other anti-social acts, sometimes of a very violent character.

Deprivation after the age of three or four, namely, in the third phase, does not have the same destructive effect on personality development and on the ability for abstract thinking. It still results, however, in excessive desires for affection and excessive impulses for revenge, which cause acute internal conflict and unhappiness and very unfavorable social attitudes.

In both the second and third phases the child's restricted sense of time and his tendency to misunderstand a situation add greatly to his difficulties. It is exceedingly difficult for grown-ups to remember that the young child's grasp of time is meager. The child of three can recall the events of a few days ago and anticipate those of a day or two hence. Notions such as last week or last month, next week or next month are incomprehensible. Even for a child of five or six, weeks are immensely long and months almost timeless. This very restricted time-span has to be understood if the despair which the young child feels at being left alone in a strange place is to be fully realized. Though to his mother it may seem not only a finite but relatively brief time, to him it is an eternity. It is this inability to imagine a time of deliverance which, together with the sense of his helplessness, accounts for the overwhelming nature of his anxiety and despair. Perhaps the nearest to it the grown-up can conceive is to imagine being committed to prison on an indeterminate sentence.

This comparison is a good one, since the notion of punishment is itself not far from many a child's mind as the explanation of events. All psychiatrists have come across children who have seriously believed that their being sent away from home was to punish them for being naughty, a misconstruction which is often made even more terrifying and distressing by being unexpressed. At other times children imagine that it has been their fault that the home has been broken up. Commonly there is bewilderment and perplexity regarding the course of events, which leads the child to be unable to accept and respond to his new environment and the new people caring for him. Naturally a child who has suffered gross privation in early infancy, or who for other reasons cannot make relationships, will not be affected in these ways, but will greet each change with genial indifference. But for the child who has had the opportunity to make relationships it is not so easy to change loyalties. Indeed, very many of the problems which arise as a result of moving an older child to a foster-home are caused by the failure to recognize the deep attachment which a child has for his parents, even if they are exceedingly bad and have given him little affection. Unless these perplexities are cleared up and these loyalties respected, the child will remain anchored in an unsatisfactory past, endlessly trying to find his mother and refusing to adapt to the new situation and make the best of it. This results in a dissatisfied restless character unable to make either himself or anyone else happy.

ANOTHER TYPE OF MOTHERING

From THE CHILDREN OF THE DREAM

Bruno Bettelheim

"What exactly constitutes the love and tender care a child needs for developing well? . . . Does something else take its place in the kibbutz which is just as effective as our type of mothering?"

These are the crucial questions posed by Bruno Bettelheim in his provocative study of kibbutz child-rearing techniques, Children of the Dream. *Bettelheim's analysis of the amazing fact that kibbutz children do* not *grow up with deformed personalities (as Bowlby suggests institution-raised children invariably do in the preceding selection) is set forth in the following two sections from the chapter "Infancy and Early Childhood."*

The most important theoretical question raised by the kibbutz method of child rearing is: What exactly constitutes the love and tender care a child needs for developing well? The view that institutional rearing creates severest pathology is so uncritically accepted by now that some observers of kibbutz children have seen the evils they expected to see where this observer did not. Does it follow then that love and tender care are not necessary, as Harry Harlow believed at first (1958), only to find, in the end, that even monkey babies cannot grow to be viable monkeys without it? (Harlow and Harlow, 1962). Or does something else takes its place in the kibbutz which is just as effective as our type

210

of mothering? And what of the fact that such mothering exists only as an ideal with us, since we often fall short of it in practice?

BASIC SECURITY

Infants do indeed need love and tender care for developing well. But the kibbutz example suggests that our view of what ingredients go into love and care are maybe parochial and not universal. According to Erik Erikson the infant needs love and tender care because it creates in him a sense of basic trust—both a trust in his own competence and a trustfulness of others. As he puts it:

The general state of trust implies not only that one has learned to rely on the sameness and continuity of the outer providers but also that one may trust oneself and the capacity of one's own organs to cope with urges; that one is able to consider oneself trustworthy enough so that the providers will not need to be on guard or to leave.

What Erikson has in mind here are the "sameness and continuity" the mother provides for her infant at this earliest period of his life. His example of why the infant has to cope with his urges to keep the provider from leaving is that of the infant who wishes to nurse at the breast and must therefore control his urge to bite the nipple.

Clearly this is pertinent for our nuclear middle-class family. But the kibbutz example suggests that the infant can achieve basic trust even if there is much less sameness and continuity of the outside provider than we assume is needed, so long as continuous providing is guaranteed. It suggests that trust in oneself can develop even if there is no threat of the outside provider being on guard or leaving; that self-control over one's asocial urges can develop out of a desire to keep the willing companionship of the peer group.

Maybe we can better understand what is needed for basic trust if we focus less on what specifics the environment must provide, and more on what the inner experience of the infant must be. Here we might also consider Erikson's important warning against an undynamic view of basic trust. It concerns what the child needs, at any given stage of development, if he is to master it successfully and hence be prepared for the next stage of growing up. And this need, according to Erikson, is for "a certain *ratio* between the positive and the negative which, if the balance is toward the positive, will help him to meet later crises with a better chance for unimpaired total development." Thus what counts at the very earliest stage of development is the ratio in the infant's experience of basic trust, versus basic mistrust.

I suggest that the inner experience of the infant leading to trust is that of security, whatever the outer experience that creates such a feeling, and whether or not it is based on any sameness in the person of the provider. And security derives from the feeling that we can safely relax, that we need not worry—provided this feeling is not delusional, but is based on a correct estimate of reality. But since we can seldom relax altogether or be wholly free of worry, what is essential is the ratio between security and insecurity. The kibbutz example suggests further that security in infancy is made up of at least two different things: physical security and companionship.

Physical security at this age derives chiefly from the fact that adults provide for the infant's essential needs such as for food, shelter, rest, and other bodily comfort, a protection from excessive stimulation, etc. It is the necessary condition for survival but is not enough by itself to assure successful growth. To it must be added *companionship*: the filling of social and emotional needs, which imply age-correct stimulation and a responsiveness from others. But again: A companionship that in one setting (ours) may consist essentially of sameness and continuity of the outer provider may in another setting (the kibbutz) be built up of other ingredients.

The dynamic counterpart of this same-and-continuous-provider is separation anxiety—the fear of desertion, or its actuality. The more crucially the child's basic trust depends on the sameness and continuity of a single provider, the more devastating the basic mistrust caused by the loss of that person. Here, too, it is the ratio that counts, a ratio between the security derived from a single provider, and the anxiety of being separated from him on whom all security depends.

Basic security, then, is the assurance of survival. Only he who has the power to assure it can truly offer security. Only with him must we come to terms (or identify) if we are utterly dependent.

Freud, in his earlier writings, stressed the utter dependence of the infant on his mother. But psychologically that situation is very different from what is stressed in the psychoanalytic literature today. Margaret Mahler, for example, speaks about "the decisive fact that . . . the survival of the human young depends on . . . the quasi-sociobiological symbiosis with the mother organism." Now a "mother organism" is quite a different thing from a mothering person. Perhaps Freud was more impressed by the infant's dependence on his caretakers, whoever they might be, than by his need for the mother's organism in particular. Because in Freud's time most middle-class children were not looked after by their mothers but by wet nurses and later on by nursemaids.

If we are less impressed by what (to me) seem somewhat mystical speculations about a symbiosis needed by the infant for survival, and more by his utter dependence on whoever can assure him satisfaction of his needs, then the kibbutz experiment may have something to teach us of what the infant must indeed have to survive.

It is true that nowadays the living-in wet nurse or nursemaid is rare, and bottle feeding is widespread. Hence for most middle-class children all pleasure and displeasure originates mainly with the mother. But both are tainted by the fact that the child is in her near absolute power. So here, too, what counts is the ratio between care given in line with the infant's needs and care imposed to satisfy needs of the mother, irrespective of the infant's needs. (There simply are no kibbutz parents who beat up their children. The phenomenon of the "battered child"—that is, of children so abused by their parents as to need hospitalization—is unthinkable in the kibbutz.)

Whatever has been said of the omnipotent beliefs of the infant and his convictions about power over his mother, such beliefs begin to break down very quickly, as soon as the mother is needed but is not there, or as soon as she fails to relieve pain or frustration. From then on and with every step he takes toward independence, the infant grows more keenly aware of the mother's power, and so does the mother.

To be dependent also means to be in the power of the one on whom we depend. And since the infant's dependence is not only physical but emotional and social, he is in another person's power on all counts. The normal mother is aware of, and afraid of misusing this power. It is this, the parent's power over the very life of his infant, that set the tragedy of Oedipus in motion. Had the father of Oedipus not had (and used) the power he held over his son's existence, his son would never have slain him. We cannot separate the receiving of dependent care from the power relations within which they are given and received.

The story in the kibbutz is entirely different. There, through a conscious act of will, parents have transferred their power to the community. All children are viewed and cared for as "children of the kibbutz." It was a strange experience, for example, to have a child introduced to me as Dalia, the daughter of Atid, and a few hours later to meet Dalia with her father, this time to be told with pride, "this is my daughter." There is no question in her father's mind that she is his daughter. But neither is there any doubt in his or her mind that she is also in a very real sense a daughter of Atid.

It took me some time to respond differently to a parent who claimed a youngster as "my" child, and another who claimed him as "ours." Each kibbutznik feels his parenthood of every kibbutz child in a deep and parental way. They are proud of the children of their kibbutz. There is deep feeling when they claim this or that child as "ours." In many ways, like an uncle, they are more straightforward, less ambivalent in their emotional attachment to such a child than in the attachment to their own child, which may be much more complex.

The difference between an American uncle's feeling for his nephew, and a kibbutznik's for a son of his kibbutz, is that the latter knows for sure, and how much, his work contributes to the well-being of all the sons and daughters of his kibbutz. He is also secure in the conviction that many of them, his sons and daughters once removed, will carry on the work of his life, as no American parent can be sure that even his own children will.

Children, for their part, do not refer to individual kibbutzniks as their parents. But to them, in an emotional sense, the kibbutz as a whole stands for the providing, controlling, and educating parent. Again and again they refer to the kibbutz as giving them all they need, and as shaping and planning their lives, just as an American child refers to his parents in this context.

In all the countless ways that a parent educates his children—from how they should spend their time, arrange their day, to how they should eat, sit at the table, talk, play alone or with others, and including such extremely intimate matters as their toilet training—the kibbutz, through its metapelets [baby nurses] and the peer group, will educate the child. Though children refer to no one but their real parents as parents, they are intensely aware, both consciously and unconsciously, that all these extremely important functions are exercised not by their parents but by the community. With the important difference that to them these are not parental but community functions.

To kibbutz children, then, basic security is provided not by their parents but the kibbutz. How early in life this is realized I cannot say. Here, unfortunately, my observations may have been hampered because I do not speak Hebrew. But my impression is that the children realize it even before they can talk. And this holds true not only for physical needs, but for social and emotional security, though we do not know as yet when and how the two blend, or when and how they separate at last.

Even in our complex world—and kibbutz life is here so much simpler—man's basic needs are still for food, shelter, and clothing, along with stimulation and companionship. All these are provided for the kibbutz child either entirely, or to a very large degree, by the community, not by his parents. He sleeps in a separate house built just for him and his age-mates; he is fed in the presence of others from the first, and soon only with them; his clothing comes from the communal supply.

Most of his stimulation comes from the metapelet and the infants he rooms with, since his mother spends at most only a few hours a day with him (and none at night), and these few hours are broken by absences. That is, she comes about four or five times a day and usually spends about half an hour, occasionally up to an hour or so, with her infant. Nevertheless, kibbutz theory holds that his emotional needs are met mainly by his parents. And this radical separation between providing for his physical and emotional needs was meant to ensure that the pleasures of the latter would not be sullied by resented controls surrounding the first. (One may wonder about the outcome of such a separation, and I shall return to this again later.)

In the nuclear family the closeness of child-parent ties depends largely on what parents do for and with their child, both materially and emotionally. That the direct emotional giving of parents to children is important for the relation between them is recognized in kibbutz theory and practice. But there is great ambivalence about material giving. While all basic material giving is to come from the kibbutz, parents in most kibbutzim get a food allowance so that they can have goodies in their room to offer their children when they visit. In quite a few kibbutzim, children and adults may also receive small presents from persons outside the kibbutz. But there is widespread dissension about this, both because it reduces equality, and because it injects economic considerations into human relations where they are not supposed to exist. . . .

CRIB MATES

[The] importance of the peer group begins in the very first days of life. We do not know whether, in the human being, something akin to the imprinting of animals takes place. But there is no doubt that the earliest experiences make a deep impact and are hence apt to shape all later ones in some measure.

Imprinting is thus nothing but an extremely important early experience. And in our own culture, at this most impressionable age, it is only or mainly the mother's image that is scanned by the infant as he nurses. In the kibbutz, by comparison, what greets the infant who wakens to feed, and looks around at his world? As likely as not, and from the very beginning, he sees just as much of the metapelets and other mothers tending their babies, as he does his own mother. She only emerges as separate and special when she puts him to breast.

Much more important in time and emotional impact are the constant companions who live in his room. Them he always sees and reacts to. Much of the waking time spent by the middle-class infant watching his parents, the kibbutz infant spends watching his roommates. As a matter of fact, so important may be the infant in the crib next to him, for example, that if his crib mate is moved to another room he may lose his appetite and get run down, a condition that improves when his "friend" or "twin" is returned.

Separation anxiety in the kibbutz is thus very typically experienced around the absence of a peer. And it can never be felt as acutely as by the middle-class infant whose mother leaves him, because however important the infant in the next crib, he is not the only one in the room, nor the only one life revolves around. At least two others are still left for companionship. And while the positive attachment to one person (the mother) seems diluted, when compared to our settings, separation anxiety is much less acute because of the continuing presence of several important others (metapelet, other infants). Thus again if we consider only the positive attachments, things seem to favor the middle-class child. But if we consider the ratio between security gained from positive attachment versus separation anxiety, it may very well be that kibbutz infants again enjoy the advantage.

While all children are "children of the kibbutz," and feel essentially like siblings, this is not just a matter of semantics. Those children who, from birth on, live together as an age-group, experience each other not only as siblings but as twins, since they were nurslings together and close crib companions. True, they do not share identical parents, and their heredity is radically different. But because of their otherwise "twinlike" existence they show some of the psychological features that characterize twins: the deep dependence and reliance on each other, the feeling that no one but their twin can ever fully understand them or share their innermost being. Only instead of one twin they have several, and of both sexes.

Because of this, though for other reasons too, the polarization, through which one twin often asserts his identity by being as different as possible from the other twin, I did not find in the kibbutz. I got to know one set of twins rather well. From all appearances (and from what I was told) they were identical twins, and by that time quite grown up. While extremely close to each other, they showed few of the characteristics I observe among identical twins in our setting. They were neither "half" a person without the other, nor did they show any need to develop in opposite ways to feel secure in their personal identity. My guess is that, having lived "like twins" from birth on with several others, and not just their own twin, they did not feel as dependent on each other as seems true of twins in our families.

Perhaps the difference in parentage and natural endowment gives enough real differentiation to those who from birth on grow up like twins so that there is no need to strive for any more on their own. It is not enough, though, to cancel out the strange situation that four or more infants share all vital steps in growing up and developing, as would be true with us only of twins or of infants growing up in institutions.

This is why the kibbutz child, in his relatedness to other children, feels closest to his very own age-group, in many ways more so than to his natural siblings, who come next, and third, to all other kibbutz children.

What does this collective life look like, for the older infant from the time he can crawl? These infants, when they wake, are placed in large playpens; then, as soon as they can walk, in rather large, fenced-in play spaces. For many periods of the day, even when the metapelets are supposedly taking care of a group of infants or toddlers, they are left to their own devices. Often this is for hours at a stretch, while the metapelets clean the house, fetch the food, sort the laundry, do the mending. During this time the infant, and later the small child, is never alone, as an infant raised at home might be even if the mother is just busy in another room.

In playpen and play yard the children crawl over each other, push each other down, and while at first the pushed down child may wail, he soon learns his place in the pecking order and adjusts accordingly. But life is not just bad times and getting pushed down; most of the time the children play successfully together. Since no parent interferes with the pecking order, and even the metapelet does so only rarely, each child stays in his given place and soon learns to play according to the hierarchy established. As long as he does, and soon they all learn to do it for most of the time, there is always someone to play with; they are never alone.

American readers will wonder what happens to the low man on the totem pole, to the weak child or the meek one who—were this a society based on nothing but the pecking order—would always come last, would never come into his own except by withdrawing or submitting. And this might well happen in our competitive society where winning is so highly valued. But things are not so in the kibbutz.

I did not see a single case of a bully or bullying. I did see the weaker infants pushed over by stronger ones, but never deliberately—if one can speak of being deliberate in such things before the age of two—nor gloatingly. And thereafter such a child was usually picked up and comforted by another child, sometimes by the one who pushed him down. Depending, of course, on the relative maturity of the child, this stage may be reached anywhere between age two and two-and-a-half.

By toddler age, then, life is truly with the group; the children are comrades, not competitors. If one is stronger, he will use and occasionally misuse his strength, but not for long. Very soon the group spirit asserts itself, and he feels the disapproval and desists. The spirit of helpfulness among them is much more evident than the desire for dominance. Since there are no parents around for whom to vie, and since the competitive spirit is frowned on, the push is toward acting like brothers and sisters, where the stronger one exerts some controlling influence, but also feels called on to use it in the interests of his brothers and sisters. And this is well established by the toddler age. But even before then, they have all learned to be self-reliant to a degree most uncommon in our middle-class settings.

How early they are forced by the arrangements to learn self-reliance may be illustrated by two observations made in one of the oldest and wealthiest of left-wing kibbutzim. The first one concerns babies and occurred while I was interviewing an elderly metapelet, in charge of the infants' house there for many years. I was asking how many babies she had in her care, and she told me there were sixteen in the nursery, but that each metapelet was only responsible for four. "I work four hours in the morning," she said, "from 7:00 to 11:00, and then I return again at 12:30."

I wondered what happens then, between 11:00 and 12:30? (The time, then, was shortly after 11:00, and the babies were in a playpen on the porch, just outside the room where we spoke.) The answer was: "They don't need anybody, they're in the playpen during that time." Nevertheless, we could hardly hear each other at times because the wailing of the babies was so loud. So I said I could hear them crying right now so they seemed to need someone to look after them, and the metapelet told me: "If they cry too long, some other metapelet will look to see what's the matter. There is always one metapelet in the house serving all four groups."

The crying continued, and I went out to see what went on. I found seven babies in a large playpen out in the sun, with some nice toys in it. Two bigger babies crawled all over a little one and took a toy away from him. He cried for a long time while the one metapelet on duty was occupied with washing furniture. Finally she came out on the porch and picked up the crying one for a moment but without comforting him. He continued to cry, but more quietly now. So she put him down at another spot in the playpen and left. And soon he stopped crying and went about his business.

As soon as the being picked up may have raised some hopeful expectations in the baby, he was returned to the old situation to fend for himself as best he could. If many such experiences are repeated, as they are, it may force the infant (and all other infants who watch it) to give up hoping for comfort from a mother figure, or any desire for her presence.

It was not that the metapelet was insensitive. She was merely convinced that the baby had to learn to get along in his group, and not to rely on the intercession of someone outside it; that her comforting would only retard a piece of learning that was more important than temporary discomfort.

And a year or two later, when they are toddlers, they have indeed learned much: how to fend for themselves, how to get along with the group, how to find comfort there and satisfaction. One day, for example, I observed an entire toddlers-house group who had been playing for quite a while in the large play space in front of their house while the metapelet was away fetching their lunch from the communal kitchen and her adolescent helper was inside setting the table. On her return the metapelet called to the children to come in for lunch.

Scrambling to get there, one little boy fell and started to cry; he had obviously hurt himself. The metapelet very nicely went over to him, picked him up, but then set him down a moment later, before she had really discovered what was wrong, and long before he had quieted down or been reassured. She then went indoors because she had to, since there were now some fourteen children inside to be taken care of and fed by her and her helper.

Eventually after some hard inner struggle the boy fought down his crying. The others were too busy with their meal and each other to offer comfort at this moment, so the best thing was to join them as soon as he could. But first he took a knife from the table and went back outside where he sat down to scrape the dirt off his slightly bleeding knee. This took some time, and quite a few minutes later, he was still there and had not yet come to the table.

The metapelet could not have returned to him easily, even had she wished. Her other duties forbade it. But after some ten minutes the boy had got complete hold of himself and rejoined the group. He really had no true choice in the matter. Had he stayed behind, he would have gotten no comfort for his hurt and would not only have missed out on lunch but also the companionship of the children and metapelet.

During this same toddler age, though, the peer group also comes to be a source of comfort in lieu of adults. It was charming, for example, to see a three-year-old come up to an age-mate who was upset about something, inviting him to play, cheering him up, leading him back to the group. But because of it, the small child is more and more relieved of having to struggle by himself with an inner experience. Because even (or especially) if no other comfort is available, the group and its doings are always there to divert his attention to an external experience with them, and away from the one with himself.

At critical times, such as at night, small children have only their mutual comforting to rely on, since it may take quite a while for the single night watch to hear a child who wakes up crying, and a bit longer till he or she comes around. Though no one in the small community is entirely a stranger, the night watch rotates among members from day to day, or week to week. So even when the night watch is finally summoned by the child's anxious cry, the person who comes when the child thus awakens from a nightmare, deeply shaken, is more or less a stranger and can therefore give only small comfort. But as likely as not, when the night watch finally gets there, he finds that some other child has already soothed the anxious one.

Thus when in deep emotional distress, the kibbutz child soon learns to rely on the help of another child for comfort and security. Later on, too, it will more likely be a more advanced or a bit older child in his peer group and not the metapelet who will help him on the toilet, with getting dressed, and at all other times when he cannot manage by himself.

Part VII

BABIES IN OTHER CULTURES

CHILD-REARING IN AN AMERICAN INDIAN TRIBE

From CHILDHOOD AND SOCIETY

Erik Erikson

Definition of an American Indian family: the mother, the father, the children, and the anthropologist. Thus went the joke in the post-Depression years when swarms of anthropology field-workers settled on the Indian reservations. It was well before this influx that the Danish-born, Freud-oriented psychoanalyst Erik Erikson did field work on two Indian reservations, bringing his special insights as a psychoanalyst to the study of two diverse cultures. The result of his studies was Childhood and Society, *a unique blending of anthropology and psychology, which remains an important contribution to both disciplines to this day.*

Here is a section from Childhood and Society *dealing with infant care among the Sioux Indians, buffalo hunters of the plains.*

As we now present a list of data significant in the Sioux system of child-rearing, the single datum owes its significance largely to the women's wish to convey a point dear to their traditional ethos, and yet sometimes also to our wish to check a point dear to our theoretical anticipations. Such a list, then, can neither be exhaustive nor entirely conclusive. Yet we thought we detected a surprising convergence between the rationale given by the Indians for their ancient methods, and the psychoanalytic reasoning by which we would come to consider the same data relevant.

The colostrom (the first watery secretion from the milk glands) was normally considered to be poison for the baby; thus the breast was not offered to him until there seemed to be a good stream of perfect milk. The Indian women maintained that it was not right to let a baby do all the initial work only to be rewarded with a thin, watery substance. The implication was clear: how could he trust a world which greeted him thus? Instead, as a welcome from the whole community, the baby's first meal was prepared by relatives and friends. They gathered the best berries and herbs the prairie affords and put their juice into a buffalo bladder, which was fashioned to serve as a breastlike nursing bottle. A woman who was considered by all to be a "good woman" stimulated the baby's mouth with her finger and then fed him the juice. In the meantime, the watery milk was sucked out of the breast and the breast stimulated to do efficient work by certain older women who had been commanded in their dreams to perform this office.

Once the Indian baby began to enjoy the mother's breast he was nursed whenever he whimpered, day or night, and he also was allowed to play freely with the breast. A small child was not supposed to cry in helpless frustration, although later to cry in rage could "make him strong." It is generally assumed that Indian mothers return to their old "spoiling" customs as soon as they can be sure they will not be bothered by the health authorities.

In the old order the baby's nursing was so important that, in principle at least, not even the father's sexual privileges were allowed to interfere with the mother's libidinal concentration on the nursing. A baby's diarrhea was said to be the result of a watery condition of the mother's milk brought about by intercourse with the father. The husband was urged to keep away from the wife for the nursing period, which, it is said, lasted from three to five years.

It is said that the oldest boy was nursed longest and that the average nursing period was three years. Today it is much shorter, although instances of prolonged nursing persist, to the dismay of those whose job it is to foster health and morals. One teacher told us that an Indian mother quite recently had come to school during recess to nurse her eight-year-old boy, who had a bad cold. She nursed him with the same worried devotion with which we ply our sniffling children with vitamins.

Among the old Sioux there was no systematic weaning at all. Some mothers, of course, had to stop nursing for reasons beyond their control. Otherwise the children weaned the mother by gradually getting interested in other foods. Before finally abandoning the breast altogether, however, the infant may have fed himself for many months on other food, allowing time for his mother to give birth to the next child and to restore her milk supply.

In this connection I remember an amusing scene. An Indian child of about three was sitting on his mother's lap eating dry crackers. He frequently became thirsty. With a dictatorial gesture and an experienced motion he reached into his mother's blouse (which, as of old, had openings on the sides from the armpits down), in an attempt to reach a breast. Because of our presence she prevented him bashfully, but by no means indignantly, with the cautious movement of a big animal pushing aside a little one. But he clearly indicated that he was in the habit of getting a sip now and then while eating. The attitude of the two was more telling than statistical data in indicating when such little fellows, once they can pursue other adventures, definitely stop reaching into their mother's blouse—or, for that matter, into the blouse of any woman who happens to have milk. For such milk, where it exceeds the immediate needs of her suckling baby, is communal property.

This paradise of the practically unlimited privilege of the mother's breast also had a forbidden fruit. To be permitted to suckle, the infant had to learn not to bite the breast. Sioux grandmothers recount what trouble they had with their indulged babies when they began to use nipples for the first vigorous biting. They tell with amusement how they would "thump" the baby's head and how he would fly into a wild rage. It is at this point that Sioux mothers used to say what our mothers say so much earlier in their babies' lives: let him cry, it will make him strong. Good future hunters, especially, could be recognized by the strength of their infantile fury.

The Sioux baby, when thus filled with rage, was strapped up to his neck in the cradleboard. He could not express his rage by the usual violent motion of the limbs. I do not mean to imply that the cradleboard or tight swaddling-clothes are cruel restrictions. On the contrary, at first they are undoubtedly comfortably firm and womblike things to be wrapped and rocked in and a handy bundle for the mother to carry around while working. But I do wish to suggest that the particular construction of the board, its customary placement in the household, and the duration of its use, are variable elements used by different cultures as amplifiers of the basic experiences and the principal traits which they develop in their young. What convergence can we see between the Sioux child's orality and the tribe's ethical ideals? We have mentioned generosity as an outstanding virtue required in Sioux life. A first impression suggests that the cultural demand for generosity received its early foundation from the privilege of enjoying the nourishment and the reassurance emanating from unlimited breast feeding. The companion virtue of generosity was fortitude, in Indians a quality both more ferocious and more stoical than mere bravery. It included an easily aroused quantity of quickly available hunting and fighting spirit, the inclination to do sadistic harm to the enemy, and the ability to stand extreme hardship and pain under torture and self-torture. Did the necessity of suppressing early biting-wishes contribute to the tribe's always ready ferocity? If so, it cannot be without significance that the generous mothers themselves aroused a "hunter's ferocity" in their teething infants, encouraging an eventual transfer of the infant's provoked rage to ideal images of hunting, encircling, catching, killing, and stealing.

We are not saying here that their treatment in babyhood *causes* a group of adults to have certain traits—as if you turned a few knobs in your child-training system and you fabricated this or that kind of tribal or national character. In fact, we are not discussing traits in the sense of irreversible aspects of character. We are speaking of goals and values and of the energy put at their disposal by child-training systems. Such values persist because the cultural ethos continues to consider them "natural" and does not admit of alternatives. They persist because they have become an essential part of an individual's sense of identity, which he must preserve as a core of sanity and efficiency. But values do not persist unless they work, economically, psychologically, and spiritually; and I argue that to this end they must continue to be anchored, generation after generation, in early child-training; while child-training, to remain consistent, must be embedded in a system of continued economic and cultural synthesis. For it is the synthesis operating within a culture which increasingly tends to bring into close-knit thematic relationship and mutual amplification such matters as climate and anatomy, economy and psychology, society and child-training.

How can we show this? Our proof must lie in the coherent meaning which we may be able to give to seemingly irrational data within one culture and to analogous problems in comparable cultures. We shall, therefore, indicate in what way various items of our material on Sioux culture seem to derive meaning from our assumptions, and then proceed from this hunter tribe to a comparison with a tribe of fishermen.

As we watched Sioux children sitting in the dark corners of their tents, walking along the trails, or gathered in great numbers around the Fourth of July dance, we noticed that they often had their fingers in their mouths. They (and some adults, usually women) were not sucking their fingers, but playing with their teeth, clicking or hitting something against them, snapping chewing-gum or indulging in some play which involves teeth and fingernails on one or both hands. The lips, even if the hand was as far inside the mouth as is at all possible, did not participate. Questioning brought the astonishing answer: yes, of course, they had always done this, didn't everybody? As clinicians we could not avoid the deduction that this habit was the heir of the biting-wishes which were so ruthlessly interrupted in early childhood—just as we assume in our culture that thumb-sucking and other sucking-habits of our children (and adults) compensate for sucking-pleasures which have been frustrated or made uncertain by inconsistent handling.

This led to an interesting further question: why were women more apt to display this habit than the equally frustrated men? We found a twofold answer to this: women, in the olden days, used and abused their teeth to chew leather and flatten the porcupine quills which they needed for their embroidery. They thus could apply the teething-urges to a toothy activity of high practicality. And indeed, I saw a very aged woman sitting in her tent, dreamily pulling a strip of moving picture film between her few remaining teeth, just as she may have flattened the porcupine quills long ago. It seems then, that tooth habits persisted in women because for them they were considered "normal," even when no longer specifically useful.

Generosity in the Sioux child's later life was sustained not by prohibition, but by the example set by his elders in the attitude which they took towards property in general and to his property in particular. Sioux parents were ready at any time to let go of utensils and treasures, if a visitor so much as admired them, although there were, of course, conventions curbing a visitor's expression of enthusiasm. It was very bad form to point out objects obviously constituting a minimum of equipment. The expectation, however, that an adult should and would dispose of his surplus caused much consternation in the early days, when the "Indian giver" offered to a white friend not what the friend needed, but what the Indian could spare, only to walk off with what he decided the white man could spare. But all of this concerned only the parent's property. A parent with a claim to good character and integrity would not touch a child's possessions, because the value of possessions lay in the owner's right to let go of them when *he* was moved to do so—i.e., when it added prestige to himself and to the person in whose name he might decide to give it away. Thus a child's property was sacrosanct until the child had enough of a will of his own to decide on its disposition.

THREE SOUTH SEA ISLAND TRIBES

From MALE AND FEMALE

Margaret Mead

The physical differences between men and women are unchangeable among humans everywhere, but what is considered appropriate male behavior and appropriate female behavior changes radically from culture to culture.

The following excerpt from Male and Female *by one of America's most popular anthropologists, Margaret Mead, compares the variations in child care among three dissimilar South Sea tribes in an effort to understand how human beings with an identical biological heritage can develop different ideas about what it is to be male and what it is to be female.*

Of the child's first experiences within the womb, and the way in which different cultures pattern these experiences, we still know very little. The Arapesh say the baby sleeps until ready for birth and then dives out. The Iatmul believe an unborn child can hurry or delay, as it wishes. "Why do you rail at me?" said Tchamwole to her husband. "This baby will be born when it likes. It is a human being, and it chooses its own time of birth. It is not like a pig or a dog to be born when others say it should." "The birth is hard," said the Tchambuli, "because the mother has not gathered enough firewood." It is probable that in different societies, by the attribution of more or less autonomy of movement to the baby, by

231

enjoining upon the mother active or placid behavior, the process of learning may begin within the womb, and that this may be interpreted differently for the two sexes. It is possible that there may be deep biochemical affinities between mother and female child, and contrasts between mother and male child, of which we now know nothing. So, at birth itself, whether the mother kneels squatting holding on to two poles or to a piece of rattan hung from the ceiling—whether she is segregated among females or held around the waist by her husband, sits in the middle of a group of gaming visitors or is strapped on a modern delivery table—the child receives a sharp initial contact with the world as it is pulled, hauled, dropped, pitched, from its perfectly modulated even environment into the outer world, a world where temperature, pressure, and nourishment are all different, and where it must breathe to live. Here there may be cultural intervention, such as to save the boy-baby and strangle the girl, but we know nothing as to whether birth itself means something different to the boy-baby and to the girl. There seems to be a differential sensitivity in the skin of males and females; and a sensitive skin is one of the clues that may make a male classify himself as a female, a hard skin may tend to get a girl dubbed masculine, in her own eyes and those of others. Skin-shock is one of the major shocks of birth, and where there is a final difference, there may be an initial one. In our own society, our images of the carefully guarded rituals of the delivery-room, in which the mind conjures up an even temperature maintained by a thermostat, the most medically perfect oils and unguents, and the softest of appropriate materials in which to wrap the baby, overlay any realization of what a shock birth is. The shock is easy enough to realize when the baby is born on an unsheltered hillside, where the mother and attending women crouch shivering over a tiny fire until finally the baby falls with a soft little thud on a cold, dew-coated leaf—to be left there, perhaps five minutes, while the mother herself cuts and ties the cord, packs up the placenta, and wipes out the baby's eyes and nose. Only then can the squirming, exposed little creature be gathered up and laid against the mother's breast. Whether or not this initial experience differs for the two sexes in any basic way, their later realization of their sex can reinvolve the experience they know has occurred. A longing for a world where pressure is even on the body and breathing is effortless, an experience that mystics of all times have sought, can be very differently woven into the fantasies of two parents expecting a child. To the expectant mother it means an increased sense of her sheltering relation to the child within her womb, to the expectant father such memories may come as a threat or as a temptation. For him, identification with the unborn child is at least partially unacceptable, for it turns his wife into his mother. For both expectant father and mother, such fantasies may arouse memories of the time before a younger child was born to his or her own mother, and then father and mother will defend themselves differently against these memories. What actual traces remain of the specificities of the birth-shock in the nervous system we do not know, but a careful examination of the ways in which new-born babies are handled—cradled gently against the breast, held up by the heels and slapped, wrapped so close that no light comes to them until they are many weeks old, stood out on the mother's iron-stiff arm to fend, like tiny frogs, for themselves— shows that these early ways of treating them are strictly congruent with later handling and later fantasies. However little the baby learns from its own birth, the mother who bears it, the midwife who assists, the father who stands by or walks the floor outside or goes off to consult a magician, all bear the marks of the birth experience and can again communicate it to the growing child. It will make a difference ultimately in our theories of human learning whether males and females are found actually to remember, differentially, their first shocking experience of temperature and breathing, or whether they learned about it from the imagery and poetry of the adult world. But in either case, whether the boy learns something different from his mother's voice because he has remembered, at some very deep level, a lesser shock upon his skin, or because he realizes that he can experience birth only once, while the girl pre-lives at that moment the day her own baby will be thrust out into the world—in either case, the birth experience becomes part of the symbolic equipment of women, who are formed to bear children, and of men, who will never bear them.

From the moment of birth—probably always from before birth also—contrasting types of behavior can be distinguished in a mother's attitude towards her child. The infant may be treated as a whole little creature—little animal, little soul, little human being, as the case may be, but whole, and to a degree capable of setting its own will and needs over against those of its mother. Such behavior may be called *symmetrical*, the mother behaves as if the child were essentially similar to herself, and as if she were responding to behavior of the same type as her own. Or she may treat the child as one who is different from herself, who receives while she gives, with the emphasis upon difference between the mother's behavior and that of the child as she cherishes and shelters and above all feeds a weak, dependent creature. This patterning of the relationship may be called *complementary*, as each of the pair is seen as playing a different rôle, and the two rôles are conceived as complementing each other. A third theme occurs when the behavior of the mother and the child is seen as involving an interchange when the child takes in what the mother gives it, and later, in elimination, makes a return. The emphasis is not on the symmetrical or the complementary character of the rôles, which include a feeling about the two personalities—as of the same kind or, in terms of the particular relationship, with different appropriate behaviors—but rather on an exchange of commodities between mother and child. Such behavior can be called *reciprocal*. In reciprocal phrasings of relationship, love, trust, tears, may become commodities, just as much as physical objects, but the interchange of physical objects remains the prototype. All these themes are present in every cultural phrasing of the mother-child relationship. To the extent that the child's whole individuality is emphasized, there is symmetry; to the extent that its weakness and helplessness are emphasized, there is complementary behavior; and to the extent that the mother gives not only her breast, but milk, there is the beginning of reciprocity. But cultures differ greatly as to which they emphasize most.

So we may contrast mothers in different societies with these different emphases. The Arapesh treat a baby as a soft, vulnerable, precious little object, to be protected, fed, cherished. Not only the mother, but the father also, must play this over-all protective rôle. After birth the father abstains from work and sleeps beside the mother, and he must abstain from intercourse while the child is young, even with his other wife. When the mother walks about she carries the child slung beneath her breast in a bark-cloth sling, or in a soft net bag in which the child still curls as he curled in the womb. Whenever it is willing to eat, even if it does not show any signs of hunger, it is fed, gently, interestedly. The receptiveness of the mouth is emphasized in both boys and girls. Through the long, protected infancy, during which children are carried, slung in bags from their mother's forehead or high on their father's shoulders, up and down the steep mountain trails, and are never asked to perform tasks that are difficult or exacting, their whole interest remains focussed on the mouth. Not even the almost ever present breast provides enough stimulation for a mouth that has been so heavily stressed, and small children sit playing endless gentle games with their lips, bubbling them, teasing them, puckering them lightly between their fingers. Meanwhile the grasping action of the mouth has never been developed. A readily offered breast does not have to be vigorously seized upon or bitten. The method of carrying places no emphasis on teaching the hands to grasp—which when it occurs can reinforce the grasping possibilities of the mouth. The Arapesh child, male and female, continues to take in, receptively, passively, what is offered it and to fly into tempers if food is ever refused—as it sometimes may be from necessity, for the people are very short of food.

Both boys and girls have learned about life from using their mouths. When they use their eyes, their eyes reflect the same passive expectancy. Eyes light up and mouths shout with excitement when some lovely color is presented to them, but hands do not reach aggressively, eyes do not probe and seek with active curiosity. The Arapesh are a people among whom communication between infants and others has been very heavily specialized to one part of the body, the mouth, and to one aspect of that part, passive receptivity. Both sexes among the Arapesh, like other human beings, have the task of eventually learning to use their whole bodies in acts of sexual maturity that will procreate children. For the Arapesh female this is easy enough. To transfer an attitude of pleasant expectancy from mouth to vulva, of soft, optimistic retentiveness, requires very little shift in attitude. Among the Arapesh, one may see a neglected wife eagerly bringing her neglectful husband food, touchingly grateful if he eats it; but I never heard a woman complain about a man's sexual competence. No accusations about low potency fill the evening air when a quarrel is on foot. When the usual pattern of marriage is followed, in which the husband as a boy of twelve or fourteen begins to feed his betrothed wife, himself playing a rôle that his mother has played to him—and his father also—and the marriage is not interrupted, the woman is in a psychological position that is the perfect development of her childhood experience—passive, dependent, cherished. In turn she treats her children in the same way.

But what happens to the Arapesh male? What kind of preparation is it for living in the rough mountain country of New Guinea, surrounded by tribes who are fierce head-hunters and blackmailing sorcerers, to have learned that the major relationship to other people is either one of passive receptivity or one of provision of food and drink? He does not, within his own society, become a homosexual, although there is great ease and warmth and much giggling puppyishness among boys. But the reverse attitude—the desire to dominate, to intrude, which would provide a basis for active homosexuality—is too slightly cultivated, nor is there enough development of assertive resentment of passivity to fit into a type of homosexuality where active and passive rôles are interchanged. The men in adulthood develop into heterosexual males, extremely distrustful of strange over-sexed women from other tribes who will take part of their semen and keep it for sorcery. Even with their own young wives, whom they have fed and cherished, there is not complete trust, but a ceremony at which the genital secretions of each are entrusted ceremonially to the other. Even copulation within the well-defined domestic circle may in the end be dangerous. They engage very little in warfare, they permit themselves to be blackmailed and bullied and intimidated and bribed by their more aggressive neighbors; they admire so deeply the artistic products of others that they have developed practically no art of their own. When they hunt, they set traps and wait until the animal falls in, or else they "walk about in the bush looking for game," and quarrels between hunting-partners come over who first caught sight of the animals. Arapesh male ceremonies, from which women are excluded, stress symbolically the nature of maternity. The men cut their arms, draw blood from them, and mix blood with coconut-milk and feed it to the novices—who thus ceremonially become their children (for the child at birth has only its mother's blood). The various sharp initiatory devices, sub-incision, beating with nettles, and so on, are all phrased as making the novices grow. Young males who have eaten carelessly of forbidden food—a phrase also used for sexual promiscuity—cut their penises and let blood from them to restore their health.

Thus the Arapesh form of child-rearing stresses complementariness in a form that is most easily transformed by women into an adult feminine sex rôle. Only that woman suffers who in spite of all this learning is still positively sexed and interested in climax for herself. But it is a society that makes it much more difficult to be a male, especially in all those assertive, creative, productive aspects of life on which the superstructure of a civilization depends. Where the upbringing fits most women, it fits only a few men.

But receptivity is only one of the two modes of behavior that are appropriate to the mouth of the young child and which may be transferred to other parts of the body. The mouth is not only soft and receptive, the infant lips are fitted for more than pressing gently against the nipple; the mouth is also a grasping, demanding organ, and the smallest infant's toothless gums are already able to chew savagely on a breast that does not yield it satisfaction. As the mother first holds her baby in her arms, she may treat it as a receptive little creature, or as an active demanding little creature already armed with a will and teeth. This active relationship is still a complementary one; the baby takes, the mother responds, either resignedly or with active interplay, or she may even angrily withdraw her breast if the child is making too great demands. We find among the Iatmul head-hunters both the receptive and the demanding behavior well developed. From birth the baby is handled as if it were a separate little entity capable of a will of its own, and immediately after birth before the mother has milk the wet nurse thrusts her nipple into its mouth with cherishing care, but also with a touch of the gesture with which mothers later stop their babies' temper tantrums by thrusting their nipples into their mouths like corks into soda-water bottles.

As soon as the Iatmul child is a few weeks old, the mother no longer carries it everywhere with her, or sits with it on her lap, but instead places it at some distance on a high bench, where it must cry lustily before it is fed. Assured that it is hungry, the mother crosses to it and feeds it generously and easily, but a baby that has had to cry hard for its food eats more definitely, and the vigor with which the mother thrusts her nipple into its mouth increases. Before the baby has any teeth, it is given pieces of hard bird-meat to gnaw on, and when its teeth begin to come in, it cuts them on round shell ornaments that hang around the mother's neck. In this interchange between mother and child, the sense of the mouth is built up as an assertive, demanding organ, taking what it can from a world that is, however, not unduly unwilling to give it. The child learns an attitude towards the world: that if you fight hard enough, something which will treat you as strong as itself will yield—and that anger and self-assertion will be rewarded. Children of each sex form images that will later inform their feeling about copulation, the girl-child forming a more active picture of her own rôle, the boy-child a more active picture of the female's rôle. Later, in the initiation ceremonies, giant model vulvas will be pushed down on the heads of the initiate males.

On a tributary of the Sepik River live the Mundugumor, among whom the active attitudes found among Iatmul women towards their nursing children are carried much farther. The Mundugumor women actively dislike child-bearing, and they dislike children. Children are carried in harsh opaque baskets that scratch their skins, later, high on their mother's shoulders, well away from the breast. Mothers nurse their children standing up, pushing them away as soon as they are the least bit satisfied. The occasional adopted new-born child is kept sharply hungry, so as to suck vigorously on a woman's breast until milk comes in. Here we find a character developing that stresses angry, eager avidity. In later life love-making is conducted like the first round of a prize-fight, and biting and scratching are important parts of foreplay. When the Mundugumor captured an enemy they ate him, and laughed as they told of it afterwards. When a Mundugumor became so angry that his anger turned even against himself, he got into a canoe and drifted down the river to be eaten by the next tribe.

In all three of these tribes, the mouth plays an important rôle as a way in which adults communicate to the growing child their own organized attitudes about the world. It seems probable that as he is fed every child learns something about the willingness of the world to give or withhold food, to give lavishly or deal out parsimoniously. But for genuine communication of a type that lays the groundwork for the child's understanding of his culture and his sex rôle, the mouth must be of interest to the adult as well as to the child. When a woman has originally formed her own picture of her feminine receptivity from the way in which she was fed as a child, this process will be present as she thrusts her erectile nipple into her new-born baby's mouth, and it is from this interchange that the basic learning seems to occur. Children will of course differ in the sensitivity of their lips, in their hunger rhythms, in the strength of the sucking impulse. These individual differences, which may in fact be systematically related to constitutional type, will be very important in laying the groundwork of individual character, but each of these individualities will develop as a version of the general attitude prevalent in that society, or that class or region, where the child is reared.

In some cultures, the adults are less interested in the mouth and may instead be more concerned with training the child to an early control of his bowels. Feeding may be done in a less involved way, while the major learning of the child is focussed on the other end of the gastro-intestinal tract, whose modes of behavior are not passive receptivity and active taking, as in the mouth, but retention and ejection. Here the emphasis shifts from the complementary relationship to an emphasis upon the relationship between the child and that which he first takes in and then gives out. Person-thing relationships are learned here, reciprocal rather than simple complementary relationships are stressed. The later transfer to the genitals of attitudes focussed on elimination makes for prudery, haste, lack of pleasure and foreplay in intercourse. This character-type in which the most emphasized communication between parent and child has been an emphasis on control of elimination is one that occurs fairly frequently in our own society. We find it writ large among the Manus tribe of the Admiralty Islands, a group of efficient puritans where women never swing their grass skirts—grass skirts after all are items in the endless exchange of goods that goes on—girls are never allowed to flirt, and all love, even the affection between brother and sister, is measured in goods. Here among these small Stone Age villages there was prostitution, and the owner of the war-captured prostitute made money. Here a woman never loosens her grass skirt even in the extremes of childbirth. Between husbands and wives sex is a hasty, covert, shameful matter; and otherwise it is adultery, heavily punished by vigilant, puritanical, ghostly guardians. Women's rôles and men's rôles are very slightly differentiated; both participate importantly in the religious system, both conduct economic affairs. If a man is stupid, his relatives seek for him a bright wife to compensate for his deficiencies. The sex act becomes a sort of shared excretion, and the attitudes that both sexes have learned during childhood come into play, not equally, for the female's sexual rôle is completely derogated, while the man is to a degree continuing an enjoined activity. But the general devaluation of sex and sex attraction is such that this difference in the images formed by males and females is less significant. A certain amount of sodomy among the young men is a natural concomitant of such a learning system.

Alternatively again, a people may show much less interest in either end of the gastro-intestinal tract. They may feed their infants in matter-of-fact fashion without emphasis, take their eliminations with the greatest casualness, and communicate with them instead by the way in which they carry them, confine their arms and legs, exert pressure on their skins, and pattern the interplay between child and carrier. The Balinese represent a people who conduct some communication with the mouth, but the emphatic part of this communication stresses pre-chewed (that is, by analogy, predigested) food, a mixture of bananas and rice piled in a little mountain on the helpless baby's mouth, and relentlessly pushed in whenever the baby opens its mouth to protest. This assault on the mouth is, not unexpectedly, followed by a great tendency to cover, or plug up, the mouth in later life. Eating is accompanied with great shame, while drinking, the prototype of which is drinking from an upturned breast, above which the infant is carried, is a matter of casual pleasure. A fundamental dichotomy runs through Balinese life between the light and the serious, heavy food and defecation on the one hand, light food and urination on the other, sleeping with one's wife and sleeping with a chance-met stranger. The infant first encounters the dichotomy in the feeding situation. But unlike the other four peoples whom I have just discussed, the Balinese place very early emphasis on the genitalia. A little boy's penis is being continually teased, pulled, flipped, flicked, by his mother, his child-nurse, and those around him. With the slight titillation go the repeated words, "Handsome, handsome, handsome," an adjective applied only to males. The little girl's vulva is patted gently, with the accompanying feminine adjective "Pretty, pretty, pretty." There is very little difference in the way in which a woman handles a male child and the way in which she handles her child's penis. The same flick, the same teasing, occur over and over again, while bystanders also handle the baby in arms just as they handle a small child's penis.

But most of the Balinese child's learning is focussed on his whole body, on his mother's carrying him as a part of her body; he is passive and relaxed, swinging in a sling as she pounds rice or works with rapid rhythmic movements. He develops a part-whole relationship to the world, in which each part of his body is a whole, and yet each is part of the whole. Valuation in sexuality is primarily a valuation of the penis itself. Male homosexuality is not a question of complementary assertiveness, but a search for as much maleness as possible, and where female homosexuality occurred— as it did in the palaces of the old rajahs—mock phalluses were part of the game. When small children put their fingers in their mouths exploringly, the emphasis seems to be on the sensation on the surface of the finger rather than upon the sensations from the lips or the mouth cavity. Love-affairs are matters of the eyes, foreplay is almost completely concentrated in a glance-exchanging courtship; the phrase for this eye-play is "as two fighting cocks looking at each other," and the sense of tension falls quickly from this first clash of feeling.

Even this very sketchy exploration of the way in which members of different cultures communicate some of their own elaborate historical cultural attitudes to their children should indicate how infinitely complicated the process of forming a picture of the adult sex rôle is for human beings who must be for so many years subjected to such elaborate adult pressures. The child's body with its orifices is open to endless pressures, stimulations, prohibitions, emphases. It may be handled only by women, or by men and women, or by little girls, or by little boys. It may be treated as part of the mother, as a whole separate person, as part of a person, as a beetle or as a god. But whatever the elaborations during learning, the adult sex act itself remains a complementary act; the male enters, the female is entered, however much these anatomical fundamentals may be overlaid and distorted. Each young child forms, from the way in which adults of each sex handle it, a picture of its own body and a picture of the body of the opposite sex, which will be in the end a part of its sex capacity and of its sex rôle. Probably emphasis on the mouth as a zone of intercommunication between adults and children gives the most vivid imagery for the sex act, but at the same time it carries extraordinary perils, because too vivid appreciation of the rewards of receptivity are incompatible with an adult male rôle, and may even lead to inversion; too much emphasis upon the assertive demanding aspects of the mouth may build a female picture that is over-active, over-demanding, and threatening. In marital quarrels among the Iatmul, the men complain bitterly that their wives demand too much of their copulatory powers.

So we have seen how emphasis on either the mouth or the genitals is basically complementary in character, and tends to build up attitudes towards activity-passivity, initiation-response, entrance and reception. We have also seen how emphasis on elimination may build most readily an emphasis on reciprocity, on taking in, retaining, and giving out, measured giving, measured receiving. To organize such behavior into symmetrical behavior, it is necessary to ignore or distort these partial relationships, all of which are essentially asymmetrical. Where the distortion is active, we find such situations as in a quarrel between Iatmul women when one says, "I'll copulate with you," and the other answers, with equal fury, "With what?" The Balinese man preserves symmetrical relationships by specific refusals of complementary situations. He covers his mouth, closes his ears, denies his responsiveness and receptivity, refuses to be worked on by oratory. He bends, and if his superior in status attempts any but the most highly stylized complementary behavior, he suddenly exaggerates his own behavior into complementary terms and offers his superior the danger of falling. The superior, to restore his own balance, must give up the complementary bit of arrogance.

But as important a set of learnings, and a set that will later be worked into the child's views of its own sex rôle, are offered to the child by the differences in size in the world around him. The differences in size between parents and children seem on the surface to be fixed, and therefore immutable; actually, however, cultures do very different things with them. The adult may stress the child's likeness to the parent, dress the child like an adult, minimize the difference in size and maximize the difference in sex. In parts of old Japan, the four-year-old male, because he was a male, could terrorize his mother and the other females of the household. His maleness overrode a difference in size that would have made it possible for any of the females to have given him a sound thrashing. Every time the sameness of sex is stressed at the expense of contrast in size, the significance and the complementary character of the two sexes are emphasized. But when children are lumped together as all inferior in status or strength to adults of both sexes, then sex differences are minimized. Some cultures play hard on one theme, others play both. So among the Iatmul, where there is a strong preference for symmetrical behavior, wherever symmetrical behavior is not possible there are elaborate devices to keep the possibilities of complementary behavior between males from getting out of hand. The young child learns simultaneously the possibilities of passivity and receptivity in the way in which his mother nurses him so assertively, and the advantages of self-assertion because he is not fed at all until he has asserted himself. Mothers not only treat their new-born as if they were separate willful beings, but it is a common sight to hear a mother pitting her will against a two-year-old who runs away shrieking in terror from her raised stick—a stick, however, which will never fall. The child is allowed to escape, strained to the utmost; the mother returns to her interrupted work muttering over his great strength and intractability. Grown men scatter small boys with showers of stones, angry fathers pace the village breathing imprecations upon their eight-year-olds, who may just have burned down a valuable sago-patch. In a thousand ways the adult world says to the child: "You are very strong. Stronger than you look, stronger than you feel. So strong that you are our possible successful rivals." And when the mother picks up food to eat, the child shrieks with rage and makes her give it a piece first.

But despite this strong premium on strength, little boys are classified with little girls and women, vis-à-vis the men, who are strongest of all, or wish to believe they are. Little boys sit with their mothers in the houses of mourning, sit with backs that curve as gracefully as any girl's above her play cooking utensils, and carry babies around affectionately. They hear any one of a dozen words for sodomy hurled about the village, irrespective of the sex of the user, but if two small boys attempt to act out what they have heard, older boys arm them with sticks and force them to fight each other. In adult life elaborate rituals in which men dress as women, caricaturing their lesserness, and women dress as men, caricaturing their glorious bombast, are a frequent feature of ceremonial life.

And still in every society men are by and large bigger than women, and by and large stronger than women, and adults are bigger and stronger than children. A little boy may be made to feel that his maleness is deeply and finally in doubt because he is so much smaller than a grown man, or he may feel that his maleness is an inalienable and absolute possession because it gives him some position of dominance or preference over a much larger woman. A girl may spend her childhood wrestling on an equal basis with boys, many of whom are smaller or weaker than she, when children of both sexes are set against the adult world, and so learn to feel that she is as strong, or stronger, than a male. A girl may be treated with such exaggerated chivalry while she is still a mite that she sets a value on her female charms that could never be learned if it were not accorded her by males of so much greater size and importance.

So the three themes, complementariness, reciprocity, and symmetry, weave in and out of the long learning process, interpenetrating and informing each other, until one side of the complementariness may be so emphasized as to become a form of symmetrical behavior, and with difference in age to provide the only asymmetry—as among the Arapesh, where husbands are ideally much older than their wives—because their receptivity and responsiveness are so much stressed. Or the assertive, invasive side of the suckling relationship may become dominant for both mother and child, with both sexes becoming assertive and demanding. Through the body, the ways of the body are learned.

THE PARENTS' CROWN

From LIFE IS WITH PEOPLE: THE CULTURE OF THE SHTETL

Mark Zborowski
and Elizabeth Herzog

The shtetls of Eastern Europe, the small Jewish towns and villages that existed as enclaves within the boundaries of Czechoslovakia, Poland, Russia, Lithuania, Bessarabia, and Slovakia until their tragic destruction in World War II, enjoyed a unique culture as rich and colorful as any that ever existed. From an anthropological study of the rapidly vanishing culture of the shtetl, *here is a description of how babies were born and cared for in the* shtetl *tradition.*

As soon as a baby is born there is great rejoicing, especially if it is a boy. Somewhat less ado is made about the birth of a girl, but a boy baby is the occasion of boundless excitement and festivity. "When my parents learned that the baby was a boy, they were so happy they danced a *kasatski* at my bedside." There is a constant stream of visitors who come to congratulate the new mother and see the new baby. Neighbors and relatives bring food, and her female relatives come in to do the work. If the baby is male, the young kheyder boys [the youngest schoolchildren] come every evening for a week to say the *krishmeh* at the bedside, the prayer that the child himself will say each evening when he is old enough. The

245

explanation for bringing in the kheyder boys is that the baby should get used to the environment of the kheyder as soon as possible. Like so many of the prayers for individual life events, the krishmeh is not personal but is the well-known affirmation, "Hear oh Israel, the Lord our God, the Lord is One. . . ."

The mother entertains from her bed, for she must remain there a week and in some regions must live entirely on liquids. Elsewhere she is indulged with delicacies and sweets. So tenderly is she pampered, that the word for a new mother, *kimpetorn*, has become a byword for indulgence. If a person demands excessive attention, he will be told, "you are not a kimpetorn." A hale adult will reject oversolicitude by protesting, "Why? Am I a kimpetorn?" After the prescribed period of rest the mother gets up from bed, purifies herself at the mikva [the ritual bath] and is ready to return to her normal life.

The baby, the center and cause of the flutter, is enfolded in precautions as palpable as its swaddling bands. Immediately after birth it is cleansed with oil, the cord severed, and the body bound in strips of soft linen from the shoulders down. Then the small human bundle is laid on a soft down pillow, its head covered by a little cap, and placed next to its mother. Perhaps a boy's forehead will be soaped and the hair removed so that he will grow up to have a high, broad brow, the symbol of wisdom.

The windows are kept closed to shut out any vestige of cold or draft. The shutters are tightly fastened to keep out the strong light of the sun, harmful to newly opened eyes. No moonlight must enter, for that brings the danger of spirits. External nature is barred from the dim, warm, draftless room almost as effectively as from the abode of the past nine months. The human contacts, however, are all-pervasive.

No less care is taken to guard against evil spirits and forces. The umbilical cord and placenta are buried in the earth where no malign influence can reach them. Throughout the first week a curtain is hung around the mother's bed where the child lies also, and curtains are hung at the windows and door. Psalms printed on pieces of paper are pinned on the curtains, in order to keep the infant from harm.

During the period before the baby is named, it is in especial danger from Lilith, Adam's first wife, who wants to snatch all babies in order to make up for her own demon children who are killed daily. If it laughs during the night, the mother must slap it quickly, for Lilith may be playing with it. The pattern of laughter swiftly followed by tears is one that will soon become familiar to any shtetl child. The baby who laughs at night, however, may be responding not to Lilith but to the angels with whom it is still on speaking terms. They come in the dark and praise a good baby, who gurgles with joy at their words. But if they say it is a bad baby, then it cries and must be comforted.

There is also especial danger from the evil eye during the first week. "Nobody is supposed to look at the child except the mother, father and the 'granny.' But if they do, they must 'spit' (say ptu!) three times and also say, 'to keep the evil eye away' and 'no evil eye!' "

Precautions against the evil eye continue throughout infancy, in fact through life, although the danger decreases with the years. Praise of the baby or boasting about him is an invitation to the evil eye, and arouses great anxiety. "The evil eye could be gotten through too much staring at the baby because of its beauty or health, from jealousy, or from excessive verbal admiration. So, if a neighbor praised the baby too much he would be warned by the parent or friend: Do not praise him so much, he may get an 'evil eye!' " Efforts are made to keep outsiders from looking at it too much. "The mother, grandmother or any person who took care of the baby at that particular time would distract his attention by turning it in another direction. The expressions most heard were, 'Look at the lamp, there is something wrong with it today,' or 'Look at the lamp, how clearly it burns today.' "

Any complimentary comment must immediately be followed by the exclamation, "No evil eye!" and this is true at any age. Moreover, any common trouble might be caused by evil eye, since nothing happens without reason. When baby yawns too much or cries too much, someone must apply the usual emergency procedure, "spitting" three times and exclaiming, "No evil eye!" Excess of any kind may be dangerous as well as unbecoming, in baby, child or grownup, and must be stopped at once.

Additional steps are taken to protect the infant. Sometimes a red ribbon is tied around one arm, or an amulet is fastened on. Girl babies may wear tiny gold earrings, perhaps set with turquoise for additional protection.

If, in spite of precautions, the baby seems to have incurred the evil eye, more drastic measures are taken. A professional "talker-away," *opshprekher*, may be called in to "talk away" the badness. On occasion a peasant woman will be summoned, just as on occasion the peasants consult the Rebbeh. There is mutual respect for magic practices and practitioners. Moreover, there is a large area shared in common. Many beliefs and usages are the same among the local peasants and the Jews, although different explanations may be given.

The difference between boy and girl—a difference that begins with their reception into the world and continues throughout their lives—is evident in attitudes, in activities and in periodic rituals. In a sense the culture ignores its females, although they are present, active and often forceful. When informants tell about babies, it is typically the boy and the boy's development that are described. "The baby" of the shtetl is a male, cared for chiefly by women and girls.

The girl has no formal *rite de passage* until her marriage, which marks her as a full adult and formally incorporates her into the community—through her husband. The boy is the center of periodic ceremonials, beginning on the first Friday night after his birth with the *ben-zokher*, "male child." The next day, on the Sabbath, is the *sholem-zokher*, "peace (and welcome) to the male child." The delighted family keeps open house, men, women and children come and go, and all are regaled with brandy, cake and cold boiled chick-peas, which are a nutlike delicacy specific to this occasion.

The circumcision ceremony that inducts the male child into the Covenant with God is known as the *bris*, or covenant. Like similar ceremonies, familiar in the Orient and Africa, it marks the formal acceptance of the male by his special group or community, and the acceptance by him of the duties and privileges attached to such membership. For the shtetl, it is a community that includes both God and man, and into which he is accepted by community representatives. The father's role is minimal in the ceremony and the mother is not even present—the excitement, it is explained, might spoil her milk.

The bris takes place on the eighth day after birth and the preceding night is known as "the watch night," during which mother and child must not be left alone for an instant. A number of men, preferably a minyan [the quorum of ten male Jews required for religious services], stand around them and pray to protect the infant from the harm that is especially potent just before the ceremonial. "Everyone" is invited to attend the celebration on the next day, and refreshments are prepared by the relatives.

To officiate at a bris is both a *mitsva* [a good deed] and an honor, and the participants are selected with utmost care—the two who present the baby, the one who holds him, the one who initiates the healing process. The more illustrious the participants, the better the auspices for the child's future. The godparents furnish the clothes in which the baby is dressed for the ceremony. Their participation sets up no mutual obligations between them and the child, but it does mark the beginning of a lasting, personal relationship.

The ceremony begins when the *kvaterin*, or godmother, brings the baby from the mother's bed to the *kvater*, the godfather, who hands him to the *sandek* or "syndicus," the one who holds him while the ceremony is performed. The sandek, wrapped in his prayer shawl, is usually seated on a special chair known as "the chair of Elijah," which is kept in the synagogue and taken to any house where a bris is to be performed.

A piece of cotton is dipped in spirits and put between the child's lips so that he will fall asleep easily. Then the operation is performed by the mohel, a pious Jew who has studied the procedure. To serve as mohel is "a big mitsva" and, although it is often done for pay, the ideal is to do it purely as a service, and to refuse any money. The operation itself is so trifling that in a society where any physical symptom provokes exaggerated anxiety, it arouses no concern. Attention is centered on the solemn prayer of dedication that accompanies the physical act. "Our God and God of our fathers, preserve this child, his father and mother, and let his name be called in Israel Mordekhay, the son of Tsvi-Hersh Halevi. Let the father rejoice in him that came forth from his loins, and the mother be glad with the fruit of her womb. . . . And it is said, He hath remembered His Covenant forever. The word which He commanded to a thousand generations; (the Covenant) which He made with Abraham, and His oath unto Isaac, and confirmed the same unto Jacob for a statute, to Israel for an everlasting Covenant. . . . This little child, Mordekhay, may he become great. And as he has entered into the Covenant, so may he enter into the Law (Torah), the nuptial canopy (khupa), and into good deeds (maasim tovim). . . ."

In the old tradition, the greatest honor of all is that of the *metsutsa*, performed by a venerable and pious man who sucks the first drop of blood. Then the wound is tied around with cotton, to be changed daily by the mohel until within a few days it has healed. Nobody worries about that part and even the baby makes little of it.

The ceremony over and the principal returned to his mother's arms, all celebrate the reception of a new member, with brandy and honey cakes, hearty "mazltovs" and innumerable toasts, "may you have pleasure in your children and your children's children, and in their children." A long line of members yet-to-be is present in spirit and hailed with enthusiasm. God is increasing the number of his Chosen. His people are fulfilling their part of the pact, the promise of the future is one step nearer to fulfillment, and in the present a living source of joy and honor to the family has been added for all to admire—"no evil eye!" As always, the festivities are accompanied by the jingle of coins, presents to the midwife and often to the mohel, contributions to community services.

For the first-born male there will be a ceremony four weeks after birth, called "the redemption of the first-born," again with feasting, toasting, and the exchange of glad congratulations. This ceremony, the *pidyan ha-ben*, is another strong link binding today with centuries long past. In ancient times the eldest male was dedicated to service in the Temple, but his father could buy him off by making a contribution to the priests, the Kohanim. Today the first-born son is also "redeemed" by a small payment to any member of the Kohanim, those who are descended from the priestly tribe. The amount is calculated to equal the five shekels originally paid to the priests of the Temple, and varies with the currency of the country. A token arrangement with the priesthood and with God, it maintains the old tradition which is viewed as merely suspended until the day when once more there will be a real Temple with its officiating attendants. The vestigial nature of the symbolism is suggested by the fact that the Kohan who receives the token payment is free to use it as he will, regarding it as a simple part of his private income.

Whatever the baby's sex, its name will be announced in the synagogue on the Sabbath after its birth, special prayers will be added to the service, and the father will be called to the reading of the Torah. In honor of the event he will donate as large a sum as he can to the community activities, although probably he will strain his resources less for a girl than for a boy. After all, he may remind himself, there is the girl's dowry to think of—a thought that will be present from the moment of her birth. Following the services he will "make a kiddush" in the synagogue, treating all the congregation to brandy and cakes.

The public announcement of the name, the special prayers of the congregation, and the series of festivities celebrating the boy, dramatize the extent to which a birth is a community affair. The child is born into a family but also into the community. If the parents are poor, clothing and food will be sent in at once, for the shtetl takes care of its children from birth to burial. The evening prayer of the kheyder boys, the "watch night," the group participation in the bris, the observances at the synagogue, the offerings to community welfare that mark the festivities, all confirm the closeness with which the strand of the individual life is woven into the texture of the group. That individual strand will always remain distinct, it will never lose its own identity and its own continuity; but as long as the newborn child remains in the shtetl, its identity will be defined as much by the fabric as by the thread.

It is customary to name the baby in honor of someone who is dead, very often a grandparent, sometimes another relative or a distinguished person, perhaps a great rabbi. It need not be a person of the same sex, for names can be masculinized or feminized. Because it is believed that the child will exhibit some of the attributes of his namesake, the name of a weak person or a failure is avoided. "I was especially interested in the Grandmother Sarah, because I was named after her. She was supposed to be a very clever and nice woman. . . . The Grandfather was . . . a sort of *shlemil*, and I remember that Mother used to wonder whether it was such a good idea to name children after him." A boy is often named for a learned member of the family, and as he grows up he will constantly be reminded to become a scholar like that one. He is named for his father only if the father is dead. It is a misfortune not to have someone named for you after you are gone, for a namesake is another link with the continuing community. . . .

The first months of the baby's life are a constant bath of warmth, attention and affection. At first it sleeps with the mother, then it is placed in its own cradle or swinging crib, near her bed. She may hold a string attached to the baby's cradle, which she rocks incessantly, even in her sleep. If the accustomed motion stops, the baby wakens and cries. Then it must be picked up, carried about and crooned to until it falls asleep again. All its wants are attended to by the mother, or by female relatives. The father may play with the infant, sing to it, talk to it, but there is a strong feeling that the serious care of a baby is woman's work, and men are incapable of handling a baby without damaging it.

The swaddling to which it is subjected is also warm, for it is laid on a pillow and wrapped with firm, soft cloths. The reason given is its welfare, and the very gestures with which it is confined convey tenderness and solicitude, although when it is done "the baby is like a mummy." Its fragile body must be protected from the rigors of a harsh world, its back and legs must be kept straight. "Mother was very careful about this swaddling. She used to put her hand on the knees and arms so as to keep him really straight. She used to show us other children who had, for instance, bad legs, or a little boy in our neighborhood who had his head a little bit inclined on the shoulder . . . and Mother used to say, 'Yes, they didn't swaddle it right. Their Mothers didn't take care of them, that's why they look this way.' "

During the first few weeks the wrappings are snug and the baby is literally "like a mummy." As protection against light, cold air and evil eye, most of the face is covered so that hardly more than the nose peeks out between the cap pulled far down over the forehead and the coverings drawn up over neck, chin and mouth. Later the whole face is exposed, the arms are freed, and the wrappings are relaxed, so that the restraint is almost cozy against the soft pillow.

Several times a day the swaddling is removed and the baby is massaged and allowed to move freely, always with an obbligato of loving coos and murmurs. Once a day it is bathed with warm water, the hair brushed, and as soon as there is enough, a boy's hair will be shaped into earlocks. These locks, *peyos*, are never to be cut as long as he lives.

Wrapped and pillowed, the baby is carried around a great deal by grownups and by older brothers and sisters, for if it lies down too much its lungs will be weak. As if to make up for the insulation and comparative immobility enforced by swaddling, it is almost never allowed to remain still or unattended. Conditioned to expect constant notice, the baby promptly signals any lapse in attentiveness, and a large part of its time is spent in motion. If it is not being carried, then it is rocked endlessly, hour after hour. The combination of swaying and singsong will be familiar from the cradle on. In the kheyder, the yeshiva [school for higher studies], the shul [synagogue], one rocks and chants as he studies or thinks, even if he is pondering a business problem. If he does not sit rocking back and forth he walks about, hands behind his back, humming a nign under his breath. To sit motionless and silent for a long time is contrary to shtetl usage.

Another familiar pattern will be the swift alternation of mood which modulates but does not interrupt a basic relationship. The mother tenderly rocking the cradle suddenly flares up at the neighbor who comes in to return a noodle-board a week later than promised. In her anger she rocks the cradle roughly, jerking it back and forth, back and forth. The startled baby cries and the mother yells, "Be quiet." Perhaps she shoves her breast into the open mouth to still the wails, holding the baby in arms tense with rage. The storm passes, the arms relax, the voice croons softly once again.

The mother talks to the baby constantly, telling it about its future as it lies in the crib, "talking out her heart" to it. It is sung to, petted, addressed with endearments that usually end in the diminutive "leh": little cat, little bird, wee one.

The father sings to it, visitors coo over it, speaking in baby talk and in a special singsong voice. "Father, mother and close relatives like brothers and sisters use baby language to the child. They say all kinds of funny things to try and make the baby laugh." Even when talk is not directed at the baby, the room is always full of words. The father murmurs to his books, prays at the wall, the mother talks to the father, everyone talks to everyone else. From the outset of life the shtetl child associates verbal expression with warmth and security, and silence comes to be equated with rejection and coldness.

The warmth and affection of this outer womb in which the baby lives comes to be associated also with food, for he is offered the breast whenever he seems to want it. The mother is proud of his appetite. "He eats so much, I don't have enough milk for him," she will boast proudly. "I'm all dried up, he sucks me dry." And visitors wanting to compliment her will exclaim, "The baby is so heavy I can't lift it."

If baby cries, the first assumption is that it must be hungry. That there must be some reason is taken for granted, just as there must be a reason for all human behavior. Crying is not "natural" nor is it naughty, but merely baby's signal—and a thoroughly effective one. If the child is not hungry, then it must be wet, cold, in pain, frightened. If no other cause appears, it must be bewitched, in which case immediate steps are taken to counteract the magic. In any case, if it cries it will at once be fussed over, cuddled, comforted, and attended to. This is not viewed as "spoiling" a baby, but merely as normal and correct procedure. That a complaint should evoke a response is always expected.

Even when the baby does not cry, there is no slackening of the anxious care for its physical well-being. It is guarded against drafts almost hysterically, for a blast of cold is the bane of the shtetl. It is guarded even against fresh air, taken outdoors only briefly, well bundled up, and merely to be whisked into the house of some friend or neighbor. Overheating can never hurt, but a chill might be fatal. It is watched for signs of stomach disorder. The big sister, who may be still a small child herself, is treated to a constant barrage of warnings when she carries the baby about—not to drop it, not to squeeze it, not to run with it, not to jar it.

To suckle one's own child, her "own flesh and blood," is regarded as a rewarding and desirable experience, pleasurable for the mother as well as for the child. "They loved to breastfeed their children. I think it's the greatest thing in the world. I'll never forget when I fed my son how he sucked and pulled that milk. . . . Modern mothers are crazy, they don't know what they are missing when they give their children bottles, not the breast. It is such a thrill, you have no idea." Moreover, the attributes of the nurse are believed to be transmitted to the child. Therefore mother's milk is better for the baby, and the milk of a Jewish woman is more desirable than that of a Gentile. It is even believed that a child knows the difference between his mother's milk and another woman's, and will choose his mother's. Human milk is obviously far better than that of an animal, which might affect the baby's character adversely. Aside from such misgivings, there is widespread belief that bottle feeding is harmful and the child would be unlikely to survive.

The wet nurse, like the midwife, has a special and lasting relationship to the child. Her own child is the "milk sibling" of the one she has nursed. Although it is better to have a Jewish nurse, in many places even the orthodox employ a peasant woman if they need, and can afford, the luxury of a wet nurse. Undoubtedly this practice has contributed to the mingling of Jewish and non-Jewish superstitions and magic practices, so that it is often difficult to tell which group has borrowed from the other. The wet nurse is a highly important personage in the house. She must be fed sturdy, milk-giving foods and plenty of them—beer, eggs, cheese, meat. Her diet may be better than the mother's, and often there is a rivalry between the two in caring for the child and winning its devotion. Everyone waits on her and she is able to become the tyrant of the house, since if she is upset her milk may be affected and if she is displeased she threatens to leave. Yet often she becomes a firm friend of the family, and the attachment between her and the child is stable and permanent.

For about six months the baby is fed only on breast milk. Then gruel and paps are added, or a brew made of water mixed with hard bread, toast or zwieback. It must be warm but not too warm, and in order to be sure the mother tastes each spoonful before putting it into the baby's mouth—just as she automatically protects her child from any threat. If any tongue is to be burned, "It should be on me!" Sometimes the baby is given a pacifier of chewed bread wrapped in a cloth. If a child learns to speak before he is weaned, he should be taught to say the "before-meals blessing" before he takes the breast, and there are legends that the great rabbis did so when they were babies.

Nursing is believed to avert pregnancy and, despite the great urge to have children, the mother who has several toddlers may prolong it for this reason. Although in theory it is impossible to have too many children, a hard-worked and impoverished mother of eight or ten may secretly feel that to be overblessed is to be overburdened. If she does become pregnant while the child is still nursing, he must be weaned at once, for otherwise he would be draining strength from the new baby. Whenever it occurs, weaning is sudden. Some hold that the best day for it is the Sabbath, and that the child should be given his mother's breast for the last time on the threshold of the door, because then he forgets it more easily. If he cries for it after that, it may be given to him, but covered with mustard or pepper in order to repel him. Then he himself will reject what he has cried for. The child is weaned directly to a cup or spoon. Solid foods are gradually introduced into the diet, and by the end of the second year the baby eats what adults eat and sits at the same table.

In keeping with the usual differentiation between strength and weakness, a boy is apt to be weaned earlier than a girl, and a strong child sooner than a sickly one. It would be dangerous to return to nursing, once the child has been weaned, and if he still needs human milk it may be fed to him from a cup or spoon. Under no circumstances may a child nurse beyond the age of four, for it is written that no "adult" may suckle at the mother's breast. It is not considered desirable to suckle a boy longer than a year, for otherwise he might become stupid.

Long before this, orderly toilet habits have probably been taught, for that begins sometime after the first six months. The training is firm and even insistent, but anxiety centers on the child's well-being rather than on repugnance for the function. If elimination is not effective, he cannot be well. It is necessary to discharge bodily excreta just as it is necessary, through verbal expressiveness, to discharge emotional tension. The great remedy is "out," *oys*—talk out, laugh out, cry out one's feelings. One should even eliminate before praying, and a blessing must be said after doing so: "Blessed be Thou, Oh Lord our God, King of the Universe, who hast created us with orifices and openings." Failure to achieve catharsis is bad, for it is dangerous to retain what should be expressed.

A child is encouraged to good performance by verbal stimulus, and praised if he does well. If he misbehaves, sounds of disapproval are made—"pheh, pheh!"—and he is shamed, though mildly, "a big boy like you, a year old, you're not a baby." If he persists in misbehavior, he may even be slapped. Basically, however, all body processes are regarded as natural and not disgusting, provided they are confined to the proper time and place. There is no need for euphemisms in referring to the toilet and "accidents" are accepted until quite late even though the child may be rebuked by the exclamation, "A kheyder boy already and look at you!"

The baby who is welcomed so eagerly and sheltered so anxiously is nevertheless hurried out of babyhood. For all the kissing and cooing, all the baby talk and coddling, there is no effort to keep him infantile. On the contrary, he is treasured as a potential adult, and the admiration of his audience is most evident when he shows signs of precocity. Early sitting, teething, creeping, crawling, standing, walking, and above all early talking, give tremendous satisfaction to parents and family. A smile, an unexpected gesture, an imitation of an adult's expression, will be taken as a sign of exceptional intelligence. "Everything the child says is a bright saying and everyone likes to hear the baby say and do things." The whole family, parents, aunts, sisters and brothers, will proudly tell neighbors and relatives, "The child has smiled." They rub his gums to make the teeth come quickly and when a baby of three months cries, someone will suggest hopefully, "Perhaps he is teething."

Slow development is a cause of serious anxiety. If a baby is late in walking or talking the family tries to cover up his deficiencies but they grieve and worry in private. Moreover, if development is out of order it causes concern. For example, the lower teeth should come in first and the upper ones later. If the order is reversed, it is bound to mean something regrettable.

Even after the baby can crawl or walk, he must never be away from a watchful elder eye, to make sure no harm comes to him. As soon as the little boy can get about by himself, he draws more attention from his father, and sometimes will be taken into father's lap to "study" with him. The bearded head in a yarmelkeh and the tiny head also in a miniature yarmelkeh bend over the "little black points" in the book. The mother is too busy to look long on this foretaste of her son's entrance into a man's world, yet she may realize that he no longer belongs exclusively to her. His body is still hers, her "own flesh and blood." But the mind and spirit belong to the father and soon they will lead the body out beyond the four safe walls of home.

A FIFTEENTH-CENTURY BEGINNING

Paulus Bagellardus

A feeling of kindly solicitude emerges in this passage from one of the earliest pediatric textbooks to be printed, written in 1472 by Paulus Bagellardus: The midwife's hand must be gentle, the receiving cloth must be smooth, the water the baby is first bathed in must be sweet and warm. And in agreement with modern theories assigning great importance to the earliest days of life, Bagellardus considers the infant's mind as well as body, requiring the mother or nurse to chant in a low voice so that "the infant's spirits, rejoicing in harmony, may become cheerful."

ON THE CARE OF INFANTS DURING THE FIRST MONTH

When the infant at the command of God emerges from the womb, then the midwife with eager and gentle hand should wrap it up in a linen cloth which is not rough, but rather smooth and old, and place it on her lap, noting whether the infant be alive or not or spotted, *i.e.*, whether black or white or of bluish color and whether it is breathing or not. If she find it warm, not black, she should blow into its mouth, if it has no respiration, or into its anus; but if, as sometimes happens, the anus is closed by a little skin, she should cut it with a sharp knife or hot gold thread or some similar instrument. If the infant is alive and of bluish color, then she should cut the umbilicus or umbilical vein, letting it out to four fingers in length and tying it with the twisted cord itself or with twisted

258

wool or silk, yet with a loose knot, lest the infant suffer pain. And thus you allow it to stay until the fall or consolidation of the umbilicus. But if the umbilicus does not consolidate, then she should cover it with powdered myrrh or aloe, or what is better, powdered myrtle.

Then having tied the umbilicus, the midwife should lay the infant in a basin or some similar vessel filled with sweet water, comfortably warm, not stinging nor cold, or salty, according to the custom of the Greeks. And she should introduce the infant into this water or bath, its head elevated with her left hand, while with her right hand she should shape its head, its sightless eyes, cleanse its nostrils, open its mouth, rub its jaws, shape its arms and its hands and everything. Next she should wrap it up in a linen cloth made comfortably warm and rub the infant's body.

After this, she should cover the infant's head with a fine linen cloth after the manner of a hood. Then secure a soft linen cloth and with the infant placed on the midwife's lap in such a way that its head is toward her feet and its feet rest upon her body, the midwife should roll it in the linen cloth, after it has been bathed, wrapping its feet. First with its arms raised above, she should wrap its breast and bind its body with a band, by three or four windings. Next the midwife takes another piece of linen or little cloth and draws the hands of the infant straight forward towards the knees and hips, shaping them evenly, so that the infant acquires no humpiness. She then, with the same assisting band, binds and wraps the infant's arms and hands, all of which will be correctly shaped.

Then she should turn the infant over on its breast with its back raised upward and, taking hold of the infant's feet, make its soles touch its buttocks to the end that its knees might be properly set. Thereupon she should straighten the infant's legs and with another band and little cloths bind and wrap up the hips. Next take the entire infant and roll it in a woolen cloth or after our manner in a cape lined with sheep skins; and this in winter, but in summer in a linen cloth simply.

Then let the midwife place it upon a bed in a room of mild temperature, not too light, nay rather inclining to darkness, lest from too much light the infant be made blind. But afterwards, let her cover it over with a light covering, wrapping a piece of linen around its head, not touching its head, lest suffocation in time follow, and so allow it to sleep. When it awakes, moreover, let the mother or attendant women place a little sugar or cooked apple with a mixture of sugar in the infant's mouth, for this is a most excellent and praiseworthy nourishment and medicine, since it incites the infant to expel by way of the bowels.

Let the infant have a nurse of from 25 to 35 years old, who is of ruddy complexion or not far from it, a moderate meat-eater also, not inclined to drunkenness, but of good morals and not exercising sexual intercourse. If the infant is poor, let it be nourished by the milk of its mother, who nevertheless should refrain from those things which can disturb or impair and modify the milk, such as all sharp-tasting things, leguminous plants, fat meat or salt meat, salt fish, salty cheese and old cheese more than fresh, anger and sexual intercourse, superfluous exercise, bath, and drunkenness. Such a nurse should feed the infant by light nursing, lest by excessive nursing she should cause coagulation of the milk in its stomach. When the nursing has been finished, let her put the infant in the cradle, placing over it a covering which does not touch its face, push the cradle to and fro and thereby with a light motion produce a gentle slumber. Let her chant in a low voice, so that the infant's spirits rejoicing in harmony may become cheerful. Let there be no noise in the room or harsh voice or anything else which might frighten the infant.

Let the midwife bathe it with an ointment two or three times, according to the present custom, although, according to the opinion of the ancients, it should be bathed up to a month. But because up to a month various diseases occur, such as constipation, crying night and day, on this account, while the constipation lasts, the nurse, taking the excrements of a mouse, should infuse it in common edible oil and insert it gently in the infant's anus, and if it suffer pains, rub the groin and ribs of the infant with oil of dill.

BAD NURSES AND GOOD

From ANATOMY OF MELANCHOLY

Robert Burton

"If she be a fool or a dolt," Robert Burton wrote in a discussion of baby nurses appearing in his seventeenth-century tour de force, Anatomy of Melancholy, *"the child she nurseth will take after her," thus seeming to ally himself with those who insist that a mother ought to be the nurse for her own child (an idea taken up by Rousseau a century later). "But why may not the mother . . . be a fool (as many mothers are)?" Burton went on to ask. What then?*

From a child's nativity, the first ill accident that can likely befall him in this kind is a bad nurse, by whose means alone he may be tainted with melancholy from his cradle. According to Favorinus, that eloquent philosopher: there is the same virtue and property in the milk as in the seed, and not in men alone, but in all other creatures. If a kid or a lamb suck of the other's milk, the lamb of the goat's, or the kid of the ewe's, the wool of the one will be hard, and the hair of the other soft.

Favorinus urgeth farther, and demonstrates it more evidently, that if a nurse be misshapen, unchaste, unhonest, impudent, drunk, cruel or the like, the child that sucks upon her breast will be so too; all other affections of the mind, and diseases, are almost engrafted, as it were, and imprinted into the temperature of the infant, by the nurse's milk, as pox, leprosy, melancholy and etc.

261

Cato for some such reason would make his servants' children suck upon his wife's breast, because by that means they would love him and his better, and in all likelihood agree with them.

A more evident example that the minds are altered by milk, cannot be given, than that of Dion, which he relates of Caligula's cruelty; it could neither be imputed to father nor mother, but to his cruel nurse alone, that anointed her paps with blood still when he sucked, which made him such a murderer, and to express her cruelty to an heir: and that of Tiberius, who was a common drunkard, because his nurse was such a one.

And if she be a fool or dolt, the child she nurseth will take after her, or otherwise be misaffected. For bodily sickness there is no doubt to be made. Titus, Vespasian's son, was therefore sickly, because the nurse was so. And if we may believe Physicians, many times children catch the pox from a bad nurse. Besides evil attendance, negligence, and many gross inconveniences, which are incident to nurses, much danger may so come to the child.

For these causes Aristotle, Favorinus, and Marcus Aurelius would not have a child put to nurse at all, but every mother to bring up her own of whatever condition soever she be; for a sound and able mother to put out her child to nurse is an outrage upon Nature, so Guatso calls it, 'tis fit therefore she should be nurse herself; the mother will be more careful, loving and attendant, than any servile woman, or such hired creatures; this all the world acknowledgeth; it is most fit, (as Rodericus a Castro, in many words, confesseth), that the mother should suckle her own infant, who denies that it should be so? and which some women most curiously observe; amongst the rest, that Queen of France, a Spaniard by birth, that was so precise and zealous in this behalf, that, when in her absence a strange nurse had suckled her child, she was never quiet till she had made the infant vomit it up again. But she was too jealous.

If it be so, as many times it is, they must be put forth, the mother be not fit or well able to be a nurse, I would then advise such mothers (as Plutarch does in his book) that they make choice of a sound woman, of a good complexion, honest, free from bodily diseases, if it be possible, and all passions and perturbations of the mind, as sorrow, fear, grief, folly, melancholy. For such passions corrupt the milk, and alter the temperature of the child, which now being moist and pliable clay, is easily seasoned and perverted.

And if such a nurse may be found out, that will be diligent and careful withal, let Favorinus and M. Aurelius plead how they can against it, I had rather accept of her in some cases than the mother herself, and (which Bonacialus, the physician approves), some nurses are much to be preferred to some mothers. For why may not the mother be naught, a peevish drunken flirt, a waspish cholerick slut, a crazed piece, a fool, (as many mothers are), unsound, as soon as the nurse? There is more choice of nurses than mothers; and therefore, except that the mother be most virtuous, staid, a woman of excellent good parts, and of a sound complexion, I would have all children in such cases committed to discrete strangers. And 'tis the only way (as by marriage they are engrafted to other families) to alter the breed, or, if anything be amiss in the mother, as Lodovicus Mercatus contends, to prevent diseases and future maladies, to correct and qualify the child's ill-disposed temperature, which he had from his parents. This is an excellent remedy, if good choice be made of such a nurse.

Part VIII

A DIM VIEW

ON BABIES

From AMERICAN WIVES AND OTHER ESSAYS

Jerome K. Jerome

Some men would rather be alone in a cage with a savage lion than alone in a room with a small baby. Unfortunately for them, they don't always have a choice. Here are the recollections of a noted American humorist about his unavoidable experiences with babies.

Oh, yes, I do—I know a lot about 'em. I was one myself once—though not long, not so long as my clothes. *They* were very long, I recollect, and always in my way when I wanted to kick. Why do babies have such yards of unnecessary clothing? It is not a riddle. I really want to know. I never could understand it. Is it that the parents are ashamed of the size of the child, and wish to make believe that it is longer than it actually is? I asked a nurse once why it was. She said:

"Lor', sir, they always have long clothes, bless their little hearts."

And when I explained that her answer, although doing credit to her feelings, hardly disposed of my difficulty, she replied:

"Lor', sir, you wouldn't have 'em in short clothes, poor little dears?" And she said it in a tone that seemed to imply I had suggested some unmanly outrage.

Since then I have felt shy at making inquiries on the subject, and the reason—if reason there be—is still a mystery to me. But, indeed, putting them in any clothes at all seems absurd to my mind.

267

Goodness knows, there is enough of dressing and undressing to be gone through in life, without beginning it before we need; and one would think that people who live in bed might, at all events, be spared the torture. Why wake the poor little wretches up in the morning to take one lot of clothes off, fix another lot on, and put them to bed again; and then, at night, haul them out once more, merely to change everything back? And when all is done, what difference is there, I should like to know, between a baby's night-shirt and the thing it wears in the day-time?

Very likely, however, I am only making myself ridiculous—I often do, so I am informed—and I will, therefore, say no more upon this matter of clothes, except only that it would be of great convenience if some fashion were adopted enabling you to tell a boy from a girl.

At present it is most awkward. Neither hair, dress, nor conversation affords the slightest clew, and you are left to guess. By some mysterious law of Nature, you invariably guess wrong, and are thereupon regarded by all relatives and friends as a mixture of fool and knave, the enormity of alluding to a male babe as "she" being only equaled by the atrocity of referring to a female infant as "he." Whichever sex the particular child in question happens not to belong to is considered as beneath contempt, and any mention of it is taken as a personal insult to the family.

And, as you value your fair name, do not attempt to get out of the difficulty by talking of "it." There are various methods by which you may achieve ignominy and shame. By murdering a large and respected family in cold blood, and afterward depositing their bodies in the water companies' reservoir, you will gain much unpopularity in the neighborhood of your crime, and even robbing a church will get you cordially disliked, especially by the vicar. But if you desire to drain to the dregs the fullest cup of scorn and hatred that a fellow human creature can pour out for you, let a young mother hear you call dear baby "it."

Your best plan is to address the article as "little angel." The noun "angel," being of common gender, suits the case admirably, and the epithet is sure of being favorably received. "Pet" or "beauty" are useful for variety's sake, but "angel" is the term that brings you the greatest credit for sense and good feeling. The word should be preceded by a short giggle, and accompanied by as much smile as possible. And, whatever you do, don't forget to say that the child has got its father's nose. This "fetches" the parents (if I may be allowed a vulgarism) more than anything. They will pretend to laugh at the idea at first, and will say: "Oh, nonsense!" You must then get excited, and insist that it is a fact. You need have no conscientious scruples on the subject, because the thing's nose really does resemble its father's—at all events quite as much as it does anything else in nature—being, as it is, a mere smudge.

Do not despise these hints, my friends. There may come a time when, with mamma on one side and grandmamma on the other, a group of admiring young ladies (not admiring you, though) behind, and a bald-headed dab of humanity in front, you will be extremely thankful for some idea of what to say. A man—an unmarried man, that is—is never seen to such disadvantage as when undergoing the ordeal of "seeing baby." A cold shudder runs down his back at the bare proposal, and the sickly smile with which he says how delighted he shall be, ought surely to move even a mother's heart, unless, as I am inclined to believe, the whole proceeding is a mere device adopted by wives to discourage the visits of bachelor friends.

It is a cruel trick, though, whatever its excuse may be. The bell is rung, and somebody sent to tell the nurse to bring baby down. Thus is the signal for all the females present to commence talking "baby," during which time you are left to your own sad thoughts, and to speculations upon the practicability of suddenly recollecting an important engagement, and the likelihood of your being believed if you do. Just when you have concocted an absurdly implausible tale about a man outside, the door opens, and a tall, severe-looking woman enters, carrying what at first sight appears to be a particularly skinny bolster, with the feathers all at one end. Instinct, however, tells you that this is the baby, and you rise with a miserable attempt at appearing eager. When the first gush of feminine enthusiasm with which the object in question is received has died out, and the number of ladies talking at once has been reduced to the ordinary four or five, the circle of fluttering petticoats divides, and room is made for you to step forward. This you do with much the same air that you would walk into the dock at Bow Street, and then, feeling unutterably miserable, you stand solemnly staring at the child. There is dead silence, and you know that everyone is waiting for you to speak. You try to think of something to say, but find, to your horror, that your reasoning faculties have left you. It is a moment of despair, and your evil genius, seizing the opportunity, suggests to you some of the most idiotic remarks that it is possible for a human being to perpetrate. Glancing round with an imbecile smile, you sniggeringly observe that "It hasn't got much hair, has it?" Nobody answers you for a minute, but at last the stately nurse says with much gravity: "It is not customary for children five weeks old to have long hair." Another silence follows this, and you feel you are being given a second chance, which you avail yourself of by inquiring if it can walk yet, or what they feed it on. By this time you have got to be regarded as not quite right in your head, and pity is the only thing felt for you. The nurse, however, is determined that, insane or not, there shall be no shirking, and that you shall go through your task to the end. In the tones of a high priestess, directing some religious mystery, she says, holding the bundle toward you, "Take her in your arms, sir." You are too crushed to offer any resistance, and so meekly accept the burden. "Put your arm more down her middle, sir," says the high priestess, and then all step back and watch you intently, as though you were going to do a trick with it.

What to do you know no more than you did what to say. It is certain something must be done, however, and the only thing that occurs to you is to heave the unhappy infant up and down to the accompaniment of "oopsee-daisy," or some remark of equal intelligence. "I wouldn't jig her, sir, if I were you," says the nurse; "a very little upsets her." You promptly decide not to jig her, and sincerely hope that you have not gone too far already.

At this point the child itself, who has hitherto been regarding you with an expression of mingled horror and disgust, puts an end to the nonsense by beginning to yell at the top of its voice, at which the priestess rushes forward and snatches it from you with, "There, there, there! What did ums do to ums?" "How very extraordinary!" you say, pleasantly. "Whatever made it go off like that?" "Oh, why, you must have done something to her!" says the mother, indignantly; "the child wouldn't scream like that for nothing." It is evident they think you have been running pins into it.

The brat is calmed at last, and would no doubt remain quiet enough, only some mischievous busybody points you out again with "Who's this, baby?" and the intelligent child, recognizing you, howls louder than ever.

Whereupon, some fat old lady remarks that "It's strange how

children take a dislike to any one." "Oh, they know," replies another, mysteriously. "It's a wonderful thing," adds a third; and then somebody looks sideways at you, convinced you are a scoundrel of the blackest dye; and they glory in the beautiful idea that your true character, unguessed by your fellowmen, has been discovered by the untaught instinct of a little child.

POOR ANDREW

From THE COMPLETE STORIES OF GUY DE MAUPASSANT

Guy de Maupassant

Matilda's husband has gone away for a few days and the handsome young captain has persuaded her to succumb at last. But there is the baby, Andrew, who also expects to share his mother's bed. How is the captain to rid Andrew of this inconvenient habit? Poor Andrew . . .

The lawyer's house looked on to the square. Behind it there was a nice well-kept garden, with a back entrance into a narrow street which was almost always deserted and from which it was separated by a wall.

At the bottom of that garden Maître* Moreau's wife had promised, for the first time, to meet Captain Sommerive, who had been courting her for a long time.

Her husband had gone to Paris for a week, so she was quite free for the time being. The captain had begged so hard, and he loved her so ardently, and she felt so isolated, so misunderstood, so neglected amid all the law business which seemed to be her husband's sole pleasure, that she had given away her heart without even asking herself whether he would give her anything else at some future time.

Then after some months of platonic love, of pressing of hands,

---

* Maître (Master) is the official title of French lawyers.

272

of kisses rapidly stolen behind a door, the captain had declared that he would ask permission to exchange and leave town immediately if she would not grant him a meeting, a real meeting, during her husband's absence. So at length she yielded to his importunity.

Just then she was waiting, close against the wall, with a beating heart; when at length she heard somebody climbing up the wall she nearly ran away.

Suppose it were not he but a thief? But no; someone called out softly, "Matilda!" And when she replied, "Etienne!" a man jumped onto the path with a crash.

It was he—and what a kiss!

For a long time they remained in each other's arms with united lips. But suddenly a fine rain began to fall, and the drops from the leaves fell onto her neck and made her start. Whereupon he said:

"Matilda, my adored one, my darling, my angel, let us go indoors. It is twelve o'clock; we can have nothing to fear; please let us go in."

"No, dearest; I am too frightened."

But he held her in his arms and whispered in her ear:

"Your servants sleep on the third floor, looking on to the square, and your room, on the first, looks on to the garden, so nobody can hear us. I love you so that I wish to love you entirely from head to foot." And he embraced her vehemently.

She resisted still, frightened and even ashamed. But he put his arms round her, lifted her up and carried her off through the rain, which was by this time descending in torrents.

The door was open; they groped their way upstairs, and when they were in the room he bolted the door while she lit a candle.

Then she fell, half fainting, into a chair, while he kneeled down beside her.

At last she said, panting:

"No! No! Etienne, please let me remain a virtuous woman; I should be too angry with you afterward, and after all, it is so horrid, so common. Cannot we love each other with a spiritual love only? Oh, Etienne!"

But he was inexorable, and then she tried to get up and escape from his attacks. In her fright she ran to the bed in order to hide herself behind the curtains, but it was a dangerous place of refuge, and he followed her. But in haste he took off his sword too quickly, and it fell onto the floor with a crash. And then a prolonged, shrill child's cry came from the next room, the door of which had remained open. .

"You have awakened the child," she whispered, "and perhaps he will not go to sleep again."

He was only fifteen months old and slept in a room adjoining hers, so that she might be able to hear him.

The captain exclaimed ardently:

"What does it matter, Matilda? How I love you; you must come to me, Matilda."

But she struggled and resisted in her fright.

"No! No! Just listen how he is crying; he will wake up the nurse, and what should we do if she were to come? We should be lost. Just listen to me, Etienne. When he screams at night his father always takes him into our bed, and he is quiet immediately; it is the only means of keeping him still. Do let me take him."

The child roared, uttering shrill screams, which pierced the thickest walls and could be heard by passers-by in the streets.

In his consternation the captain got up, and Matilda jumped out and took the child into her bed, when he was quiet at once.

Etienne sat astride on a chair and made a cigarette, and in about five minutes Andrew went to sleep again.

"I will take him back," his mother said, and she took him back very carefully to his bed.

When she returned the captain was waiting for her with open arms and put his arms round her in a transport of love, while she, embracing him more closely, said, stammering:

"Oh, Etienne, my darling, if you only knew how I love you; how—"

Andrew began to cry again, and he, in a rage, exclaimed:

"Confound it all, won't the little brute be quiet?"

No, the little brute would not be quiet but howled all the louder, on the contrary.

She thought she heard a noise downstairs; no doubt the nurse was coming, so she jumped up and took the child into bed, and he grew quiet directly.

Three times she put him back, and three times she had to fetch him again, and an hour before daybreak the captain had to go, swearing like a proverbial trooper, and to calm his impatience Matilda promised to receive him again the next night. Of course he came, more impatient and ardent than ever, excited by the delay.

He took care to put his sword carefully into a corner; he took off his boots like a thief and spoke so low that Matilda could hardly hear him. At last he was just going to be really happy when the floor, or some piece of furniture or perhaps the bed itself creaked; it sounded as if something had broken, and in a moment a cry, feeble at first, but which grew louder every moment, made itself heard. Andrew was awake again.

He yapped like a fox, and there was not the slightest doubt that if he went on like that the whole house would awake, so his mother, not knowing what to do, got up and brought him. The captain was more furious than ever, but did not move, and very carefully he put out his hand, took a small piece of the child's skin between his two fingers, no matter where it was, the thighs or elsewhere, and pinched it. The little one struggled and screamed in a deafening manner, but his tormentor pinched everywhere, furiously and more vigorously. He took a morsel of flesh and twisted and turned it and then let go in order to take hold of another piece and then another and another.

The child screamed like a chicken having its throat cut or a dog being mercilessly beaten. His mother caressed him, kissed him and tried to stifle his cries by her tenderness, but Andrew grew purple, as if he were going into convulsions, and kicked and struggled with his little arms and legs in an alarming manner.

The captain said softly:

"Try and take him back to his cradle; perhaps he will be quiet."

And Matilda went into the other room with the child in her arms. As soon as he was out of his mother's bed he cried less loudly, and when he was in his own he was quiet, with the exception of a few broken sobs. The rest of the night was tranquil.

The next night the captain came again. As he happened to speak rather loudly, Andrew awoke again and began to scream. His mother went and fetched him immediately, but the captain pinched so hard and long that the child was nearly suffocated by its cries; its eyes turned in its head, and it foamed at the mouth. As soon as it was back in its cradle it was quiet, and in four days Andrew did not cry any more to come into his mother's bed.

On Saturday evening the lawyer returned and took his place again at the domestic hearth and in the conjugal chamber. As he was tired with his journey he went to bed early, but he had not long lain down when he said to his wife:

"Why, how is it that Andrew is not crying? Just go and fetch him, Matilda; I like to feel that he is between us."

She got up and brought the child, but as soon as he saw that he was in that bed in which he had been so fond of sleeping a few days previous he wriggled and screamed so violently in his fright that she had to take him back to his cradle.

M. Moreau could not get over his surprise. "What a very funny thing! What is the matter with him this evening? I suppose he is sleepy?"

"He has been like that all the time that you were away; I have never been able to have him in bed with me once."

In the morning the child woke up and began to laugh and play with his toys.

The lawyer, who was an affectionate man, got up, kissed his offspring and took him into his arms to carry him to their bed. Andrew laughed with that vacant laugh of little creatures whose ideas are still vague. He suddenly saw the bed and his mother in it, and his happy little face puckered up, till suddenly he began to scream furiously and struggled as if he were going to be put to the torture.

In his astonishment his father said:

"There must be something the matter with the child," and mechanically he lifted up his little nightshirt.

He uttered a prolonged "O—o—h!" of astonishment. The child's calves, thighs and buttocks were covered with blue spots as big as halfpennies.

"Just look, Matilda!" the father exclaimed; "this is horrible!" And the mother rushed forward in a fright. It was horrible, no doubt the beginning of some sort of leprosy, of one of those strange affections of the skin which doctors are often at a loss to account for. The parents looked at one another in consternation.

"We must send for the doctor," the father said.

But Matilda, pale as death, was looking at her child who was spotted like a leopard. Then suddenly, uttering a violent cry as if she had seen something that filled her with horror, she exclaimed:

"Oh, the wretch!"

In his astonishment M. Moreau asked: "What are you talking about? What wretch?"

She got red up to the roots of her hair and stammered:

"Oh, nothing, but I think I can guess—it must be—we ought to send for the doctor. It must be that wretch of a nurse who has been pinching the poor child to make him keep quiet when he cries."

In his rage the lawyer sent for the nurse and very nearly beat her. She denied it most impudently but was instantly dismissed, and the municipality having been informed of her conduct, she will find it a hard matter to get another situation.

ADVICE TO THOSE VISITING A BABY

From MINCE PIE

Christopher Morley

> *Some useful hints from one who has obviously had much experience with new babies and their parents.*

Interview the baby alone if possible. If, however, both parents are present, say, "It looks like its mother." And, as an afterthought, "I think it has its father's elbows."

If uncertain as to the infant's sex, try some such formula as, "He looks like her grandparents," or "She has his aunt's sweet disposition."

When the mother only is present, your situation is critical. Sigh deeply and admiringly, to imply that you wish *you* had a child like that. Don't commit yourself at all until she gives a lead.

When the father only is present, you may be a little reckless. Give the father a cigar and venture, "Good luck, old man; it looks like your mother-in-law."

If possible, find out beforehand how old the child is. Call up the Bureau of Vital Statistics. If it is two months old, say to the mother, "Rather large for six months, isn't he?"

If the worst has happened and the child really does look like its father, the most tactful thing is to say, "Children change as they grow older." Or you may suggest that some mistake has been made at the hospital and they have brought home the wrong baby.

If left alone in the room with the baby, throw a sound-proof rug over it and escape.

278

TRAITOR'S THROAT AND OTHER RARE AFFLICTIONS

From WHAT DR. SPOCK DIDN'T TELL US

B. M. Atkinson, Jr.

Arcaro's Disease, Durante's Frenzy, Vesuvian Bladder—these are some of the common afflictions of infancy that are not to be found in Dr. Spock's famous baby book. B. M. Atkinson, Jr., used his own experiences as a father to compile a supplement to Dr. Spock that fills in some of the more obvious gaps. He prefaces his book with a warning to parents not to expect that any of the various afflictions he is setting down will follow any definite chronology. "A child of three may take such delight in the suffering that one of his infantile afflictions is causing his parents," writes the author, "that he will cling to it for years—or until such time as he is big enough to hit."

The first time my wife announced that I was in a fatherly way, I bought a book on the care and maintenance of babies. I wanted to find out if a baby would upset the even tenor of a parent's ways, etc.

The book was quite thick but most comforting. There were chapters on breast feeding, weaning, bowel training, diets, schedules, the standard childhood diseases and such fancy extras as pro-

truding navels and undescended testicles, but nothing, I felt, that a child, a mother and a good pediatrician couldn't handle. I was quite relieved. As was my wife. She felt there was nothing that a child, a good pediatrician and a *father* couldn't handle.

In due time the child arrived, a fine baby daughter, and for three weeks we hewed to the line laid down in the baby book.

"My, but I was smart buying that book," I told my wife. "When you know what to expect from a baby, it isn't bad at all."

But shortly thereafter I noticed something rather strange. I was getting up with the baby at night much more often than was my wife. She said she hadn't noticed this, but I insisted, and called in our neighbor, John Blackheart, a bitter old man with five children.

Upon hearing my story, he brightened considerably.

"The reason you're getting up so much at night," he said, "is that your baby has got a bad case of TRAITOR'S THROAT."

"Traitor's Throat?" I said. "I never heard of such a thing!"

"Traitor's Throat," he said, brightening even more, "is what a baby has when she cries just loud enough to wake her father up but not loud enough to wake her mother up. The father can either get up and change her or he can lie there half the night waiting to see if she won't wake the mother up. With Traitor's Throat, she never does."

"What a diabolical disease!" I exclaimed. "But why isn't there something about it in my baby book?"

"For the same reason there is nothing about POTTY ARM in your baby book!"

"Potty Arm?" my wife wheezed.

"Potty Arm," John explained, "is a compulsion all children get when they're about two years old. They start throwing stuff in the potty. Mostly the mother's stuff. Her toothbrush, her face cloth, her powder puff, her girdle. It's almost as bad as VESUVIAN BLADDER."

"My God!" I said. "There are more of these things?"

"Hundreds more! Physical *and* mental. And every one is this catalytic type thing. The child has the affliction but only the parents suffer from it."

"I repeat," I said. "*Why* isn't there something about it in my baby book?"

"Don't be silly!" he said. "If those experts told *everything* about children, there wouldn't *be* any more children, and without any more children there wouldn't be any more books about children."

"But," I whimpered, "if the experts won't tell *all* about children, why doesn't some victim do it? Why doesn't some poor beat-up father catalogue the strangest of these afflictions, the grisliest of these surprises, and put humanity in his debt forever?"

"Well," John smirked, "all you need is a few more years and a notebook. Why don't you do it?"

Now that was some time ago—fifteen years, four children, twenty notebooks and 823 afflictions ago, to be exact—and I am now prepared to put humanity in my debt, but not at the risk of discontinuing humanity. I realize now that the technical experts on child maintenance are right: Tell new parents, potential parents *everything* they can expect from children and there won't be any more children. (And God forbid that I should deprive our deserving teen-agers of the joys of parenthood.)

Therefore I am cataloguing only a fraction of the afflictions in my vast collection: not enough to frighten man and wife away from the Trap completely, but still enough so that the Trap won't be too much of a shock once they're in it.

I have arranged the afflictions in alphabetical rather than chronological order for a very simple reason: a catalytic type affliction follows no set chronological pattern. A child of three may take such delight in the suffering that one of his infantile afflictions is causing his parents that he will cling to it for years—or until such time as he is big enough to hit.

ARCARO'S DISEASE

A temporary form of insanity in which a crib-bound baby supposes himself to be Eddie Arcaro. The baby will place himself on all fours somewhat in the manner of a jockey astride a horse and then will commence to ride this imaginary horse as though he is Mr. Arcaro aboard a Kentucky Derby winner. The rocking of the crib can be heard throughout the house and quite often in the next block. Upon first hearing this noise, a new father immediately assumes that at least eight burglars are breaking into the house. Especially is this true if the child suffers a seizure between midnight and 4:00 A.M. Technically the disease at this hour is known as REVERE'S VISITATION. Instead of thinking he is Eddie Arcaro, the child thinks he is Paul Revere and acts accordingly.

DURANTE'S FRENZY

A violent thrashing of a baby's arms, legs, head, feet, rib cage and buttocks, punctuated by shrieks from the baby and profane mutterings from attendant parents seeking to control the thrashing.

Caused by belief among babies that the human nose is a fit depository for anything but nose drops. The average eighteen-month-old will, without a qualm, introduce into his nostrils peas, marbles, collar buttons, cigarette butts and carpet tacks, but when asked to submit the same organ to four drops of nasal balm, immediately fears for his life, evidently confusing the nosedropper with a suctional device for removing the brains. Administering the nose drops against the child's wishes is the equivalent of force-feeding a python and, unless the mother outweighs the child by 150 pounds or has recourse to a vise, strait jacket and leg irons, the assistance of the father will be required. The father should first gird himself with ear muffs, raincoat and catcher's mask, because in the ensuing struggle there is always considerable doubt as to who will wind up with the drops and where. In administering suppositories the father should exercise even more care.

GOAT MOUTH

A dietary phenomenon in which babies, usually from nine to twenty-four months, are possessed of a great appetite for everything but food, showing a marked preference for coffee grounds, egg shells, lamp cords, soap, soil, crib railings, dog biscuit and quite often the ear of the dog itself. Just how the infant, with his small and limited number of teeth, can chew his way through crib railings, spaniel ears, etc., will forever remain a mystery to the parent *unless* in an effort to remove splinters, dog hair, egg shells, etc., the parent is stupid enough to stick a finger in said infant's mouth. Not all nine-fingered fathers have power saws.

LAP LEG

A violent neuromuscular disorder marked by a series of jumps, bounces, lurches, squirms, handsprings, push-ups and other such attempts on the part of a baby to turn his mother's lap into a gymnasium. Occurs when the baby is being "rocked to sleep" by a doting mother who has seen too many pictures of doting mothers rocking babies to sleep. Unbeknownst to the mother, all such pictures are either fakes or possess tragic overtones, as any baby who allows himself to be rocked to sleep without a fight should be placed under a physician's care immediately. A healthy baby at six months, while lacking the strength to walk around in the mother's lap unaided, will compensate for it by digging his head and heels into the mother's lap, arching his back, and attempting a back jackknife onto the floor, thus giving the mother a feeling of Togetherness matched only by cuddling alligators. At nine months the baby *will* be able to walk around in his mother's lap, but due to the smallness of his feet and the sharpness of his heels the mother will feel more as if he is traveling by Pogo stick than by foot. At twelve months the child will enter the critical phase of the affliction known as HILARY'S URGE. In this phase, the child, having tired of the mother's lap, will attempt to climb her head, the technique being to dig his toes into her ribs, grab two handfuls of hair and

heave. Once the head has been scaled, the next step is to try and dismantle it. Should the mother still think a baby can be peacefully rocked to sleep, her head *should* be dismantled.

———

MISER'S BURP

A hardening of the head and heart in which a baby, whose mother is trying to burp him at two o'clock in the morning, will ignore all her patting and pleading and fiendishly refuse to part with the bubble of gas in his stomach that would then permit the poor, groggy woman to deposit him in his crib and stagger back to bed. Fathers caught up in the same situation must exercise the greatest of self-control, as there will be a growing temptation to help the bubble along by gently dangling the little ingrate by his heels.

TARZAN'S GLUT

A dietary hallucinosis occurring when a baby is allowed to feed himself at too early an age. In this, the baby sees all his food as alive and believes that it must be killed before it can be devoured. Given a piece of cake, a nine-month-old baby, before putting it in his mouth, will either strangle it or beat it to death. Strangling is the more common of the two techniques and only when the cake is shooting out between his fingers does he consider it dead enough to eat. The cake is thus transformed from a three-inch square into a coil and looks more like something that came out of an innerspring mattress than a cake box. To properly eat a piece of cake squeezed into this shape, the baby should screw it into his mouth but invariably he will attempt to put it in sideways, resulting in an earful of crumbs and an iced nostril. The baby who prefers beating his food to death is generally considered the more savage and should never be left alone with kittens, puppies or fathers. This child's favorite food is a jelly sandwich. Invariably he will place the sandwich upon the highchair tray and, in a flash, give it a murderous whack with the flat of his hand. As the jelly quite often shoots some thirty feet, this child is popular only with ants, dogs and linoleum salesmen.

VESUVIAN BLADDER

A spectacular urethral expulsion of bodily liquids, resulting from sudden pressure of the bladder. Occurs exclusively among boy

babies, usually from one to six months of age, and most often at bathtime when the child is without clothing and lying flat on his back. The expulsion takes the form of an arching stream and may attain a height of six to eight feet. Such heights, however, are rarely achieved, the stream generally arching only a few feet before striking the hovering parent between the eyes or, should the head be turned, in the ear. A new father, thus anointed for the first time, will usually back over a table or out the nearest window. His amazement, however, immediately gives way to parental pride, and for weeks the father will speak of the boy's feat in terms usually reserved for men who put satellites in orbit.

VIGILANTE'S DILEMMA

Metamorphosis in which a child's powers of locomotion vary in direct ratio to a parent's vigilance or lack thereof. A year-old child being watched by his mother will waddle about the room for hours with all the sure-footedness of a drunken midget, his top speed never exceeding two feet per second. The moment the mother turns her back, however, he immediately assumes all the grace of a gazelle and moves at a speed exceeding sound. Thus the mother, before hearing the patter of little feet, will first hear the crash of her best lamp. Escaped children heading for freshly frosted cakes, antique vases and open wall sockets have been clocked at Mach 3.

WEISSMULLER'S AMNESIA

A mystifying lapse of memory in which a year-old child, normally obsessed with the fear that he can be drowned by as little water as

that contained in a damp washrag, will, upon being placed in a tub of it, suddenly forget this fear and begin disporting himself with all the enthusiasm of a drunken hippopotamus. Any parental joy at the child's change in attitude toward water is always dampened by the ensuing splashing and thrashing which leaves the parent in attendance wetter than the child and the bathroom floor under enough water to plant rice.

Attempts to control the splashing by maintaining a firm hold on the child are seldom rewarded, as a fat, active baby, on being lathered with soap, is rendered so slippery that the parent comes to believe that she is no longer dealing with flesh and blood but so much okra. Looking back on this phase, parents will remember it as something of a cross between wrestling alligators and Simonizing seals.

KILLING IS MURDER

From PEREGRINE PICKLE

Tobias Smollett

One of the most amusing scoundrels in English literature is the picaresque hero of Tobias Smollett's eighteenth-century novel Peregrine Pickle. *Could it be that all of Peregrine's adult misdeeds were but his means of getting even with the world for the morning baths he was subjected to as an infant, described in the following episode?*

The child was christened by the name of Peregrine, in compliment to the memory of a deceased uncle. While the mother was confined to her bed and incapable of maintaining her own authority, Mrs. Grizzle (his aunt) took charge of the infant by a double claim; and superintended with surprising vigilance the nurse and the midwife in all the particulars of their respective offices, which were performed by her express direction. But no sooner was Mrs. Pickle in a condition to re-assume the management of her own affairs, than she thought proper to alter certain regulations concerning the child, which had obtained in consequence of her sister's orders, directing, among other innovations, that the bandages with which the infant had been so neatly rolled up, like an Egyptian mummy, should be loosened and laid aside, in order to rid nature of all restraint, and give the blood free scope to circulate; and with her own hands she plunged him headlong every morning in a tub-ful of cold water. This operation seemed so barbarous to the tender-hearted Mrs. Grizzle that she not only opposed it with all her

293

eloquence, shedding abundance of tears over the sacrifice when it was made; but took horse immediately, and departed for the habitation of an eminent country physician, whom she consulted in these words:

"Pray, doctor, is it not both dangerous and cruel to be the means of letting a poor tender infant perish, by sousing it in water as cold as ice?"

"Yes, (replied the doctor) downright murder, I affirm."

"I see you are a person of great learning and sagacity; (said the other) and I must beg you will be so good as to signify your opinion in your own handwriting."

The doctor immediately complied with her request, and expressed himself upon a slip of paper to this purpose:

These are to certify whom it may concern, that I firmly believe, and it is my unalterable opinion, that whosoever letteth an infant perish, by sousing it in cold water, even though the said water should not be so cold as ice, is in effect, guilty of the murder of said infant, as witness my hand
                                                            Comfit Colocynth

Having obtained this certificate, for which the physician was handsomely acknowledged, she returned in triumph, hoping, with such authority, to overthrow all opposition; and accordingly next morning, when her nephew was about to undergo his diurnal baptism, produced the commission, whereby she conceived herself impowered to overrule such inhuman proceedings. But she was disappointed in her expectation, confident as it was; not that Mrs. Pickle pretended to differ in opinion from Dr. Colocynth, "for whose character and sentiments (said she), I have such veneration, that I shall carefully observe the caution implied in this very certificate, by which, far from condemning my method of practice, he only asserts that killing is murder; an asseveration the truth of which, it is to be hoped, I shall never dispute."

Mrs. Grizzle, who, sooth to say, had rather too superficially considered the clause by which she thought herself authorized, perused the paper with more accuracy, and was confounded at her own want of penetration. Yet, though she was confuted, she was by no means convinced that her objections to the cold bath were unreasonable; on the contrary, after having bestowed sundry opprobrious epithets on the physician, for his want of knowledge and candour, she protested in the most earnest and solemn manner against the pernicious practice of dipping the child; a piece of cruelty, which with God's assistance, she should never suffer to be inflicted on her own issue; and washing her hands of the melancholy consequence that would certainly ensue, shut herself up in her closet, to indulge her sorrow and vexation.

She was deceived, however, in her prognistic; the boy, instead of declining in point of health, seemed to acquire fresh vigour from every plunge, as if he had been resolved to discredit the wisdom and foresight of his aunt, who, in all probability, could never forgive him for this want of reverence and respect.

Part IX

EARLY LEARNINGS

INFANT CONDITIONING

From BRAVE NEW WORLD

Aldous Huxley

Aldous Huxley's Brave New World, *with its predictions of the direction civilization might take in an increasingly mechanized and computerized society, is a frightening book. It is also, many people forget, a very funny book.*

Here is a chapter from Brave New World *describing how infants of Huxley's Utopia are trained to take their proper place in their well-planned society—a society where babies are made in bottles and the greatest obscenity of the English language is the word . . .* Mother!

Mr. Foster was left in the Decanting Room. The D.H.C. and his students stepped into the nearest lift and were carried up to the fifth floor.

INFANT NURSERIES. NEO-PAVLOVIAN CONDITIONING ROOMS, announced the notice board.

The Director opened a door. They were in a large bare room, very bright and sunny; for the whole of the southern wall was a single window. Half a dozen nurses, trousered and jacketed in the regulation white viscose-linen uniform, their hair aseptically hidden under white caps, were engaged in setting out bowls of roses in a long row across the floor. Big bowls, packed tight with blossom. Thousands of petals, ripe-blown and silkily smooth, like the cheeks of innumerable little cherubs, but of cherubs, in that bright light, not exclusively pink and Aryan, but also luminously Chinese, also Mexican, also apoplectic with too much blowing of celestial trumpets, also pale as death, pale with the posthumous whiteness of marble.

The nurses stiffened to attention as the D.H.C. came in.

"Set out the books," he said curtly.

In silence the nurses obeyed his command. Between the rose bowls the books were duly set out—a row of nursery quartos opened invitingly each at some gaily colored image of beast or fish or bird.

"Now bring in the children."

They hurried out of the room and returned in a minute or two, each pushing a kind of tall dumbwaiter laden, on all its four wire-netted shelves, with eight-month-old babies, all exactly alike (Bokanovsky Group, it was evident) and all (since their caste was Delta) dressed in khaki.

"Put them down on the floor."

The infants were unloaded.

"Now turn them so that they can see the flowers and books."

Turned, the babies at once fell silent, then began to crawl to-wards those clusters of sleek colors, those shapes so gay and bril-liant on the white pages. As they approached, the sun came out of a momentary eclipse behind a cloud. The roses flamed up as though with a sudden passion from within; a new and profound significance seemed to suffuse the shining pages of the books. From the ranks of the crawling babies came little squeals of excitement, gurgles and twitterings of pleasure.

The Director rubbed his hands. "Excellent!" he said. "It might almost have been done on purpose."

The swiftest crawlers were already at their goal. Small hands reached out uncertainly, touched, grasped, unpetaling the trans-figured roses, crumpling the illuminated pages of the books. The Director waited until all were happily busy. Then, "Watch care-fully," he said. And, lifting his hand, he gave the signal.

The Head Nurse, who was standing by a switchboard at the other end of the room, pressed down a little lever.

There was a violent explosion. Shriller and ever shriller, a siren shrieked. Alarm bells maddeningly sounded.

The children started, screamed; their faces were distorted with terror.

"And now," the Director shouted (for the noise was deafening), "now we proceed to rub in the lesson with a mild electric shock."

He waved his hand again, and the Head Nurse pressed a second lever. The screaming of the babies suddenly changed its tone. There was something desperate, almost insane, about the sharp spasmodic yelps to which they now gave utterance. Their little bodies twitched and stiffened; their limbs moved jerkily as if to the tug of unseen wires.

"We can electrify that whole strip of floor," bawled the Director in explanation. "But that's enough," he signalled to the nurse.

The explosions ceased, the bells stopped ringing, the shriek of the siren died down from tone to tone into silence. The stiffly twitching bodies relaxed, and what had become the sob and yelp of infant maniacs broadened out once more into a normal howl of ordinary terror.

"Offer them the flowers and the books again."

The nurses obeyed; but at the approach of the roses, at the mere sight of those gaily-colored images of pussy and cock-a-doodle-doo and baa-baa black sheep, the infants shrank away in horror; the volume of their howling suddenly increased.

"Observe," said the Director triumphantly, "observe."

Books and loud noises, flowers and electric shocks—already in the infant mind these couples were compromisingly linked; and after two hundred repetitions of the same or a similar lesson would be wedded indissolubly. What man has joined, nature is powerless to put asunder.

"They'll grow up with what the psychologists used to call an 'instinctive' hatred of books and flowers. Reflexes unalterably conditioned. They'll be safe from books and botany all their lives." The Director turned to his nurses. "Take them away again."

Still yelling, the khaki babies were loaded on to their dumb-waiters and wheeled out, leaving behind them the smell of sour milk and a most welcome silence.

One of the students held up his hand; and though he could see quite well why you couldn't have lower-caste people wasting the Community's time over books, and that there was always the risk of their reading something which might undesirably decondition one of their reflexes, yet . . . well, he couldn't understand about the flowers. Why go to the trouble of making it psychologically impossible for Deltas to like flowers?

Patiently the D.H.C. explained. If the children were made to scream at the sight of a rose, that was on grounds of high economic policy. Not so very long ago (a century or thereabouts), Gammas, Deltas, even Epsilons, had been conditioned to like flowers—flowers in particular and wild nature in general. The idea was to make them want to be going out into the country at every available opportunity, and so compel them to consume transport.

"And didn't they consume transport?" asked the student.

"Quite a lot," the D.H.C. replied. "But nothing else."

Primroses and landscapes, he pointed out, have one grave defect: they are gratuitous. A love of nature keeps no factories busy. It was decided to abolish the love of nature, at any rate among the lower classes; to abolish the love of nature, but *not* the tendency to consume transport. For of course it was essential that they should keep on going to the country, even though they hated it. The problem was to find an economically sounder reason for consuming transport than a mere affection for primroses and landscapes. It was duly found.

"We condition the masses to hate the country," concluded the Director. "But simultaneously we condition them to love all country sports. At the same time, we see to it that all country sports shall entail the use of elaborate apparatus. So that they consume manufactured articles as well as transport. Hence those electric shocks."

"I see," said the student, and was silent, lost in admiration.

There was a silence; then, clearing his throat, "Once upon a time," the Director began, "while Our Ford was still on earth, there was a little boy called Reuben Rabinovitch. Reuben was the child of Polish-speaking parents." The Director interrupted himself. "You know what Polish is, I suppose?"

"A dead language."

"Like French and German," added another student, officiously showing off his learning.

"And 'parent'?" questioned the D.H.C.

There was an uneasy silence. Several of the boys blushed. They had not yet learned to draw the significant but often very fine distinction between smut and pure science. One, at last, had the courage to raise a hand.

"Human beings used to be . . ." he hesitated; the blood rushed to his cheeks. "Well, they used to be viviparous."

"Quite right." The Director nodded approvingly.

"And when the babies were decanted . . ."

" 'Born,' " came the correction.

"Well, then they were the parents—I mean, not the babies, of course; the other ones." The poor boy was overwhelmed with confusion.

"In brief," the Director summed up, "the parents were the father and the mother." The smut that was really science fell with a crash into the boys' eye-avoiding silence. "Mother," he repeated loudly, rubbing in the science; and, leaning back in his chair, "These," he said gravely, "are unpleasant facts; I know it. But then most historical facts *are* unpleasant."

He returned to Little Reuben—to Little Reuben, in whose room, one evening, by an oversight, his father and mother (crash, crash!) happened to leave the radio turned on.

("For you must remember that in those days of gross viviparous reproduction, children were always brought up by their parents and not in State Conditioning Centers.")

While the child was asleep, a broadcast program from London suddenly started to come through; and the next morning, to the astonishment of his crash and crash (the more daring of the boys ventured to grin at one another), Little Reuben woke up repeating word for word a long lecture by that curious old writer ("one of the very few whose works have been permitted to come down to us"), George Bernard Shaw, who was speaking, according to a well-authenticated tradition, about his own genius. To Little Reuben's wink and snigger, this lecture was, of course, perfectly incomprehensible and, imagining that their child had suddenly gone mad, they sent for a doctor. He, fortunately, understood English, recognized the discourse as that which Shaw had broadcasted the previous evening, realized the significance of what had happened, and sent a letter to the medical press about it.

"The principle of sleep-teaching, or hypnopedia, had been discovered." The D.H.C. made an impressive pause.

The principle had been discovered; but many, many years were to elapse before that principle was usefully applied.

"The case of Little Reuben occurred only twenty-three years after Our Ford's first T-Model was put on the market." (Here the Director made a sign of the T on his stomach and all the students reverently followed suit.) "And yet . . ."

Furiously the students scribbled. *"Hypnopedia, first used officially in A.F. 214. Why not before? Two reasons. (a) . . ."*

"These early experimenters," the D.H.C. was saying, "were on the wrong track. They thought that hypnopedia could be made an instrument of intellectual education . . ."

(A small boy asleep on his right side, the right arm stuck out, the right hand hanging limp over the edge of the bed. Through a round grating in the side of a box a voice speaks softly.

"The Nile is the longest river in Africa and the second in length of all the rivers of the globe. Although falling short of the length of the Mississippi-Missouri, the Nile is at the head of all rivers as regards the length of its basin, which extends through 35 degrees of latitude . . ."

At breakfast the next morning, "Tommy," someone says, "do you know which is the longest river in Africa?" A shaking of the head. "But don't you remember something that begins: The Nile is the . . ."

"The - Nile - is - the - longest - river - in - Africa - and - the - second - in - length-of-all-the-rivers-of-the-globe . . ." The words come rushing out. "Although-falling-short-of . . ."

"Well now, which is the longest river in Africa?"

The eyes are blank. "I don't know."

"But the Nile, Tommy."

"The-Nile-is-the-longest-river-in-Africa-and-the-second . . ."

"Then which river is the longest, Tommy?"

Tommy bursts into tears. "I don't know," he howls.)

That howl, the Director made it plain, discouraged the earliest investigators. The experiments were abandoned. No further attempt was made to teach children the length of the Nile in their sleep. Quite rightly. You can't learn a science unless you know what it's all about.

"Whereas, if they'd only started on *moral* education," said the Director, leading the way towards the door. The students followed him, desperately scribbling as they walked and all the way up in the lift. "Moral education, which ought never, in any circumstances, to be rational."

"Silence, silence," whispered a loud speaker as they stepped out at the fourteenth floor, and "Silence, silence," the trumpet mouths indefatigably repeated at intervals down every corridor. The students and even the Director himself rose automatically to the tips of their toes. They were Alphas, of course; but even Alphas have been well conditioned. "Silence, silence." All the air of the four-teenth floor was sibilant with the categorical imperative.

Fifty yards of tiptoeing brought them to a door which the Director cautiously opened. They stepped over the threshold into the twilight of a shuttered dormitory. Eighty cots stood in a row against the wall. There was a sound of light regular breathing and a continuous murmur, as of very faint voices remotely whispering.

A nurse rose as they entered and came to attention before the Director.

"What's the lesson this afternoon?" he asked.

"We had Elementary Sex for the first forty minutes," she an-swered. "But now it's switched over to Elementary Class Con-sciousness."

The Director walked slowly down the long line of cots. Rosy and relaxed with sleep, eighty little boys and girls lay softly breathing. There was a whisper under every pillow. The D.H.C. halted and, bending over one of the little beds, listened attentively.

"Elementary Class Consciousness, did you say? Let's have it re-peated a little louder by the trumpet."

At the end of the room a loud speaker projected from the wall. The Director walked up to it and pressed a switch.

". . . all wear green," said a soft but very distinct voice, begin-ning in the middle of a sentence, "and Delta children wear khaki. Oh no, I don't want to play with Delta children. And Epsilons are still worse. They're too stupid to be able to read or write. Besides they wear black, which is such a beastly color. I'm *so* glad I'm a Beta."

There was a pause; then the voice began again.

"Alpha children wear gray. They work much harder than we do, because they're so frightfully clever. I'm really awfully glad I'm a Beta, because I don't work so hard. And then we are much better than the Gammas and Deltas. Gammas are stupid. They all wear green, and Delta children wear khaki. Oh no, I *don't* want to play with Delta children. And Epsilons are still worse. They're too stupid to be able . . ."

The Director pushed back the switch. The voice was silent. Only its thin ghost continued to mutter from beneath the eighty pillows.

"They'll have that repeated forty or fifty times more before they wake; then again on Thursday, and again on Saturday. A hundred and twenty times three times a week for thirty months. After which they go on to a more advanced lesson."

Roses and electric shocks, the khaki of Deltas and a whiff of asafetida—wedded indissolubly before the child can speak. But wordless conditioning is crude and wholesale; cannot bring home the finer distinctions, cannot inculcate the more complex courses of behavior. For that there must be words, but words without reason. In brief, hypnopedia.

"The greatest moralizing and socializing force of all time."

The students took it down in their little books. Straight from the horse's mouth.

Once more the Director touched the switch.

". . . so frightfully clever," the soft, insinuating, indefatigable voice was saying. "I'm really awfully glad I'm a Beta, because . . ."

Not so much like drops of water, though water, it is true, can wear holes in the hardest granite; rather, drops of liquid sealing-wax, drops that adhere, incrust, incorporate themselves with what they fall on, till finally the rock is all one scarlet blob.

"Till at last the child's mind *is* these suggestions, and the sum of the suggestions *is* the child's mind. And not the child's mind only. The adult's mind too—all his life long. The mind that judges and desires and decides—made up of these suggestions. But all these suggestions are *our* suggestions!" The Director almost shouted in his triumph. "Suggestions from the State." He banged the nearest table. "It therefore follows . . ."

A noise made him turn round.

"Oh, Ford!" he said in another tone, "I've gone and woken the children."

INSTRUCTIONAL WORK IN THE WAKING HOURS

From SOVIET PRESCHOOL EDUCATION, Volume II

Ten percent of all Soviet children under the age of two and twenty percent of children between three and six are currently enrolled in public nurseries, all of which, from Tallin in Estonia to Alma Alta in Soviet Asia, and from Moscow to Tiflis are governed by identical principles and procedures carefully outlined in a single text: The Kindergarten Teacher's Manual. *In America, a growing interest in preschool education and an increasing need for nationwide day-care centers has heightened curiosity and interest in the Soviet preschool program. At last a recent translation has made the* Manual *available to a wide American audience in* Soviet Preschool Education.

In the following portion of the Soviet Kindergarten Teacher's Manual, *a striking contrast to traditional American child-care beliefs is seen in the Soviet teachers' active and systematic encouragement of learning from the earliest months. It has been suggested that the American approach to child-rearing is characterized by a concern to avoid pathology (". . . if you encourage him to try you may make him feel incompetent. This does more harm than good") while the Soviet approach is aimed at developing talent. More and more American educators are beginning to lean in the direction of earlier educational intervention and are finding the Soviet* Manual *a surprisingly sound model for an early childhood program.*

307

In working with the youngest babies (3 to 5 weeks to 3 to 5 months), the nurse must remember that they need not only hygienic care and breast feeding but also the development of their neuropsychological activity.

At this age, the main attention must be directed toward the formation of audiovisual reflexes, and the development of the positive happy emotions which determine the general animation of the baby and improve all of his physiological processes.

When the children are awake, it is important that they be put in a playpen. There should never be more than six to eight children in a playpen at one given time. Moreover, those who cannot move about must be placed in different areas of the playpen.

One should put children up to 2 months in the playpen immediately after feeding, having previously wrapped them in a blanket up to the underarms and having put a flat pillow or a folded diaper under their head. Toward the end of the waking period, overalls should be put on the babies to enable them to move about freely.

It is very important to take care that the child does not catch cold. Therefore the baby must not be put down right away on a spread covered with oilcloth, but rather on a blanket a corner of which is folded over to cover the baby. Two- to 3-month-old babies wear playsuits during their waking hours.

It is healthful for the child to be in different positions, that is, lying not only on his back, but also on his stomach. This contributes to the strengthening of the body muscles. Children must be put down on their stomachs before meals or toward the end of the waking period. After meals, this position might cause vomiting. If a baby who, lying on his stomach, gets tired of the same position and begins to fret, he must be turned over on his back.

As a result of lying down on his stomach every day, after two or three months the baby learns how to raise and hold up his head.

From time to time, the nurse does exercises with the babies who know how to hold their head erect (at 2 to $2\frac{1}{2}$ months) to prepare them for more complicated movements, such as standing and walking. Holding the baby under the armpits, she gives the baby a chance to stretch out his legs from the hips and touch a table or the adult's knees, to do a sort of dance. In doing this, however, the nurse does not allow a baby under 4- or 5-months-old to stand on his legs. A playful exercise like this is not only healthful but gives the babies a great deal of pleasure.

While the babies are awake, the nurse keeps in close contact with them. She plays with them, talks affectionately to each of them, sings nursery rhymes, and endeavors to induce in the babies a happy mood. The nurse sees to it that the children who are lying down in the playpen are kept active and busy. Constant affection of the staff toward the babies creates in them a happy state. Seeing the nurse, the baby begins to smile and move about energetically, stretching out and bending his arms and legs and making sounds which are of great significance for the later development of speech. The person in charge must remember at all times that a prevailing state of happiness in small children is vital for their proper physical and psychological development.

From the very first months of life, the baby begins to be aware of surrounding sounds, and he reacts to them in different ways. Loud, shrill sounds usually evoke crying, while melodious sounds he will listen to attentively. For this reason, the nurse and her assistant must speak to the children in an even voice with a calm, soothing intonation. By calling the child's name and then coming up to him, the nurse and her assistant develop in the baby the ability to determine from which direction a sound is coming.

In the second month of life the baby begins to focus his sight on surrounding objects, especially on those which attract his attention by their bright color, as well as on the faces of adults when they are talking to him. Gradually babies begin to follow moving objects with their gaze. In order to help develop the ability to concentrate visual attention on objects and their movement, it is recommended that some bright large toy (balloon) be suspended above the baby's chest, at a distance of about 70 centimeters, or, if the toy is smaller, at a distance of 50 to 60 centimeters.

Pictures on the walls of the babies' rooms, large bright toys on the shelves, and low flowering plants at the windows all attract the babies' attention; the babies look at them while in a variety of different positions (lying on their backs, on their stomachs, or in a vertical position in the arms of an adult).

With babies from 3- to 3½-months-old the nurse continues to develop the ability to see and distinguish objects, and to listen and distinguish (and even imitate) sounds; she encourages attempts by the baby to use vocal chords. It is essential to encourage the development of the grasping movements of the hands as well as those movements which prepare the baby for crawling, sitting, and standing.

Babies at this age continue to be put in playpens while they are awake, but they need more space. As they are able to change their position, and later to move a little, they must be given this opportunity. For babies of this age (up to 7 months), experiments have demonstrated the convenience of a playpen on legs with sides made of vertical and horizontal boards.

Dressed in a baby's vest, a warm jacket and a playsuit, children can move their legs and arms around freely.

Celluloid rings with balls and other toys should be hung up above 3-month-old babies not only so that they can look at them, but also so that they can occasionally grasp them when their hands accidentally knock against them. Later on when, toward the age of 4 months, the baby can extend his arms all the way, the toys should be hung higher. At that point, the baby's movements can be made more complicated by providing such toys as parrots and rattles, which require greater coordination of movement.

Beginning when he is 3-months-old, each baby must be given, besides the suspended toys, something to hold in his hands such as pleasant sounding rattles of various shapes. From 5 to 6 months on, when the babies are able to grasp and hold an object in their hands, they no longer need the suspended toys.

While they are awake, the nurse keeps the babies happy by talking to them in a gentle voice, encouraging response, and giving them toys corresponding to their stage of development. She makes sure that the babies are all spread out in the playpen so that they will not get in each other's way. The nurse helps those babies who still do not know how to change their position: some are put on their stomachs, others are turned over on their backs; the 5- to 6-month old babies are encouraged to crawl by having brightly colored toys placed within easy reach.

With the help of the nurse in charge the baby gradually masters the movements preparatory to crawling: by the age of 4 months he begins to turn from his back onto his side; by 5 months, from his back onto his stomach; and by 6 months, from his stomach onto his back. A 5-month baby can stay a long time on his stomach with his arms extended, propping himself up with the palms of his hands, raising the upper part of his body, and arching his back. By the age of 6 months he stands on all fours, leaning on the palms of his hands and his knees. At that stage some children begin to crawl.

As of 4 to 5 months of age, a baby recognizes and distinguishes adults close to him (his mother, the nurse and her assistants). The nurse, taking advantage of the mother's arrival at the kindergarten (when the baby is brought to the kindergarten, is being breast fed or is about to leave), turns to the baby affectionately and says, "Mommy has arrived, let's go to Mommy," or "Mommy will come again for her little girl Olya," or "Misha will go home with Mommy now."

The nurse must do her best to see that all the time which the mother spends at the kindergarten is used for close personal contact between her and the baby. Suitable conditions must be established to permit the mother to spend a little time talking and playing with the baby after feeding.

Infants from 6 to 9 months develop the ability to perform a series of movements: crawling and changing position at will; sitting without the help of adults; lying down and then standing up; walking while leaning on something. For children over 7 months, the playpen must be replaced by a sufficiently large area of the floor which is covered with an oilcloth-covered spread. A specially made fence or various pieces of furniture (such as tables, sofas and climbing horses) may serve to enclose the area.

The nurse, leading various activities, encourages the children to be physically active. Pointing to a toy placed at some distance from the infant, the nurse gently urges him on: "Ivan, here is a ball, come on, crawl to it, come on!" She thereby stimulates in the baby the desire to get close to it.

A toy, placed on top of the railing, encourages the baby to stand up. If the toy is moved, the baby will try to move step by step to follow the toy. He will experience a great sense of satisfaction if, reaching the toy, he is able to take it in his hands.

Babies of 6 to 9 months of age show noticeably increased interest in their surroundings; they can, by moving around, get familiar with a large number of objects. By the age of 9 months, babies begin to walk holding on to surrounding objects.

The nurse then makes the babies' handling of toys more precise and intricate. If at the beginning the baby limits himself to inspecting the toy, shaking it, banging it, and shifting it from one hand to the other, then by eight or nine months of age, as a result of training, he masters various actions suggested by the object itself: he shakes a rattle, he rolls a ball, he squeezes a squeaking toy. The baby's interest in toys will increase significantly; he is able to play with them for a longer period, and when he drops them he is distressed.

The nurse develops the babies' speech and familiarizes them with the names of surrounding objects, pointing to them and naming them as she goes along: "clock," "cat," "dog." Changing the usual position of an object, she challenges the baby to find it. The baby will remember the names of things better if he is given an opportunity not only to look at them, but also to use them (to roll a ball, to shake a rattle).

If, wishing to attract a child's attention, the nurse calls him by his name, the baby begins to respond first by turning his head, and then later with sounds. Children recognize the names of the nurse and her assistant if they call themselves by name when playing hide and seek with the babies ("Where's Auntie Ann?") or challenge the baby to "give Auntie Mary the toy."

Babies of this age are not only interested in adults, people who are around them constantly, but also in babies their own age. The interest of a baby in the one next to him in the playpen is already obvious. A baby can, although not for very long at the beginning, observe what his neighbor does with this or that toy, the way he laughs or moves about. In answer to his laugh, the baby smiles and tries to get closer to him. These attempts at mutual communication are to be encouraged provided that they are inspired by good will and friendliness and give the babies pleasure.

These efforts will only be successful in cases where the mutual relationships are developed under the constant influence and guidance of the nurse. At this age, negative relationships between babies may also appear; a baby seeing a toy in the hands of another baby begins to take it away from him. One should then divert his attention to some other toy, take the baby into one's arms or talk to him gently.

To arouse the babies' interest in each other and to acquaint them with each other's names, the nurse may use various games such as hide and seek. She puts a muslin napkin over a baby's head and, turning to the other babies, says: "Where is Alyosha? Alyosha's gone, gone!"; then, taking off the napkin, she exclaims, "Here is our Alyosha." In this kind of game, the attention of a small group of babies is attracted toward a specific baby, and they hear and remember his name.

If the nurse accompanies with words the baby's actions, as well as her own when handling objects, the babies then quickly assimilate the name of these actions. Holding the baby in her arms, the nurse brings him up close to various objects and attracts his attention to their functions: "The clock goes tic-toc." Such instruction gives the babies new impressions and evokes a happy mood. On being told by the nurses "Give me your hand," "Bring me the ball," "Bring me the rattle," the baby begins actually to carry out the simple actions involved.

To give the babies practice in pronouncing sounds and syllables, the nurse encourages them to imitate. Some games will be found very useful for this purpose, especially those based on nursery rhymes.

To further improve the ability of the babies to look and listen, the teacher shows them winding toys and fish swimming in an aquarium, and hums or sings songs. The nurse's singing lends a special emotional feeling to her relationship with each baby, as well as to the games which she plays with the babies in small groups. At the beginning, the babies listen attentively, then begin to indicate their pleasure with a smile, a "coo," and animated movements.

The babies who already know how to follow moving objects with their eyes particularly enjoy it when the teacher shows them some bright shining toy and sings a song at the same time. For example, one may sing a song and at the same time wave a flag or shake a rattle.

Babies at this age usually have three musical activities a week. Half an hour after feeding time, the babies are brought closer together in the playpen and everything that may distract their attention is removed, for example, suspended toys and the toys lying around in the playpen.

At the beginning of this period, the teacher sings or plays on some instrument (mirliton, mouth organ, metallophone), then for no more than five to six minutes performs rhythmical movements using any sort of toy, little flag, or rattle. This demonstration should proceed without hurry, so that all the babies can follow the moving object with their eyes.

In order for the teacher's singing to be enjoyed by the babies, it must be soft and melodious. Loud singing deafens babies and prevents them from listening attentively. Singing should be heard in the kindergarten not only during special activities, but also when relating to the babies individually, whenever they are being undressed, and on walks during the summer.

From 9 to 10 months up to 12 months of age, children must be taught to walk by themselves and to pronounce consciously about ten very simple words, such as mommy, pussy, and so on. . . . As of 10 or 11 months, the babies move from one support to another, crawl, and climb up and down a three-step climber, while at about 12 months, they begin to walk without using any support.

At this age babies master movements in independent activity and therefore must have at hand suitable toys and sufficient room to be able to move about. For this reason, a space must be set aside which is partitioned off from the rest of the room by a railing. The furniture placed in this area, for instance a climber, a play table, or a little couch, will be used by the teacher for the babies' physical development and play.

It is also important that the babies be provided with brightly colored, pretty, washable toys: large and small colored balls for rolling, rings to lower onto a pole, rattles, rubber toys, and, later on, celluloid and rubber dolls as well as bits of colored materials.

Besides, it is important that toys should be so selected that the baby can use several of them at the same time. Examples are a box with two or three balls (so that babies can put the balls into the box, then take them out), a little stand with rings attached, and so forth.

Not all available toys should be given to the babies for play: some of them should be stored in a closet. From time to time it is good to change the set of toys with which the babies play. Otherwise they will no longer hold their attention. A baby should not be allowed to play with a broken toy. So that each baby can choose a toy easily, they should be spread out on tables, on the climber, on the couch, on top of or inside the toy box. The babies crawl or walk up to the toys and take them in their hands. While playing, the babies move about, take toys from one place to another, climb up on the little couch, or sit down on the floor.

If, by the age of 11 months, a baby does not make any attempts to walk, special exercises should be done with him. The nurse or assistant, sitting down in front of the baby, holds out her hands toward him and calls him to her: "Masha, come to me!" This encourages the child to walk by himself.

It is also possible, holding a toy in one's hands, to stimulate the baby's desire to come toward it and take it. It is very important to encourage the child at such a time, as this helps him to overcome the fear of falling. It is good to attract the attention of children and adults present to the success of the baby: "Look, children, how nicely Ivan is walking." One can also sing or beat out rhythmically "See how our Masha walks, top-da-top," etc. Giving him attention and encouraging his first steps makes the baby happy and stimulates his desire to move by himself.

From time to time, the nurse draws several babies into a motion game, for example "Hide and Seek." She "hides" right in front of the children and asks: "Who will go and look for Auntie Anya?" Some of the babies will set out to look for her.

The nature of the independent activity depends mainly on the way it is organized by the adults. Although the babies at this age are given enough time for such activity and have acquired some ability to move about and handle toys by themselves, they still cannot play for any length of time without the participation of adults. Therefore, the nurse must have her mind on the babies who are playing, mix with them, introduce variety into their activities and prevent negative relationships from springing up between them.

After some time the baby will attempt to carry over the actions he has learned to other similar objects; for instance, he will put together the two halves of a *matreshka*,* he will put the lid on a saucepan after looking for the lid by himself, etc. The nurse encourages the babies to play independently, but comes to the rescue herself when this seems necessary.

One cannot expect babies at this age to put the toys away. This the nurse and her assistant must do, and toys with which the babies are not playing should not be allowed to remain scattered on the floor. While the babies are asleep, the nurse or her assistant washes the toys and puts them back in their proper place.

A baby who has learned to move about independently has an opportunity to get better acquainted with surrounding objects, and to associate more with other babies his age as well as with adults. Babies enjoy this immensely. One should help babies at this

---

* A *matreshka* is a container in the shape of a peasant woman, containing smaller containers of the same shape, sometimes as many as twelve and as few as two.

age to develop their ability to see and distinguish objects, and to observe. This is an indispensable condition for the development of the children's speech.

Working with each baby individually and with small groups of babies (no more than five), the nurse strives to improve the babies' understanding of adult speech, and at the same time develops their own speech and their ability to communicate with adults for various reasons and on different occasions. To make the babies familiar with the names of objects, the nurse shows various objects to the baby and names them. Then she asks him to give her a toy, the name of which the baby knows by that time, and gives the name of a toy that is still unfamiliar to the baby.

A series of games can also be organized to this effect. For example, the nurse suggests that the babies bring this or that toy which is placed within easy view. When the baby brings the toy to the teacher, she names it, saying: "Here, Sergei has just brought the cat, purr-purr. Good boy, Sergei." In another variation, the nurse, together with the babies, "hides" toys, naming the toys and the place where they are hidden: "Let's put the chicken on the table, let's put the ball on the couch," and so on; then the group of babies, together with the nurse, "look for" the toys, each time naming them.

After some time, the nurse begins to work on developing the babies' ability to generalize, having them find objects similar in name but different in appearance and in the material of which they are made. For instance, she asks them to bring dolls (made of rubber, celluloid, rag) or dogs (of papier-mâché, rubber, wood).

The teacher names the actions with which the babies are very familiar: the ball rolls, the rattle rattles, and so forth. Just as she did in the previous subgroup, the nurse continues to acquaint the babies with the names of the surrounding children and adults, and to develop in them friendly attitudes toward each other.

Further improving their babbling is very significant for the development of the active speech of the babies. The particular sounds uttered by the babies must be clearly and slowly repeated (*ma-ma, ba-ba*). New sounds are then introduced as well as such words as are within the ability of the baby to repeat, frequently those linked by similarity in sound: doggy (*av-av*), etc.

In order to arouse the babies' interest in the imitation of sounds and the pleasurable experiences related to this type of exercise, a simple dramatization can be organized using various toys. For example, holding a doll wrapped up in a blanket, the nurse sings a lullaby. Showing the babies a toy rooster, she says: "Here is our rooster! How beautiful he is! He sings loudly: 'koo-ka-re-koo.' The rooster wants to peck grain. Peck, Peter (the rooster), peck, peck. And now he sings his song again, 'koo-ka-re-koo.' Children, how does the rooster sing?"

Similar dramatizations may be shown with other toys. Doing this, one must keep in mind that the babies will want to play with the toy which has been shown, so it is important to prepare ahead of time a sufficient number of such toys to satisfy the desire of all the babies who want to play with them.

Much laughter and joy is brought about by showing winding toys. The nurse lets a winding car go on a slide or on the table. "Here goes the car, too-too-too," she says. The babies go on repeating the simple sounds, such as too-too, which the nurse pronounces with particular emphasis.

If the teacher-nurse sings or dances with little flags or a bright kerchief, tambourine or rattle, the babies will look on with great interest, laugh, babble and hop around, and, sitting either in the playpen or standing by a railing, draw close to the nurse, expressing their desire to dance. Imitating the nurse, the babies also try to hit the tambourine which is brought to them. When mixing with the children, the nurse sings songs, clapping the babies' hands or, having taken a baby in her arms, raises and lowers him gently in time with the dance music. Later, the baby will begin to make dancing movements as soon as he hears gay music.

In connection with such activities for babies of this age, the songs in the collection of Babadjan can be used. The best for listening are the following: "Ladooshki (Palms)," arranged by Rimsky-Korsakov, "The Rooster," arranged by Krasev, "The Little Bird" by Raukhverger, words by Barto, etc.

With babies of this age group, the teacher spends five to seven minutes doing musical exercises. If such training was performed regularly when the babies were in the previous age group, then the babies listen eagerly and look for the teacher who is playing or singing. At the age of nine to ten months the babies turn their head toward the side of the room from which the sound of song or music is coming.

The listening attention of babies at this age continues to develop.

They can be attentive to music for 20 or 30 seconds without a break, and listen in a general way to music (with breaks) for two or three minutes. Singing, when accompanied by the showing of bright objects and toys or movements by the teacher, stimulates in the babies the desire to be active.

Much interest and happiness is experienced by the babies when observing animals: chickens, pigeons, sparrows, hens, a cat, a puppy, a rabbit, or a baby goat. The process of getting acquainted with these animals is usually accompanied by certain movements and the pronouncing of various sounds.

Gradually the babies must be acquainted with pictures of the objects and animals with which they are familiar. Pictures for babies must be drawn beautifully, clearly, and in bright colors (*Pictures for the Little Ones*, cardboard cubes with pictures on them, may be used).

In addition to the regular activity periods, the nurse takes advantage of each time she is in close contact with the babies to develop their active speech and their understanding of adult speech.

THE EDUCATION OF BABY ANNE

From CHEAPER BY THE DOZEN

Frank B. Gilbreth, Jr., and Ernestine Gilbreth Carey

*Anne was the first of that jolly one-family popu-
lation explosion immortalized in* Cheaper by the
Dozen. *Being the first, she had to bear the brunt of
Dad Gilbreth's insatiable curiosity about children,
later to be dissipated among eleven additional
Gilbreth offspring.*

*Curiously, Dad Gilbreth's ideas about early learn-
ing, so delightfully absurd at the beginning of the
twentieth century when he tried to put them in
practice, and still preposterous in 1948 when*
Cheaper by the Dozen *was published, are beginning
to be confirmed by scientists today, who agree that
babies start learning from their very first days.*

Dad had long held theories about babies and, with the arrival of
Anne, he was anxious to put them to a test. He believed that
children, like little monkeys, were born with certain instincts of
self-preservation, but that the instincts vanished because babies
were kept cooped up in a crib. He was convinced that babies
started learning things from the very minute they were born, and
that it was wrong to keep them in a nursery. He always forbade
baby talk in the presence of Anne or any of his subsequent offspring.

319

"The only reason a baby talks baby talk," he said, "is because that's all he's heard from grownups. Some children are almost full grown before they learn that the whole world doesn't speak baby talk."

He also thought that to feel secure and wanted in the family circle, a baby should be brought up at the side of its parents. He put Anne's bassinet on a desk in his and Mother's bedroom, and talked to her as if she were an adult, about concrete, and his new houseboat, and efficiency, and all the little sisters she was going to have.

The German nurse whom Dad had employed was scornful. "Why, she can't understand a thing you say," the nurse told Dad.

"How do you know?" Dad demanded. "And I wish you'd speak German, like I told you to do, when you talk in front of the baby. I want her to learn both languages."

"What does a two-week-old baby know about German?" said the nurse, shaking her head.

"Never mind that," Dad replied. "I hired you because you speak German, and I want you to speak it." He picked up Anne and held her on his shoulder. "Hang on now, Baby. Imagine you are a little monkey in a tree in the jungle. Hang on to save your life."

"Mind now," said the nurse. "She can't hang on to anything. She's only two weeks old. You'll drop her. Mind, now."

"I'm minding," Dad said irritably. "Of course she can't hang on, the way you and her mother coddle her and repress all her natural instincts. Show the nurse how you can hang on, Anne, baby."

Anne couldn't. Instead, she spit up some milk on Dad's shoulder.

"Now is that any way to behave?" he asked her. "I'm surprised at you. But that's all right, honey. I know it's not your fault. It's the way you've been all swaddled up around here. It's enough to turn anybody's stomach."

"You'd better give her to me for awhile," Mother said. "That's enough exercise for one day."

A week later, Dad talked Mother into letting him see whether new babies were born with a natural instinct to swim.

"When you throw little monkeys into a river, they just automatically swim. That's the way monkey mothers teach their young. I'll try out Anne in the bathtub. I won't let anything happen to her."

"Are you crazy or something," the nurse shouted. "Mrs. Gilbreth, you're not going to let him drown that child."

"Keep quiet and maybe you'll learn something," Dad told her.

Anne liked the big bathtub just fine. But she made no effort to swim and Dad finally had to admit that the experiment was a failure.

"Now if it had been a boy," he said darkly to the nurse, when Mother was out of hearing.

The desk on which Anne's bassinet rested was within reach of the bed and was piled high with notes, *Iron Age* magazines, and the galley proofs of a book Dad had just written on reinforced concrete. Mother utilized the "unavoidable delay" of her confinement to read the proofs. At night, when the light was out, Dad would reach over into the bassinet and stroke the baby's hand. And once Mother woke up in the middle of the night and saw him leaning over the bassinet and whispering distinctly:"Is ou a ittle bitty baby? Is ou Daddy's ittle bitty girl?"

"What was that, dear?" said Mother, smiling into the sheet.

Dad cleared his throat. "Nothing. I was just telling this noisy, ill-behaved, ugly little devil that she is more trouble than a barrel of monkeys."

"And just as much fun?"

"Every bit."

THE CASE FOR BABY TALK

From LEARNING TO TALK

Margaret C. L. Greene

An educator and expert on children's speech presents a convincing argument in favor of a much-maligned dialect: baby-talk.

I have spoken of the mother's investing her baby's babble syllables or vocables with meaning, of helping him to use the first words meaningfully by teaching him nursery words at first. It is fashionable nowadays among educated parents to reject with disgust the time-honored custom of using nursery words in this way to help an infant to talk. In a broadcast in which I advocated the use at a year old of this method of baby talk, or the child's "little language" as it has been called, I received a deluge of indignant letters from parents and schoolteachers who were genuinely shocked that a speech therapist of all people could recommend such harmful teaching methods. They obviously regarded the acceptance of nursery words as the primary cause of defective speech in children. These parents saw nothing inconsistent, incidentally, in allowing themselves to be called "Daddy" and "Mommy," or of referring to "baby," "teddy," or "golliwogg," which have no adult equivalent.

Of course to use baby talk when addressing a child, such as "Did Mommy's ikkle darling want an itsy-bitsy chockie before her dindin," is revolting at any time, and is a sentimental debasement of the human language. I certainly do not advocate this. However, the use of nursery words such as "choo-choo," "moo," "baa,"

322

derived from baby's own babbling, serves a good purpose at the right time. The most important thing at nine to twelve months is to encourage the small child to use articulate syllables with meaning, to communicate with words. It does not matter particularly what the sound is nearly so much as that the sound should be used consistently to refer to a toy, object or person. As soon as a child uses a syllable intelligently in this way, he is at one stroke lifted far above any other animal in creation. He thereby in fact qualifies as a human being, for only man can speak. Birds learn to imitate words and even nursery rhymes with extraordinary accuracy, but this is not speech because it has no meaning for the bird. The parakeet has no idea of the symbolism of any word or sentence he chirps forth.

Attempting to teach a one-year-old exact articulation is a waste of time. Try to teach him to say "dog," for instance, which necessitates the lifting of the tongue tip for "d" and a swift change to "o" and the lifting of the back of the tongue for "g." He cannot possibly manage this with his immature muscular co-ordination. Why not let him say "wow-wow," which he can manage with ease? The use of word pictures like "moo-cow," "baa-lamb," "choo-choo-train" and so forth is a great help in teaching the most important principle in learning to speak, which is that a vocal symbol stands for an object. He will soon discard the "moo," "baa" and "choo-choo" and use "cow," "lamb" and "train" when he is ready and especially if his parents discard the nursery props altogether by eighteen months. After all, you help baby with his first steps in walking, why not in talking?

It is extraordinary how hard it is to convince some parents that they may discourage their babies from trying to talk altogether by not using nursery words in this way at first. Going hand in hand with this intransigent attitude of course is a refusal to accept and understand baby's first crude attempts at naming things, so the poor mite may lose confidence in speaking and give up trying. The parents of one little girl declared that they would on no account allow Jane of nine months to say "bye-bye" but she must say "good-bye," and not "Mommy and Daddy" but "Father and Mother." Since they endeavored to elicit these words from Jane and corrected all her spontaneous attempts at utterance and refused to understand *her* baby talk (the immature attempts at talking perfectly natural to every infant), this little mite grew so discouraged and frustrated she ceased to talk to her parents altogether. At two years she would only chatter freely to her grandmother, who was so old-fashioned that she had no notion of the new-fangled ideas concerning learning to talk. She understood baby talk and never drew attention to its deficiencies, and she also knew the arts of mothercraft and how to talk to little children— simply, sympathetically, matter-of-factly, using little words and sentences as she and Jane did odd jobs together round the house. Jane's parents realized the damage they were doing eventually, but Jane suffered a real setback and good, clear speech developed slowly as a result.

Rigid four-hourly feedings became the fashion this century and it was until recently considered a fearful breach of discipline to lift a wailing child up and pet him and give him a little snack between times. Now doctors and psychiatrists tell mothers to cuddle their babies when they need it and to feed them when they are hungry. This is no new idea but an incredibly old one. To my mind the idea that one should not use nursery words in teaching baby to talk is as unnatural as four-hourly feedings, and I look forward to the day when baby talk is once more discovered to be the right way of helping to get baby to talk.

A REMARKABLE BUSINESS

From HOW CHILDREN LEARN

John Holt

John Holt's thesis in How Children Learn, *that children have a natural style of learning too often warped or destroyed by grown-up intervention, places him in the forefront of the romantic movement in American education, a movement with roots going back to Tolstoy and Rousseau. But rather than trying to prove his point with rhetoric and polemics, he advances his case convincingly by means of detailed and sympathetic observations (sympathetic to the young subjects, that is—parents and especially teachers are frequently objects of distrust and scorn).*

Sitting in his stroller, in a local store the other day, was a child about a year old. His mother was busy in the store, and he was absorbed in his own affairs, playing with his stroller, looking at cans of fruit and juice. I watched him. Suddenly he said to himself, "Beng-goo." After a few seconds he said it again, then again, and so perhaps ten times. Was he trying to say "Thank you"? More probably he had hit on this sound by accident and was saying it over and over because he liked the way it sounded, and felt in his mouth.

A few months ago, I saw quite a bit of another one-year-old. She liked to say "Leedle-leedle-leedle-leedle." It was her favorite sound, and she said it all the time; indeed that was about all she said. Now and then she would add an emphatic "a!" (as in cat)—"Leedle-leedle-leedle-a!" I asked her father how she had come to make that sound. Was she imitating a sound that someone had made to her? No; apparently she had learned to stick her tongue out and bring it back in quickly, and liked the feel of it. (Babies like all tongue-waggling games.) One day, as she was doing this, she made a sound with her voice, and was amazed and delighted to hear what the movement of her tongue did to that sound. After much practice she found that she could make the sound without having to put her tongue outside her mouth. It felt good, and it sounded good, so she kept it up for a month or two before moving on to something else.

How a sound feels seems to be as important as the sound itself. Everyone who has watched babies knows how pleased they are when they first discover how to make a Bronx cheer. And they do discover it; this sound, at least, is one that their mothers would never teach them.

In France, some years ago, I was surprised to hear an 18-month-old boy, while babbling away, make the sound of the French "u." Perhaps there was no reason to be surprised; everyone who talked to him called him "tu." But I had never heard a baby make that sound before, and had had a very hard time to get even a few of my French students to make it. Of course, my students were anxious and self-conscious, and this baby was not—which makes a world of difference.

Why does a baby begin to make sounds in the first place? Is it instinctive, like crying? It seems not to be. A puppy raised apart from other dogs will know how to bark when he gets old enough. But the few children we know of who grew up without human contact, grew up almost wholly mute. Babies in understaffed foundling hospitals, who see very little of older people, are said, except for crying, to be almost silent. Apparently it is from hearing people speak around them that babies get the idea of "speaking." When they make their first sounds, are they imitating the sounds they hear around them? Or are they inventing, so to speak, from scratch? Perhaps at first they mostly invent, and imitate more later.

It is a remarkable business. We are so used to talking that we forget that it takes a very subtle and complicated coordination of lips, tongue, teeth, palate, jaws, cheeks, voice, and breath. Simply as a muscular skill it is by far the most complicated and difficult that most of us ever learn, at least as difficult as the skill required to master a serious musical instrument. We realize how difficult speech is only when we first try to make the sounds of a language very different from our own. Suddenly we find that our mouths and tongues won't do what we want. Yet every child learns to make the sounds of his own language. If he lives where more than one language is spoken, he makes the sounds of them all. How does he do it? His coordination is poor to start with; how does he manage to do what many adults find so difficult?

The answer seems to be by patient and persistent experiment; by trying many thousands of times to make sounds, syllables, and words; by comparing his own sounds to the sounds made by people around him; and by gradually bringing his own sounds closer to the others; above all, by being willing to do things wrong even while trying his best to do them right.

Bill Hull once said to me, "If we taught children to speak, they'd never learn." I thought at first he was joking. By now I realize that it was a very important truth. Suppose we decided that we had to "teach" children to speak. How would we go about it? First, some committee of experts would analyze speech and break it down into a number of separate "speech skills." We would probably say that, since speech is made up of sounds, a child must be taught to make all the sounds of his language before he can be taught to speak the language itself. Doubtless we would list these sounds, easiest and commonest ones first, harder and rarer ones next. Then we would begin to teach infants these sounds, working our way down the list. Perhaps, in order not to "confuse" the child—"confuse" is an evil word to many educators—we would not let the child hear much ordinary speech, but would only expose him to the sounds we were trying to teach.

Along with our sound list, we would have a syllable list and a word list.

When the child had learned to make all the sounds on the sound list, we would begin to teach him to combine the sounds into syllables. When he could say all the syllables on the syllable list, we would begin to teach him the words on our word list. At the same time, we would teach him the rules of grammar, by means of which he could combine these newly-learned words into sentences.

Everything would be planned with nothing left to chance; there would be plenty of drill, review, and tests, to make sure that he had not forgotten anything.

Suppose we tried to do this; what would happen? What would happen, quite simply, is that most children, before they got very far, would become baffled, discouraged, humiliated, and fearful, and would quit trying to do what we asked them. If, outside of our classes, they lived a normal infant's life, many of them would probably ignore our "teaching" and learn to speak on their own. If not, if our control of their lives was complete (the dream of too many educators), they would take refuge in deliberate failure and silence, as so many of them do when the subject is reading.

Last summer, in a supermarket, a young mother came with her baby to the meat counter, and began to discuss with him, in the most lively and natural way, what meat they should get for supper. This piece of meat looked nice, but it was too expensive—terrible what was happening to food prices. This piece might be all right, but it would take too long to cook; they had many other errands to do and would not get home before four o'clock. These chops looked good, but they had had them just two nights ago. And so on. There was nothing forced or affected in her words or her voice; she might have been talking to someone her own age.

A year or more ago, some friends and I dropped in on some people who had a six-month-old baby. She was well-rested and happy, so they brought her in to see the visitors. We all admired her before going on with our talk. She was fascinated by this talk. As each person spoke, she would turn and look intently at him. From time to time she would busy herself with a toy in her lap; then after a few minutes she would begin watching and listening again. She seemed to be learning, not just that people talk, but that they talk to each other, and respond to each other's talk with smiles, and laughter, and more talk; in short, that talk is not just a kind of noise, but messages, communication.

Babies and young children like to hear adult conversation, and will often sit quietly for a long time, just to hear it. If we want to help little children as they learn to talk, one way to do it is by talking to them—provided we do it naturally and unaffectedly— and by letting them be around when we talk to other people....

One winter morning, when we were eating breakfast, Tommy began to say "Toe! Toe! Toe!" Putting helpful expressions on our faces, we said, "Toe?" It was clear that we did not know what he meant. Again he said, "Toe! Toe! Toe!," looking furiously at us. We knew that he had been using the word to mean toe, coat, cold, and toilet. So we said, pointing at his toe, "Does your toe hurt?" Wrong. "Do you want your coat? Your blue coat?" Wrong again. "Do you want to go towet?" (family expression inherited from previous baby). Still wrong. "Are you cold?" Now we were on the right track. Asking more questions, we eventually found that someone had left an outside door open, letting in a draft, and that Tommy wanted us to close the door—which we did. This shows that a baby's speech may be more varied than it sounds. He may *know* the difference between a number of words, even if he cannot say the difference.

When a baby shows us, by his expression, by the insistent tone of his voice, and by repeating his words over and over, that he is trying hard to tell us something, we must try just as hard to understand what he is saying. Often it will not be easy. Some people, if they don't understand the first or second time, say, "I don't know what you're saying," and give up. But we must not give up. It sometimes helps to ask the next oldest child in the family. He may be able to interpret, perhaps because he knows the smaller child better and hears him talk more, perhaps because he himself is closer to early speech and remembers what it is like. Or, if there is no other child to interpret for us, we can say to the child who is speaking, "Can you show me?" I remember seeing one mother do this with her little boy. At first he did not understand her question, and looked puzzled. She then took a step or two in one direction, pointing, and saying, "Is it in here? Is it this way?" Then she went in another direction and asked again, while the child watched, puzzled and intent. After a while he saw what her question meant, and was soon able to lead her to what he wanted to tell her about.

Once, when Tommy was very little, he came to tell me that his teddy bear was stuck between the bars of his crib. Since I couldn't understand him at first, I went through the "show-me" routine. As soon as he understood me, he led me to the scene of the tragedy. I said, "Oh, I see. Your poor teddy bear has got stuck in the crib. His head is stuck in the bars. Well, the thing for us to do is to get him unstuck and pull him out. First we have to turn him a little bit, so that his head is pointing the narrow way, and then we just slide him out." I continued to talk about the bear, and how it feels to be stuck, etc. What was the point of this talk? First, just to make some conversation, and secondly, to show Tommy our ways of saying what he was trying to say, and to assure him that we do have words for talking about such things.

FROM NOTHING TO EVERYTHING

From THE ABSORBENT MIND

Maria Montessori

At the heart of Maria Montessori's educational theories lies her conviction that the learning process is very different for very young children than it is for older children and grown-ups. The following excerpt from The Absorbent Mind *proposes a question so simple and obvious and yet a question few had considered before Montessori: how does a baby create something out of nothing—emerging at the end of his second year with a thinking mind where no thoughts had existed before?*

Why should it be necessary for the human being to endure so long, and so laborious a babyhood? None of the animals has so hard an infancy. What happens while it is going on? Beyond question, there is a kind of creativeness. At first, nothing exists, and then, about a year later, the child knows everything. The child is not born with a little knowledge, a little memory, a little will power, which have only to grow as time goes on. The cat, after a fashion, can mew from birth; the newly hatched bird, and the calf, make the same kind of noises as they will when adult. But the human baby is mute; he can only express himself by crying. In man's case, therefore, we are not dealing with something that develops, but with a fact of formation; something nonexistent has to be produced, starting from nothing. The wonderful step taken by the baby is to pass from nothing to something, and our minds find it very hard to grapple with this conundrum.

A mind different from ours is needed to take that step. The child has other powers than ours, and the creation he achieves is no small one; it is everything. Not only does he create his language, but he shapes the organs that enable him to frame the words. He has to make the physical basis of every moment, all the elements of our intellect, everything the human being is blessed with. This wonderful work is not the product of conscious intention. We adults know what we want. If we desire to learn something, we set ourselves to learn it consciously. But the sense of willing does not exist in the child; both knowledge and will have to be created.

If we call our adult mentality conscious, then we must call the child's unconscious, but the unconscious kind is not necessarily inferior. An unconscious mind can be most intelligent. We find it at work in every species, even among the insects. They have an intelligence which is not conscious though it often seems to be endowed with reason. The child has an intelligence of this unconscious type, and that is what brings about his marvelous progress.

It begins with a knowledge of his surroundings. How does the child assimilate his environment? He does it solely in virtue of one of those characteristics that we now know him to have. This is an intense and specialized sensitiveness in consequence of which the things about him awaken so much interest and so much enthusiasm that they become incorporated in his very existence. The child *absorbs* these impressions not with his mind but with his life itself.

Language provides the most obvious example. How does it happen that the child learns to speak? We say that he is blessed with hearing and listens to human voices. But, even admitting this, we must still ask how it is that, among the thousands of sounds and noises that surround him, he hears, and reproduces, only those of the human voice? If it be true that he hears, and if it be true that he only learns the language of human beings, then it must be that the sounds of human speech make on him a deeper impression than any other sounds. These impressions must be so strong, and cause such an intensity of emotion—so deep an enthusiasm as to set in motion invisible fibers of his body, fibers which start vibrating in the effort to reproduce those sounds.

By way of analogy, let us think of what happens at a concert. A rapt expression dawns on the faces of the listeners; heads and hands begin to move in unison. What can be causing this but a psychic response to the music? Something similar must be happening in the unconscious mind of the child. Voices affect him so deeply that our response to music is nothing to it. We can almost see the vibrant movements of his tongue, the trembling of the tiny vocal cords and cheeks. Everything is in motion, trying in silent preparation to reproduce the sounds which have caused such turmoil in his unconscious mind. How does it happen that the child learns a language in all its detail, and so precisely and fixedly that it becomes a part of his psychic personality? This language he acquires in infancy is called his mother tongue, and it is clearly different from all the other languages which he may learn later, just as a natural set of teeth is different from a denture.

How does it happen that these sounds, at first meaningless, suddenly bring to his mind comprehension and ideas? The child has not only absorbed words and their meanings; he has actually absorbed sentences and their constructions. We cannot understand language without understanding the structure of sentences. Supposing we say, "The tumbler is on the table," the meaning we give those words derives partly from the order in which we say them. If we had said "On tumbler the is table the," our meaning would have been hard to grasp. We draw meaning from the arrangement of the words, and this is also something the child can absorb.

And how does all this happen? We say: "The child remembers things," but, in order to remember something, it is necessary to have a memory, and this the child has not. On the contrary, he has to construct it. Before one can appreciate how the ordering of words in a sentence affects its meaning, one must be able to reason. But this also is a power which the child has to make.

Our mind, as it is, would not be able to do what the child's mind does. To develop a language from nothing needs a different type of mentality. This the child has. His intelligence is not of the same kind as ours.

It may be said that we acquire knowledge by using our minds; but the child absorbs knowledge directly into his psychic life. Simply by continuing to live, the child learns to speak his native tongue. A kind of mental chemistry goes on within him. We, by contrast, are recipients. Impressions pour into us and we store them in our minds; but we ourselves remain apart from them, just as a vase keeps separate from the water it contains. Instead, the child undergoes a transformation. Impressions do not merely enter his mind; they form it. They incarnate themselves in him. The child creates his own "mental muscles," using for this what he finds in the world about him. We have named this type of mentality, *The Absorbent Mind*.

WHY WE FORGET OUR INFANCY

From AT LIFE'S BEGINNING

Samuel Marshak

> *The Russian poet and children's writer Samuel Marshak proposes a theory for why grown-ups remember so little of their early childhood, a theory in complete harmony with Montessori's concept of "the absorbent mind."*

No matter how you exert your memory, it is almost impossible to reach back to the beginnings of your life and to early childhood. All we are left with of those first years are two or three episodes, isolated moments picked out from the darkness.

Why is it that we remember so little of our infancy? Because it was so long ago and has been wiped out by subsequent decades? But usually memory retains impressions of the distant past more firmly than imprints of our recent, later years.

Perhaps we do not remember our first years simply because we ourselves were too stupid at that time to see, or notice, or understand things? No, surely everyone who has watched children of two or three years—let alone four-year-olds—knows how observant they are, how resourceful and imaginative, how complicated their feelings and experiences.

The first childhood years are the hardest of all the universities a person has to go through. Schoolchildren spend several years learning languages, and rarely succeed in mastering one of them by the time they leave. Yet a child has to assimilate the whole wisdom of speech—at least enough to talk quite fluently and correctly—by the time he is two. He studies a language without the medium of another, already familiar one and at the same time acquires a mass of the most important basic knowledge of the world: he comes to know from experience what is cold or hot, hard or soft, high or low. It is impossible to list all that enters a child's consciousness in the course of those years. His life is a series of discoveries. The most humdrum details of everyday life are for him events of enormous significance.

And so why is it that these events which impress the two- or three-year-old so profoundly are only seldom, and accidentally, retained by his memory? I think it is because the child yields to his every impression and experience directly, without consideration, in other words without the elaborate system of mirrors which builds up in his consciousness at a later age. He does not see himself from the outside, and is swallowed up in the current of events and impressions; he is unaware of himself, just as a person "forgets himself" when he is in a rage or in a state of dizzy excitement.

ABOUT THE AUTHORS

LOUISA MAY ALCOTT (1832-1888) was a daughter of Bronson Alcott, noted American transcendentalist and educational theorist. Raised in Boston and Concord and educated by her father, she received additional instruction and guidance from such family friends as Emerson and Thoreau. She achieved immediate success with the publication of *Little Women* (1868), a fictionalized account of her own early life in New England. She continued writing in the same vein, in *An Old Fashioned Girl* (1870), *Little Men* (1871), *Eight Cousins* (1875), *Rose in Bloom* (1876), and many other works, mainly for children, as well as participating in the temperance and women's suffrage reform movements.

B. M. ATKINSON, JR., was born in Georgia in 1918 and graduated from Emory University. He was a sports writer with the *Atlanta Journal* and the *Macon Telegraph* and has been writing a column for the *Louisville Times* for more than twenty-five years. He has written more than fifty short stories that have appeared in various magazines, including *Ladies' Home Journal, Esquire*, and *Collier's*, as well as several television plays. He is the father of four children, three girls and one boy.

PAULUS BAGELLARDUS (?–1492) was born and educated in Padua, where he studied philosophy and medicine. He practiced medicine in Padua for many years and is said to have been most popular both with the common people and with the rulers of that city. His book on the diseases of children was a compendium of pediatric opinions of his time, as well as a result of his own experiences in medical practice. The book was written in medieval Latin, interspersed with words of local origin, and was printed by the still-new printing process in Padua in 1472, one of the earliest books ever printed, and certainly the first printed book on pediatrics.

SIMONE DE BEAUVOIR (born in 1908), French existentialist writer and novelist, was born in Paris and studied with Jean Paul Sartre at the Sorbonne, where she became closely associated with his literary activities. Among her works are *The Second Sex* (1949), *The Mandarins* (1954), *Memoirs of a Dutiful Daughter* (1959), and *The Coming of Age* (1972).

ARNOLD BENNETT (1867-1931), one of the great triumvirate of late nineteenth-century British writers with Galsworthy and H. G. Wells,

337

was born and raised in modest surroundings in Hanley, Staffordshire, one of the "five towns of the Potteries" that figure prominently in his works. His reputation as a novelist was firmly established with the publication of *Old Wives' Tale* (1908), a chronicle of the lives of two daughters of a draper from Bursley, another of the five towns. His other novels include *Clayhanger* (1910), *Hilda Lessways* (1911), and *These Twain* (1916), a trilogy that centered again on the ugly, banal features of life in the pottery centers Bennett knew well. Collections of his short stories have appeared with the titles *The Grim Smile of the Five Towns* (1907) and *The Matador of the Five Towns* (1912).

BRUNO BETTELHEIM was born in Vienna, where he began his career in the arts, winning a doctorate in aesthetics before switching to psychology. He later studied with Sigmund Freud. Dr. Bettelheim emigrated to the United States in 1939, where he wrote his first book, *Individual and Mass Behavior in Extreme Situations*, based on his experiences in concentration camps. The book was a forerunner of his series of seven books dealing with adult and adolescent psychological problems and the treatment and rehabilitation of mentally ill children. Among his books are *The Empty Fortress* (1967), *Dialogues with Mothers* (1962), *Symbolic Wounds* (1962), *The Informed Heart* (1960), *Truants from Life* (1961), *Love Is Not Enough* (1950) and *The Empty Fortress* (1967), based on his experiences at the University of Chicago Orthogenic School, a renowned treatment center for childhood schizophrenia. His latest book, *The Children of the Dream* (1969), analyzes communal child-rearing methods on a kibbutz in Israel.

WILLIAM BLAKE (1757-1827), son of a London shopkeeper, received no formal schooling, but showing artistic talents, was apprenticed at the age of fourteen to an engraver. Throughout his life he earned his living by book illustrations, and gained renown for employing a new engraving process. But it is for his poetry that he is celebrated today, the most beloved being lyrics that appeared in the volumes *Songs of Innocence* (1789) and *Songs of Experience* (1794). The poems in these books are written with great simplicity and economy, using a childlike voice and easily understandable symbolism. Blake's later works became increasingly metaphysical and mystical, with much of the symbolism remaining obscure to the reader. Among the volumes of Blake's poetry are *Poetical Sketches* (1783) and *The Marriage of Heaven and Hell* (1790).

JOHN BOWLBY was born in 1907 and educated at Dartmouth and Trinity College, Cambridge. After medical qualification at University College Hospital, he specialized in psychiatry, child psychiatry, and psychoanalysis. Since 1946 he has worked at the Tavistock Clinic and Tavistock Institute of Human Relations as Director for Children and Parents and of the Child Development Research Unit. Among his publications before the war are *Personal Aggressiveness and War* (with Evan Durbin), *Personality and Mental Illness,* and *Forty-four Juvenile Thieves* (1944). In 1950 he was appointed consultant in mental health to the World Health Organization, for whom he wrote *Maternal Care and Mental Health* (1950). His most recent book is *Attachment* (1969).

ROBERT BURNS (1759-1796), the greatest and most popular poet of Scotland, was the first of seven children of a peasant family in Alloway. Educated by his father, he soon showed a talent for literature. He wrote many of his best songs and poems before he was thirty while working as a laborer on his father's farm. He achieved immediate literary success with the publication of his first collection of songs and poems in 1786, acquiring a reputation as well for his many (frequently fruitful) love affairs and his cheerful flaunting of conventional morality. His most beloved poems, written in a vernacular style uncharacteristic for the times, celebrated love and freedom and laughter above all. Among them might be mentioned "The Twa Dogs," "Corn Rigs," "Green Grow the Rashes," "Tam o' Shanter," and "The Mouse."

ROBERT BURTON (1577-1640) was born in Leicestershire, England, educated at Oxford, and elected to Christ Church, Oxford, in 1599, where he lived, studied, and wrote for his entire life. Prevented by circumstances from taking a place in the world of affairs, for which he was temperamentally well-suited, Burton turned to books, reading a phenomenal quantity of works from classical literature, as well as medical, astrological, and magical books then extant. His great work *Anatomy of Melancholy* (1621), one of the most amazing and entertaining books of all times, while ostensibly a medical treatise upon the causes, symptoms, and cures of melancholy, is in reality a wild compendium of his readings, containing thousands of excerpts (paraphrased in most cases into his own, individual voice) from classical and post-classical writers on poetry, theology, morals, food, travel, love, pride, astrology, and more—virtually no topic is left uncovered—providing an excellent picture of contemporary life and thought of his day.

ERNESTINE GILBRETH CAREY was born and raised in Montclair, New Jersey, a childhood familiar to the many thousands of readers of her best-selling book (written with her brother Frank B. Gilbreth, Jr.) *Cheaper by the Dozen* (1948). After graduating from Smith College she entered the retail merchandising field, serving as a buyer for a New

York department store for many years. *Cheaper by the Dozen* was followed by an equally beloved sequel, *Belles on Their Toes* (1950).

ANTON CHEKHOV (1860-1904), one of the most important writers of pre-Revolution Russia, was born in the south of Russia, studied medicine but never became a practicing physician, deciding to devote his time to his writing. Most at home in the shorter forms of literature—short stories and plays—Chekhov began to produce his greatest works early in his literary career, firmly establishing his literary reputation with the publication of his second collection of short stories, *Motley Stories* (1886), at the age of 26, and winning the Pushkin Prize of the Academy of Sciences. His tragically premature death from tuberculosis came at the very apex of his fame and literary powers. Among his best-known short stories, for skill and polish sometimes compared to those of Maupassant, may be mentioned "The Duel," "A Dreary Story," "Ward No. 6," "Peasants," and "My Life." His greatest plays, made famous by productions of Stanislavski at the Moscow Art Theater, include *The Sea-Gull* (1896), *The Three Sisters* (1899), *Uncle Vanya* (1902), and *The Cherry Orchard* (1904).

GILBERT KEITH CHESTERTON (1874-1936) was born in Kensington, England, studied art at the Slade School, and began his diversified literary career as an art critic for *The Bookman* magazine. His prolific literary output includes works in most major literary subdivisions: novels and short stories—*The Napoleon of Notting Hill* (1904), *The Man Who Was Thursday* (1908), *The Innocence of Father Brown* (1911); drama—*Magic* (1913); poetry—"The Ballad of the White Horse" (1911), "Wine, Water and Song" (1915); essays—*Heretics* (1905), *Generally Speaking* (1928); biography—*Robert Browning* (1910), *Charles Dickens* (1906); criticism—*G. F. Watts* (1904) and *William Blake* (1910).

SAMUEL TAYLOR COLERIDGE (1772-1834), English poet and literary critic, was born in Devonshire and educated at Jesus College, Cambridge. After a period of quixotic utopianism, including plans for a communistic community in Susquehanna, Pennsylvania, he began a precarious livelihood as a poet, publishing his first volume in 1796. Shortly thereafter he began a long and intimate association with William and Dorothy Wordsworth, during which period most of his important works were written. Among his best-known poems are *The Ancient Mariner, Christabel,* and *Kubla Khan,* all characterized by a sense of mystery and foreboding. Apart from his poetry, Coleridge produced a body of important and influential critical works, notably *Biographia Literaria,* or a *Literary Biography* (1817), and *Aids to Reflection* (1825), in which he introduced ideas of German idealistic philosophy to English thinkers, as well as presenting his own original critical theories.

COLETTE (1873-1954) was born Sidonie-Gabrielle Colette in the Burgundy district of France. Her first novels about a semi-autobiographical heroine, Claudine, were published under her first husband's pen name of "Willy," and aroused a certain amount of scandal as well as much admiration for their odd combination of naïve freshness and perverse sensuality. After the marriage ended in divorce, she began to use the single name Colette to sign a large body of literary works of sufficient distinction to secure her a place as one of the most outstanding French writers of modern times. In 1954 she was elected the first woman president of the powerful Académie Goncourt. Her best-known works include the three *Claudine* novels (1900-1903), *Chéri* (1920), *Le Blé en Herbe* (1923), *La Chatte* (1933), and *Gigi* (1944).

JOSEPH CONRAD (1857-1924) was born Teodor Jezef Konrad Korzeniowski, of Polish parents in the Russian Ukraine. At the age of seventeen Conrad shipped aboard a French vessel, thus beginning twenty years of a seafaring life, during which time he mastered the English language and became a British citizen. In 1895 he published his first novel, *Almayer's Folly*, to be followed by a steady succession of narratives, including *The Outcast of the Islands* (1896), *The Nigger of the "Narcissus"* (1898), *Lord Jim* (1900), *Chance* (1913), *Victory* (1915), and *The Arrow of Gold* (1919), as well as a great number of short stories and an autobiography. Conrad is generally considered one of the greatest modern English novelists, with a particular skill at evoking an atmosphere, and a thematic preoccupation with human isolation and loneliness.

WHITNEY DARROW, JR., whose cartoons have enlivened the pages of *The New Yorker* magazine for over three decades, is well known for his portrayal of fiendish children. He is a graduate of Princeton University, where he was Art Editor of the *Tiger*. He is married, has two children, and lives in Wilton, Connecticut.

CHARLES DICKENS (1812–1870) was born in Portsmouth, England, and spent a childhood of hardships and humiliations not unlike those suffered by the hero of *David Copperfield*. He began his literary career as a journalist, and most of his great novels were first published in serial form in various monthly periodicals. He achieved fame and financial success at the age of twenty-four with the publication of *The Pickwick Papers* (1836), and continued to produce a steady succession of important works for the rest of his life. Among these are *Oliver Twist* (1837), *Nicholas Nickleby* (1838), *A Christmas Carol* (1843),

Dombey and Son (1848), *David Copperfield* (1849), *Bleak House* (1852), *A Tale of Two Cities* (1859), and *Great Expectations* (1860). Of his ten children, only one was successful in literature, his next-to-youngest son Henry Fielding Dickens, who was the author of *Memories of My Father* (1929).

MARGARET DRABBLE was born in Sheffield in 1939, and went to Newnham College, Cambridge, on a major scholarship when she was eighteen. Following a spectacular academic success at Cambridge, she acted with the Royal Shakespeare Company. She is married to Clive Swift, an actor, and is the mother of three children. Her novel *The Millstone* (1965) was awarded the John Llewelyn Rhys Memorial Prize in England, while each of her other novels met with critical acclaim. Among her books are *A Summer Birdcage* (1963), *The Garrick Year* (1964), *Jerusalem the Golden* (1967), *The Waterfall* (1969), and *The Needle's Eye* (1972).

ISADORA DUNCAN (1878-1927) was an influential figure in the evolution of modern dance. Born in San Francisco, she developed her novel theories of interpretive dance based on classic forms and modern aesthetic thought during her long residence in Europe. She founded schools of dance in Berlin, Salzburg, Vienna, and Moscow, where she met the experimental "imagist" poet Sergei Esenin, whom she subsequently married. She was strangled to death in a bizarre accident when her long scarf caught in the wheels of her car while she was driving. Her autobiography, *My Life*, was published in 1927.

NELL DUNN was born in London in 1936. Educated at a convent, she left school at fourteen, spending the next three years traveling around Europe and reading Russian novels. She is married to Jeremy Sanford, a writer, and has a young son called Roc. She is the author of *Poor Cow* (1967), an earthy and realistic picture of lower-class life in today's London that was made into a popular motion picture. Her second book, *Talking to Women*, was published in 1965.

ERIK ERIKSON was born in Frankfort, Germany, in 1902, of Danish parents, and emigrated to the United States at the age of thirty-two. Having acquired extensive training at the Vienna Psychoanalytic Institute, he soon established himself in this country as one of the foremost figures in the field of psychoanalysis. His first book, *Childhood and Society* (1950, revised 1963), was a unique application of the concepts of clinical psychology to the study of society and history. *Young Man Luther* (1958) examined the intersection of development and history in the youth of the great religious reformer. *Insight and Responsibility* (1964) dealt with the growth of ego strength in the young in light of the relation between the generations, and *Identity: Youth and Crisis* (1968) was concerned with the relationship of the historical and the individual. His latest work, *Gandhi's Truth* (1970), a psychohistorical study of the origins of Gandhi's theory of militant non-violence, was awarded the National Book Award in the category of philosophy and religion in 1970.

GUSTAVE FLAUBERT (1821–1880) was born and educated at Rouen, where his father was chief surgeon of the hospital. He briefly studied law in Paris, but soon abandoned it to devote himself to literature. For most of his life he led a hermit-like existence, subordinating everything else to his writing and laboring endlessly to secure the precisely right word in the right place. He struggled for over five years on *Madame Bovary* (1857), his first published work. This, perhaps the most famous French novel, with its romantically minded heroine at odds with her environment, and its devastating portrait of the dullness, vulgarity, and pettiness of middle-class provincial life, brought the author and publisher legal prosecution on the grounds of immorality, but after a trial that was a literary sensation of the day, Flaubert was acquitted. Among his other works are *Salammbo* (1862); *L'Education Sentimentale* (1869); *Three Stories* (1877), containing "A Simple Heart," "St. Julian the Hospitaller," and "Herodias"; *Bouvard et Pecuchet* (unfinished, published posthumously 1881).

SELMA H. FRAIBERG was born in Detroit and studied at Wayne State University. Presently Professor of Child Psychoanalysis at the University of Michigan Medical School and Director of the Child Development Project of Children's Psychiatric Hospital of the University of Michigan Medical Center, Mrs. Fraiberg has published widely on the problems of early childhood in professional journals and in lay magazines. Her book *The Magic Years* (1959) is considered one of the best and most useful guides to the early childhood years, both for parents and professionals.

DR. ARNOLD GESELL (1880–1961) was born in Alma, Wisconsin, and educated at the University of Wisconsin, Clark University and Yale University. A pioneer in the field of child development, he established and directed the Clinic of Child Development at the Medical School of Yale University and headed a research staff that attempted to chart the behavior characteristics of thirty-four advancing age levels from birth to age ten. The results of these studies were reported in numerous works, among them *The First Five Years* (1940), *Infant and Child in the Culture of Today* (with F. Ilg, 1943), and *The Child from Five to Ten* (with F. Ilg, 1946). Upon the termination of the Yale Clinic in

1948 its studies were continued at the newly founded Gesell Institute of Child Development.

FRANK B. GILBRETH, JR., is presently assistant publisher of *The News and Courier* and *The Charleston Evening Post* in South Carolina. Besides the immensely successful books about his childhood co-authored with his sister Ernestine, he has written a biography of his mother, *Time Out for Happiness* (1970).

MAXIM GORKY (1868-1936) was born Alexei Maximovich Peshkov in the Russian city of Nizhni Novgorod (renamed Gorki in his honor in 1932), but began using the pen name Maxim Gorky (Maxim the bitter one) at the start of his literary career at the age of twenty-four. He was noted for his realistic stories and plays depicting the lives and sufferings of poor and downtrodden people; the revolutionary nature of his writings as well as his political activities led to his arrest and exile in 1904. He returned after the Bolshevik revolution to become the central figure of Soviet literature, and his particular blending of romanticism and realistic observation, along with a certain optimistic rationalism, became the basis of the theory that was given the name Socialist Realism, the officially sanctioned literary style of the Soviet Union. Among his works are many collections of stories, most notably *Twenty-six Men and a Girl* (1901), several novels including the prototypal proletarian and revolutionary novel *Mother* (1907). His plays include *The Lower Depths* (1903) and *The Night Lodgings* (1905). Among the huge body of Gorky memoirs are found three widely read autobiographical novels—*Childhood* (1913), *In the World* (1918), and *My Universities.*

MARGARET C. L. GREENE is an English speech therapist and Fellow of the College of Speech Therapists, having qualified in 1949. She is at present the head of the Department of Speech Therapy of St. Bartholomew's Hospital in London. Besides her guide to parents on children's speech, *Learning to Talk* (1960), she is the author of *The Voice and Its Disorders* (1957) and many articles on children's speech and language disorders. In 1968 she founded the Association for All Speech Impaired Children (AFASIC) in England and remains active in its affairs. She is the mother of two daughters and the grandmother of six children.

ELIZABETH HERZOG is a graduate of the University of Chicago and did graduate work at Yale and Columbia Universities in anthropology, sociology and psychology. Formerly the chief of the Youth and Child Studies branch of the Research Division, Children's Bureau, in Washington D.C., she is presently the Project Director of the Social Research Group at George Washington University in Washington. Earlier work included participation in a project of cultural anthropology headed by Ruth Benedict and Margaret Mead at Columbia University, one product of which was the book *Life Is with People* (1962), of which she is the co-author. She has published many monographs for the Children's Bureau, including *Some Guidelines for Evaluative Research* (1959) and *About the Poor: Some Facts and Some Fictions* (1968), and has written many articles that have appeared in various professional publications. Many of her articles have been reprinted in collected readings, one of them appearing in at least fourteen different collections.

JOHN HOLT was born in New York City in 1923. Asserting that a person's schooling is as much a part of his private business as his politics or religion, he does not answer questions about it, stating instead that most of his education has taken place outside of school. He has worked as a teacher for many years in elementary and high schools in Colorado, Cambridge (Massachusetts), and Boston. Based on his teaching experiences, he has written four books on education, as well as many articles and reviews. After his first book, *How Children Fail* (1964), established him as a leading educational critic and innovator, he has published *How Children Learn* (1967), *The Underachieving School* (1969), *What Do We Do Monday* (1970), and *Freedom and Beyond* (1972).

ALDOUS HUXLEY (1894-1963), grandson of the eminent British biologist Thomas Huxley, was born in Surrey, England, and educated at Eton and Oxford. Best known as a novelist, and also noted for his satiric, at times outrageous humor, Huxley was a prolific writer of essays, biography, drama, and verse. His first novel, *Crome Yellow* (1921), established him as one of the most accomplished writers of his generation. His best-known books are *Antic Hay* (1923), *Point Counter Point* (1928), and *Brave New World* (1932), as well as later works marked by a growing seriousness and tendency toward mysticism, such as *Eyeless in Gaza* (1936), *Ape and Essence* (1949), and *The Doors of Perception* (1954), a study of the hallucinogenic drug mescaline.

SHIRLEY JACKSON (1919-1965), California-born author, lived in Bennington, Vermont, with her husband, the critic Stanley Edgar Hyman, and her large brood of children. Her literary output was great, including many stories and novels frequently characterized by bizarre, savage happenings taking place in realistic, commonplace settings. Many of her best-known stories are collected in *The Lottery* (1949). Other works include the novels *The Sundial* (1958), *The Haunting of Hill*

House (1959), *We Have Always Lived in the Castle* (1962), and two amusing accounts of her own family life, *Life Among the Savages* (1953) and *Raising Demons* (1957).

JEROME K. JEROME (1859-1927), English humorist, novelist and playwright, was born of Hungarian origin in Walsall, Staffordshire, England. Brought up and educated in London, he began his working life as a clerk and went on to become a teacher, a reporter and an actor. His literary career was launched in 1889 with the publication of two highly successful books: *Three Men in a Boat*, a humorous account of a boat cruise to Hampton Court, and *Idle Thoughts of an Idle Fellow*, a collection of light essays. With others he founded a popular monthly magazine, *The Idler*, in 1892, which continued to be published for almost twenty years. He achieved fame as a dramatist with his first play, *The Passing of the Third Floor Back* (1908). His autobiography, *My Life and Times*, was published in 1926, shortly before his death.

JAMES JOYCE (1882-1941) was born in Dublin, and though Ireland remained the setting of his great works, he left it as a young man of twenty, never to return. He lived and wrote chiefly in Trieste, Zurich, and Paris, struggling for many years to get his writings published and supporting his family by teaching languages. The publication of *Ulysses* (1922), with its striking use of the "stream of consciousness" technique, brought Joyce to the attention of the world, and secured him a life-long patron whose financial aid allowed him to devote the rest of his life to his writing. *Ulysses*, an infinitely detailed picture of a single day in the lives of two middle-class Irishmen, Leopold Bloom and Stephen Dedalus, began to exert a tremendous influence on modern literature which obtains to this day. Joyce's other principal works are *Dubliners* (short stories, 1914), *Portrait of the Artist as a Young Man* (1916), and *Finnegans Wake* (1939).

MARTIN LUTHER (1483-1545), German religious reformer and father of the Reformation in Germany, was born in Eisleben and became an Augustinian friar and ordained priest at the age of twenty-two. Increasingly critical of the Roman Catholic Church, he attacked church policies in his famed gesture of 1517, nailing ninety-five theses to the church door at Wittenberg. Excommunicated by Pope Leo X in 1520, Luther was forced to go into hiding in the castle of his friend Frederick of Saxony. Two years later Luther returned to Wittenberg and devoted himself to the organization of a new church he had inaugurated, now known as the Lutheran Church.

KATHERINE MANSFIELD (1888-1923) was born in New Zealand, but left for England at the age of nineteen to establish herself as a writer.

Her ambition was realized with the publication of her first collection of short stories, *The Aloe* (1916), later revised and reprinted as *Prelude* (1918). A second collection, *Bliss* (1920), secured her reputation as a master of the short story genre, and was perhaps the first appearance of the "stream of consciousness" technique in the short story. She was at the height of her creative powers in *The Garden Party* (1922), published shortly before her tragically premature death from tuberculosis. Her final work, *The Dove's Nest*, was published posthumously in 1923.

SAMUEL MARSHAK (1887-1964), Russian poet, children's writer and translator, was born in Voronezh and received part of his education at London University from 1913 to 1914. In the Soviet Union he is equally famed for his translations from English literature, especially of Shakespeare, Burns and Byron, as well as for his many children's books, fairy tales and plays, including *The Silly Bear Cub* (1923), *Mister Twister* (1933), *Ice Island* (1947), *The Forest Book* (1950), *My Horse* (1963). He also wrote various critical articles and was awarded four Stalin prizes and the Lenin Prize in 1963. His autobiographical work *At Life's Beginning* was published in an English translation in 1964.

GUY DE MAUPASSANT (1850-1893) was born and educated in Normandy, the setting of a great number of his famous short stories. After serving in the army (1870) and taking a job as a government clerk, he became a disciple of Flaubert, joining an eminent literary circle that included Turgenev, Daudet, and Zola, among others. He began to practice the literary craft under Flaubert's guidance, learning much of Flaubert's technique of objectivity and stylistic precision. In 1880 he contributed a short story to an anthology, *"Boule-de-suif"* (Butterball), and with its publication became a celebrity virtually overnight. His phenomenal output during the next ten years (three hundred stories, six novels, and some dramatic works) established him as a superb craftsman and an unequaled master of the short story. Collections of his stories published during his lifetime include *La Maison Tellier* (1881), *Mademoiselle Fifi* (1882), *Yvette* (1885), *Monsieur Parent* (1886), and many others.

MARGARET MEAD, one of America's best-known anthropologists, was born in Philadelphia in 1901 and educated at Barnard College and Columbia University. After finishing her university work Dr. Mead spent many years living with various South Seas peoples, in the course of which she learned to use seven primitive languages. Her field work formed the basis of a number of highly successful books written in a style accessible to the general public. Among these are *Coming of Age in Samoa* (1928), *Growing Up in New Guinea* (1930), *Sex and Temperament in Three Primitive Societies* (1935), *Male and Female* (1949). She has written other books studying contemporary cultures in the light of perspectives gained by the study of small, homogenous stable societies. These include *The School in American Culture* (1951) and *Culture and Commitment* (1970). Dr. Mead is at present Curator Emeritus of Ethnology at the American Museum of Natural History in New York and Adjunct Professor of Anthropology at Columbia University.

MARIA MONTESSORI (1870-1952), Italian physician and educator, was born and educated in Rome, where she became the first woman in Italy to receive a medical degree in 1894. She first became interested in education while working at the University psychiatric clinic, and first put her pedagogic ideas into practice while working with feeble-minded and defective children. She opened her first school for normal children in a slum district of Rome in 1907, featuring the development of a child's initiative and intellectual understanding by means of specially prepared teaching materials and games. Her educational ideas became widely accepted, and the number of "Montessori" schools for young children are increasing to this day, in the United States and many parts of the world. Among Maria Montessori's published works are *The Montessori Method* (1912), *Pedagogical Anthropology* (1913), *Advanced Montessori Method* (1917).

CHRISTOPHER MORLEY (1890-1957) was born in Pennsylvania and educated at Haverford College and as a Rhodes Scholar at Oxford in 1913. A journalist for many years on the *Philadelphia Evening Public Ledger* and the *New York Evening Post*, and a contributor to the *Ladies' Home Journal* and the *Saturday Review of Literature*, his prolific output includes more than fifty books on widely diverse subjects, collections of poetry as well as a revised edition of *Bartlett's Familiar Quotations*. Among his best-known novels are *Parnassus on Wheels* (1917), *Kitty Foyle* (1939), and *The Man Who Made Friends with Himself* (1949). His nonfiction works include a collection of poetry, *The Rocking Horse* (1919), and *Shandygaff* (1918), *History of an Autumn* (1938), and *The Ironing Board* (1949), collections of essays.

EDITH NESBIT (1858-1924) was nearly forty, married for seventeen years to Hubert Bland (one of the founders of the Fabian Society, later joined by G. B. Shaw and Sidney Webb), and the mother of four children when she first began transmuting her own childhood experiences into the beloved and enduring stories of the Bastable family. The first of these books, *The Story of the Treasure Seekers* (1889), was immediately successful and was followed by *The Would-be Goods* (1901) and *The New Treasure Seekers* (1904).

FRANÇOIS RABELAIS (1494-1553) was born in the Loire Valley of France, son of a country lawyer. He entered a Franciscan monastery in his early youth and in due course was ordained a priest. He subsequently studied medicine, was granted permission to practice while wearing his priestly garb, and achieved great renown for his skills as a physician. Both these sober professions form an unlikely background for his literary career, pursued simultaneously with his medical and theological ones, the principal literary products being two outrageous masterpieces of grotesque, earthy, frequently obscene humor: *Pantagruel* (1532) and *Gargantua* (1534). These works aroused the anger of the theological authorities and were condemned, but important connections with the royal family helped Rabelais escape official censure and continue his medical career and his writings unhindered. The unabashed focus of great parts of his works on specific facts of human physiology, especially the functions of digestion, elimination, and reproduction, have given rise to the adjective "rabelaisian" to describe gross or earthy writings focusing on bodily functions.

CARL SANDBURG (1878-1967) was born in Galesburg, Illinois, of a Swedish immigrant family. He is noted as a poet with a special interest in capturing the distinctive flavor of the American idiom. His poetry includes the volumes *Chicago Poems* (1916), *Cornhuskers* (1918, special Pulitzer Prize 1919), *Smoke and Steel* (1920), *The People, Yes* (1936), *Complete Poems* (1950, Pulitzer Prize), and *Honey and Salt* (1953). His interest in American folklore led to the compilation of a collection of ballads and folk songs, *The American Songbag* (1927), and to several children's books, including *Rootabaga Stories* (1922) and *Potato Face* (1930). He devoted many years and much effort to his great biography of Abraham Lincoln that appeared in two parts: *Abraham Lincoln: The Prairie Years* (two volumes, 1926), and *Abraham Lincoln: The War Years* (four volumes, 1939, Pulitzer Prize). His other prose works include *The Chicago Race Riots* (1919); *Steichen the Photographer* (1929); *Mary Lincoln, Wife and Widow* (1932); a novel, *Remembrance Rock*; and a memoir about his youth, *Always the Young Strangers* (1953).

ELINOR GOULDING SMITH was born in New York City in 1917. After attending New York public schools and Cornell University, and selling twenty-five-cent perfumes at Liggett's Drug Store, she sold her first magazine article in 1943 and has since had well over a hundred articles in most of the national magazines. Among her books are *The Complete Book of Absolutely Perfect Housekeeping* (1956), *The Complete*

Book of Absolutely Perfect Baby and Child Care (1957), *Confessions of Mrs. Smith* (1958), *The Great Big Messy Book* (1962), *Nobody Likes a Nervous Cow* (1965), *That's Me, Always Making History* (1967), and *Horses, History and Havoc* (1969).

TOBIAS SMOLLETT (1721-1771) was born in Dumbartonshire, England, and educated at Glasgow University. After serving several years at sea as surgeon's mate, he returned to London, taking up a practice as a surgeon, and began the writing of his novels, which have established him as one of the four great English writers of the eighteenth century (with Richardson, Fielding, and Sterne). His novels, distinguished by a strong, earthy humor, and usually following the adventures of a picaresque hero, include *Roderick Random* (1748), *Peregrine Pickle* (1751), *Ferdinand Count Fathom* (1753), *Sir Launcelot Greaves* (1760-62), and his best-known work, *Humphrey Clinker* (1771).

LINCOLN STEFFENS (1866-1936), born in San Francisco, educated at the University of California, began his career in journalism as city editor of the *New York Commercial Advertiser*. Best known as a leader of the "muckraking" movement that undertook to expose corruption in politics and business by means of sensational journalism, his articles were collected in *Shame of the Cities* (1904), *The Struggle for Self Government* (1906), and *Upbuilders* (1909). His best-known work remains his *Autobiography*, which not only describes the career of an eminently successful journalist but gives a unique picture of American life and politics at the beginning of the twentieth century.

LEO TOLSTOY (1828-1910), the first Russian writer to achieve worldwide fame, was born on his family estate, Yasnaya Polyana (serene meadow), where he later wrote many of his great works. His literary career began with the publication of his reminiscences *Childhood* (1852), *Boyhood* (1854), and *Youth* (1856). In 1862 he married Sonya Andreevna Behrs and a year later began work on his monumental novel *War and Peace*, often spoken of as the greatest novel ever written. His literary works were gigantic in scope and length—*War and Peace* (1866), *Anna Karenina* (1875-77), *Resurrection* (1899), dozens of volumes of minor novels, plays, short stories, essays, religious tracts and educational treatises. His personal life was also larger than life, as it were, marked by riotous passions, spiritual upheavals, religious conversions, domestic dramas, and not the least impressive statistic—thirteen children.

HENRI TROYAT, biographer and novelist, was born in Russia in 1911, but was educated in France, earning a law degree, later becoming an editor and finally establishing his own career in literature with the publication of his first novel in 1935. Though fourteen of his novels have been published in the United States, it is as a biographer that he has made his mark in America, notably with *Firebrand: The Life of Dostoevsky* (1946), *Tolstoy* (1967), and most recently, *Pushkin* (1970). He is a member of the Académie Française and a winner of the Prix Goncourt (1938).

MARK TWAIN (Samuel Langhorne Clemens, 1835-1910) grew up in Hannibal, Missouri, where he experienced many of the adventures described in *Tom Sawyer* (1876) and *Huckleberry Finn* (1885). Beginning his literary career as a journalist, he soon won recognition for his humorous sketches, first collected in 1867 in the volume *The Celebrated Jumping Frog of Calaveras County and Other Sketches*. Carrying on a tradition of Western humor and frontier realism, Twain's particular blending of factual material and humorous exaggeration became hallmarks of a style uniquely his own, but underlying the humor of his greatest works is a current of indignation at injustice and a profound appreciation of the human values of friendship and loyalty. Other works include *The Innocents Abroad* (1869), *Roughing It* (1872), *The Prince and the Pauper* (1882), *Life on the Mississippi* (1883), and *A Connecticut Yankee in King Arthur's Court* (1889).

JOHN UPDIKE was born in 1932 in Shillington, Pennsylvania, and attended Harvard College and the Ruskin School of Drawing and Fine Arts in Oxford, England. He worked for *The New Yorker* magazine before publishing his first novel, *Poorhouse Fair* (1959), and many of his stories, poems, and essays have first appeared there. Considered one of the most important young writers in America today, Updike is the author of nine works of fiction, which include *Rabbit Run* (1960), *The Centaur* (1963), and *Couples* (1968), as well as three books of poetry, a collection of essays, and four children's books.

KURT VONNEGUT, JR. (born in 1923), a writer most popular with today's college generation, lives in West Barnstable, Cape Cod, Massachusetts, with his wife and six children. While many of his early stories are written in a conventional style, all his novels are characterized by a wild blending of fantasy and comic realism that refuses to fit neatly into any critical pigeonhole, though his work has been described variously as science-fiction or black comedy. His best-known novels include *Piano Player* (1952), *Cat's Cradle* (1963), *Mother Night* (1965), and *Slaughterhouse-Five* (1969). His short stories appear in the collection *Welcome to the Monkey House* (1968).

WILLIAM CARLOS WILLIAMS (1883-1963) was born in Rutherford, New Jersey, where he lived his whole life and practiced medicine as a pediatrician. A prize-winning poet (Pulitzer Prize, 1963), his poetry was marked by his use of vernacular American speech and observations of ordinary people and their lives. Among his prolific literary output are many volumes of poetry, including the monumental five-volume poem *Paterson* (1946, 1958); *In the American Grain* (1925), a collection of impressionistic, biographical essays; *Many Loves* (1961), a collection of plays; stories collected in *Life Along the Passaic River* (1938), *Make Light of It* (1950), and *The Farmers' Daughters* (1961); and four novels: *A Voyage to Pagany* (1928), *White Mule* (1937), *In the Money* (1940), and *The Build Up* (1952). Also among his works are an *Autobiography* (1951), *Selected Letters* (1957), and a memoir of his mother, *Yes, Mrs. Williams* (1960).

MARK ZBOROWSKI was born in 1908 in Uman, Russia. A graduate of the University of Paris, Dr. Zborowski's academic affiliations in this country have included Columbia University, Cornell University Medical College and Harvard University, where he was a Research Associate in Anthropology. Dr. Zborowski's investigations in the field of cultural anthropology have focussed on the subjects of aging, rehabilitation of the physically disabled and cultural components in responses to pain, as well as Eastern European culture. He is the author of *Life Is with People* (1952, with Elizabeth Herzog) and *People in Pain* (1969). He is at present Cultural Anthropologist and Research Associate in Medicine at Mount Zion Hospital in San Francisco.

MIKHAIL ZOSHCHENKO (1895-1958) was born in the Ukraine, the son of a painter of noble descent. He studied at the University of St. Petersburg, served as an officer in World War I, and began publishing in 1921. Zoshchenko's sly irreverence and satirical mockery of human pretensions and bureaucratic imbecilities made him one of the most popular humorists in Russia in the nineteen twenties and thirties, but these were the very qualities that brought him into inevitable trouble with the Soviet authorities. After a twenty-year silence he was publicly vindicated in the famous "thaw" of 1956, and posthumously honored with new editions of his works in 1959. The amazing success of these works proved that Soviet readers' affection for Zoshchenko's works had never waned. His works include *The Merry Life* (1924), *The Joyous Adventure* (1927), *The Woman Who Could Not Read and Other Tales* (1940).